I0380390

JOHN R. TORRANCE

PRODUCTIVITY POWER PACK

4 BOOKS IN 1

SUPERCHARGE PRODUCTIVITY HABITS,
PROVEN SPEED READING TECHNIQUES,
ACCELERATED LEARNING UNLOCKED,
EATING FOR COGNITIVE POWER

BOOKS

Supercharge Productivity Habits

50+ Simple Hacks to Organize Your Tasks,
Overcome Procrastination, Increase Efficiency
and Work Smarter to Become a Top Performer

John R. Torrance, Productivity Coach

TABLE OF CONTENTS

INTRODUCTION

Your Current Status

Today's workplace or business environment has become ever more demanding and competitive. Irrespective of the type of work you do, your job designation and industry, everything seems to be moving so fast. To add to that, advancements in technology and our near-total dependence on it, and it's easy to see how becoming more productive in today's world is increasingly complicated. In other words, the tools to achieve productivity keep evolving, but the human capacity to meet them appears to be dwindling.

Everyone has the same amount of time: 24 hours a day, 7 days a week, and 365 days a year. However, the ability to get the most out of each day is not common to all. You wake up daily, hurriedly get out of bed, get dressed, and rush off to work. Now, if you are someone who sets daily, weekly, or monthly goals for success, you may actually get some things done. However, most people get bogged down by a myriad of problems and interruptions while at work. Others get into the workplace with personal issues and work-related problems.

In the end, many become demotivated, stressed, and dejected due to the inability to complete the task for each day. The annoying thing is, as the days and weeks go by, the pressure begins to mount. Deadlines are fast approaching, the board meeting is two days away, and the details required for your reports are still on the drawing board. No matter how hard you work, things somehow happen to spiral out of control.

Yes, you are diligent, astute, and hardworking, but everything does not seem to add up for you sometimes. To worsen issues, you still have to take work home in order to meet deadlines. As much as you don't like it, you feel burnt out and are losing steam, yet you cannot stop to catch a breath. The sad news is, the constant running around could be counterproductive to your health, further reducing your productivity levels.

Where You Want to Be

The rules of engagements in the workplace have changed. You must be swift and decisive to stay on top of your game. Two decades ago, it would have been okay to work hard to attain success. However, today's world thrives on the principles of working smarter rather than harder to excel. That's not to say the business environment condones laxity, but due to interactions with human environments, better ways to get tasks done have evolved.

Productivity depends largely on the efficient utilization of your limited time for task optimization. There are time tested tools, productivity systems, and principles to increase your personal effectiveness at work. Working smarter helps channel your energy and resources, leading to increased focus. What you have at last is an adjusted schedule with a better outlook that results in increased productivity and fewer burnouts.

Overall, your focus should be on possessing the ability to identify time wasters in your daily work routine. Next, you want to be in a position to determine how your workflow should proceed, increasing the value of time spent. In the end, you increase your chances of becoming one of the top performers in your industry.

Supercharge Productivity Habits offer you over two decades of my personal experience and knowledge as a productivity coach. It contains time-tested systems and life hacks to help you improve productivity levels considerably. It provides practical steps, principles, and experiences that have shaped my past and helped me to achieve peak performance in all spheres of life.

This book can serve as a personal guide in your journey to self-mastery and improved productivity.

Reading *Supercharge Productivity Habits* will help you to:

- Overcome procrastination.
- Increase your efficiency by helping you focus on what's vital to your success.
- Help you develop strategies to work smarter instead of harder.
- Place you on a journey to becoming a top performer in the workplace.
- Take more pleasure in your work.
- Accelerate your learning potential.
- Achieve more from the limited work hours of the day.
- Re-organize work and study time to make you an expert in your field.
- Follow your dreams passionately.

How Realistic Is *Supercharge Productivity Habits?*

Supercharge Productivity Habits contains the principles that have shaped my life for several decades now. Reading these truths will make all the difference in your rise to a more productive life. Most of these principles helped in increasing my productivity by at least 80%. A lot of times, authors and public speakers offer impractical solutions to sound good or to sell an idea. However, this book does not sell hogwash. No, it does not try to build castles in the air by promising unrealistic steps and principles. That's because the bulk of what you will read here revolves around real-life experiences and proven scientific hacks. Other related views are from reliable productivity experts and industry leaders from all walks of life.

Supercharge Productivity Habits: What's In It for You?

My recommendations and tips for working smarter and not harder can make you a top performer in your workplace. Consider the purchasing and reading of this book as an investment. As such, the primary aim of this book is to ensure you derive maximum value to boost your productivity measurably.

However, to achieve the best from each chapter and exercise found in this book requires consistency and unrelenting effort. Put into practice the valuable lessons in this book and, over time, you will see immense productivity output. In the end, you have the potential to become one of the top performers in your workplace or industry.

The Promise

If you promise to read carefully with an open mind the information (or hacks, if you will) contained in this book, and put them into practice, I guarantee that within the next few days to four weeks you will see at least a 45% improvement in your productivity level. At the end of one year, your potential and productivity will know no limits!

What to Do Now

To enable you to get the most out of *Supercharge Productivity Habits*, you must create a plan of action on how to read this book. Considering your schedule, set out a specific time during the day to read. As a rule of thumb, the early hours of the day usually offer an excellent opportunity to learn with minimal distractions. Also, determine how many minutes each morning you want to set aside to finish reading this book. You could do a 14 to 40 days challenge to finish this book. It all depends on how fast a reader you are. However, it is not about speed, but about being able to learn and apply the valuable resources found in this book. When reading, I suggest you arm yourself with a pen and a jotter to take down salient points. If you have sticky notes and a board within your room or office, you can stick essential points you do not want to forget to your mirror or door, somewhere within easy view.

Last, but not least, once you learn a new idea, get to work immediately to put it into practice. Please do not wait to finish reading this book before implementing it. Take the learning process one step at a time.

Keep reading now to start supercharging your productivity habits using these 50+ time-tested and actionable steps today.

CHAPTER ONE

Decide What You Want

Life is about decision making. You can only rise in life to the extent to which you make up your mind. Therefore, you must decide what you want out of life. Whatever goals you have set for your life or career can only become a reality after you make firm decisions. Life will not bequeath to you what you think you deserve. You only get out of life what you put into it. In most cases, an increase in productivity and any success you will enjoy in life starts in the mind.

Whatever your pursuit in life, work or personal, you first must evaluate your course. Next, you need to set meaningful goals for attaining them. Such goals must also include an action plan for actualizing them. To become more productive, these 6 steps to successful goal setting can help ensure you reach top performance:

Belief

Having strong confidence in the process is a vital part of goal setting. If you do not have faith in what you do, then the process of achieving it will wear you out more quickly. Deciding what you want should be predicated on having ample knowledge of what is required.

"Whenever you see a successful business, someone once made a courageous decision." -Peter F. Drucker

Nothing meaningful happens by chance, it takes goal setting and action to see success. A belief in your abilities serves as gasoline for achieving your goals. When you believe in the process, you will strive to own or personalize it. Having faith in the process does not remove the challenges or pitfalls that go with any endeavor. It can, however, help strengthen your resolve to look beyond the temporal setbacks and to focus on what's most important. A firm belief in yourself can help release the energy required to follow the process through. Your thought process can serve as the building blocks to achieving your goals.

Certain lines of thought can only serve as self-limiting. Such self-limiting thoughts are mostly negative thoughts. Positive thoughts and beliefs will help channel your energy toward the attainment of your goals. Once you have decided what you want, having faith in the process makes achieving your goal simpler.

"Happiness is not the absence of problems, it's the ability to deal with them." -Steve Mariboli

"Once you make a decision, the universe conspires to make it happen." -Ralph Waldo Emerson

You are in the best position to inspire yourself to achieve your goals in life, therefore, believe in yourself.

Limiting Beliefs

"Every person takes the limits of their own field of vision for the limits of the world." -Arthur Schopenhauer

Certain beliefs are self-limiting thoughts. Limiting beliefs usually send negative vibes that make achieving your personal or work goals impossible. These limiting thoughts come from your past experiences, environment, and norms. Such limiting beliefs include:

Everything or nothing belief

The all or nothing belief is an extremist mindset seated on two opposite ends. It's like thinking in black and white without room for a midpoint or balance. In other words, it is either you have everything or you have nothing.

Exaggeration belief

Persons with an exaggerated belief tend to magnify events or incidences out of proportion. It's okay to think positively and aim for the best, but having an exaggerated belief makes it difficult to set and achieve your work or personal goals.

Minimalist belief

A minimalist mindset tends to expend energy on small things. It may also involve paying little attention to the intricate details of a particular goal. A minimalist can put off pursuing a goal or consider it as not something significant.

Labeling and Mislabeling

Labeling is stereotyping yourself based on a past incidence, usually using negative terms. Giving yourself names due to what did or did not occur is another form of labeling. It involves overgeneralizing a situation or experience that could put you in a negative light.

Mislabeling

Mislabeling is a form of misrepresentation of yourself. It involves using an inappropriate description of an occurrence or event. Such misrepresentation does not sync adequately with your workplace or personal goals.

Hasty Conclusions

Decisions or judgments made in haste without rational evidence could result in negative outcomes. Making snap judgments based on a person's actions or reactions can lead to inaccurate assumptions. Such assumptions could result in complications in the workplace or in your personal goals.

Pessimistic thoughts

Some lines of thought can only produce negative outcomes. Always seeing the wrong in situations and people can only produce negativity in your personal and work life. People sometimes hold negative feelings and accept them as fact. When this happens, they discredit the truth and choose to believe the negative situations about work, their environment, or themselves. Negative emotional reasoning makes you see a situation as negative because you feel bad about it.

How to Get Rid of Limiting Beliefs

Your belief shapes the person you have become.

"Learning too soon our limitations, we never learn our powers."
-Mignon McLaughlin

The only way to make meaningful changes in your life is by making certain adjustments in your belief system. Here is what to do to make the needed change in your belief system:

Self-Reappraisal

Start first by re-appraising your life. In what specific areas do you feel like you are stuck? What aspect of your goal isn't exactly working for you? To get rid of self-limiting beliefs, you need to identify the likely problems in achieving your goals. State these problems in as few sentences as possible.

What Are Your limiting Beliefs?

You need to write down the particular belief systems you perceive as the limiting factors. Identify how each particular belief has prevented you from achieving your goals. For instance, you need to take certain actions to get to the next stage of your goal. However, being pessimistic is limiting you from achieving your personal or work goals. In this case, in order to succeed, you must know the causes of pessimistic feelings and how to deal with them.

Sometimes, a limiting belief can help protect you from certain dangers or actions. They could also become detrimental to achieving another goal. For example, if you are a person who believes in being frugal and must save up as many funds as possible, spending a lot on vacation might appear wasteful. It will take a clear understanding of your goals and the purpose of the vacation to convince such a person to spend more. A vacation trip, for instance, could be a source of relaxation, education, or career pursuit. Therefore, you could tie spending on vacation to a specific goal to challenge this limiting belief.

"I am not interested in your limiting beliefs; I'm interested in what makes you limitless." -Brendon Burchard

One of the best ways to challenge or get rid of a limiting belief is to find a purpose. When the purpose aligns with your goals, then it becomes easier to push yourself toward attaining it. For a limiting belief, therefore, we must look for ways to overcome them. Certain habits need to change to see the realization of your goals. Does the belief help you achieve your goal at the desired level? If not, then think of ways to get rid of it. Sometimes, the belief might work perfectly for a particular level of your goal. At other stages of your goal, it could become counter-productive. Then, you need to re-appraise the goal and make adjustments.

Purpose

"The secret of success is constancy to purpose." -Benjamin Disraeli

John was living the American dream we all look forward to achieving. Immediately after college, he got a job with a high-powered company in the Manhattan area. Within the space of three years, he was promoted to a managerial role. With that position came a car and other benefits, including yearly vacations. It seemed as if John was living the life of his dreams. The next thing for John was to get married and start raising kids.

Eight years down the line and after three kids, it didn't take long before John began feeling overwhelmed. Endless pressure from work and home, unending bills screaming louder than the American dream were too much for John. Feeling frustrated, he decided to take the subway home instead of driving. Boldly written on an electronic billboard on the way home was this commercial from a popular beverage brand: "Find your sparks, make it real!"

Taking a long walk home, John began to think. He examined his work and personal life over the past 8 years. He felt empty inside. *My 9-5 job sucks!* said, John. He wanted more out of life, but couldn't place his hand on what exactly he wanted. As he walked, John kept asking himself the century-long questions most people ask when life seems not to make sense anymore. *What's my spark? Who am I? What's my life really about?*

At one time or the other, we all get to that point in life where the feeling of emptiness steps in. At this point, we begin to ask meaningful questions just begging for answers. Sometimes, the answers to these questions take us on a ride of self-discovery.

"There is no greater agony than bearing an untold story inside." -Maya Angelou

Understanding the reason for setting a goal is a powerful tool. It helps you to keep the goal in focus and align your activities towards attaining that goal. Knowing the reason for your goal will serve as a motivation for achieving it. Finding your purpose in life gives you the springboard to fulfill your life's dream. Your purpose helps define your personal and career choices.

To live a life of fulfillment and enjoy inner peace, you must find out your purpose. Your purpose serves as a compass that guides your life.

"What am I living for and what am I dying for are the same question." -Margaret Atwood

Questions to Avoid in Finding Purpose:

- Can I do it?
- Will it work?
- Who will come to my aid?
- What if I fail?
- What if I lose interest?
- What if I don't make a profit?
- What if I am wrong?

Honest Questions for Finding Your Purpose in Life:

- What would you do even without being paid?
- What exactly do you want?
- What do you find so easy to do?
- What are you passionate about?
- What will you do if you know you can't fail?
- What do you do that makes you come alive?
- What one thing makes you forget to eat or even poop?
- What one thing are you willing to do repeatedly even when people make fun of you?

- What can keep you up so late at night without feeling bored or discouraged?
- What problem do you think you are best suited for in saving the world?
- If you had one year left on earth, how would you use it for? How would you wish to be remembered?

How to Discover Your Purpose in Life

Explore Your Passion

What are you passionate about? The honest questions expressed above provide an easy way to answer the question of life's purpose. Everyone has an innate ability that inspires us to act. There is a deep connection between what you are passionate about and your purpose in life. You cannot create a purpose for yourself, it is already within you.

All you need is to discover your purpose. However, you will not be the best in any discipline because it is in line with your purpose, but you will find it easier to cope and more exciting once it is your life's purpose. Training and development can help hone your skills to make you a top performer in your field.

Therefore, exploring those things that excite you can help you to discover purpose, in finding your sparks. What talents and gifts can you express or explore?

What most people don't understand is that passion is the result of action, not the cause of it.

Take action

"The experience is the reward; clarity comes through the process of exploring." -Shannon Kaiser

Once you know what you are passionate about, it's time to take action. It is only in trying things in the area of your passion that you can discover what you are truly good at.

If you spend the bulk of your time thinking about what your purpose should be, you might become frustrated. Finding your purpose is in the doing, not in the asking alone. Relate with others. Utilize those qualities, gifts or talents, even for free. Try out new things. Then you will discover what you love best. The more you utilize your gifts, the more you will discover about you. Over time, your innate abilities become glaring to you.

Do not overthink your purpose—just do it!

Visualizing What You Want

"Visualization is daydreaming with a purpose." -Bo Bennett

As of the early 1990s, the film camera was a popular means of taking photos of your family and friends at events. At the time, film cameras made use of transparent films to capture images in the process, making a 'click-click' sound when you snapped a photo. Before that, however, you needed to insert the film into the appropriate slot. The film was made by popular brands like AGFA, Kodak, and more.

To take a photo, you needed to look into the viewfinder to ensure the subject was at the center. You could also zoom in or out to ensure you were getting the best positioning. Once you had completed about 36 shots, then it would be time to bring out the film. You then took the film to the lab to convert into a negative. The negative was a reel of film for creating a blur expression of the images you snapped. With that, you could identify the best films to print into clear photos.

The journey from having a desire or goal to the actualization of your dreams looks a lot like this process.

21

"You can't depend on your eyes when your imagination is out of focus." -Mark Twain

In other words, visualization involves creating a mental picture of what you want or where you want to be in life. It is a powerful success tool anyone who wants to become a top performer must possess. Everything you wish to accomplish in life first starts as a picture in the mind.

"A picture is worth a thousand words." -Arthur Brisbane

To accomplish your personal or work goals you need adequate focus. At first, the picture will not be clear and appear like a negative. Once you carefully set your goals, just like identifying the right film or exposure to print, then you can work toward actualizing your dreams. Each goal or aspiration has its own specifications to make a beautiful picture. The better you know how to centralize before taking a shot, the better the photo's output. Also, the better the mental picture you create, the better your chance of success.

"Visualization helps our brain send a signal to our body to start behaving in a way consistent with the images in our head." - New York City therapist Kimberly Hershenson

Everyone dreams or creates mental pictures in the mind daily. However, not all mental pictures can produce positive outcomes in your life. Sometimes people use the power of visualization to create a life they don't want. They imagine the worst situations and end up with ugly photos.

"If you can dream it, you can do it." -Walt Disney

Value of Visualization

- It brings your creative sense to life. It won't take long before you start having creative ideas related to your goals.

- Visualization helps channel your mental energy to identify the resources required for achieving your goals.
- Your mental visual picture puts to motion the law of attraction. This law is what causes the people, resources, and situations needed to bring your goals to reality.
- Visualization creates the inner strength or motivation to pursue your dreams.

Tips to Visualizing and Actualizing Your Goals

Know what you want. In clear terms, state what you want. What do you value the most? What is that thing that can give you the most joy? Create a mental blueprint of what your life will look like after achieving this goal.

Describe the Goal in Detail

The secret to describing your goal in detail is to ask yourself: if nothing is stopping you, how would you go about achieving your goal? This has to do with the process of attaining your goal. Create a clear mental photo of what exactly you want. You can write down the process involved in achieving the goals. Act as if you already have all you need to implement the goal when writing.

Create an Emotional Scene of Your Goal

Try to picture the mood, scenes and other scenarios that will accompany the goal once you achieve it. To help inspire you, create a vision board with the relevant images and quotes. Write the short and long term goals associated with the vision.

Get to Work

Start taking small steps daily toward achieving your goals. Don't let the enormity of the goal scare you. Draw an action plan with a timeline to achieve daily, weekly, and monthly goals.

Say Aloud Your Goals

Saying your goals out loud can also help spur creative actions. You can face the mirror or wherever you like and speak your goals, declaring them into life.

Go the Long Hall

Understand that visualizing your goals is not a sprint, but a journey. Along the way, you will face challenges and discouragement from friends and family. But you must learn to stick to your goal, even when it looks like nothing seems to be working.

"All successful men and women are big dreamers. They imagine what their future could be, ideal in every respect, and then they work every day toward their distant vision." -Brian Tracy

Writing Down Your Goal

Everyone can have a dream or carry a mental picture of what they want to achieve in life, but not everyone takes the time to write down their goals in clear terms. Writing down your goals helps you see what it looks like on paper. It becomes easier to re-focus or adjust any aspect that does not make complete sense.

When it has to do with writing down goals, there are three categories of people you will discover. The first set of people do not write down their goals. The second set writes their goals, but without a clear blueprint on how to achieve them. The third set of people write their goals down and set a clear plan of action on how to achieve them. This third group of people does what is known as SMART Goals.

Research shows that less than 20% of people write down their goals in clear terms. One study also states that those who wrote their goals are 1.2 to 1.4 times more likely to achieve them than others.

Why Should You Write Down Your Goals?

Increases Your Chance of Success

Dr. Gail Matthews, a Psychology Professor at Dominican University, California, conducted a study on 270 participants on goal setting. The results showed that people have a 42% higher chance of achieving their goals when they write them down.

Creates Clarity of Goals

Writing down your goals helps you identify in vivid terms what exactly you want. When you write your goals down, you naturally begin to think about the resources you have and the strategies to accomplish them. However, writing down 'I want to be a millionaire when I'm 30 years old' is not enough. You must identify what exactly you will be doing and how you intend on making the millions.

When writing down your goals, you must make sure they are SMART goals. We'll talk more about SMART goals later in this chapter.

It Motivates You to Success

Seeing your goals written down on paper will serve as a motivation to accomplishing them. You can assess how far you are away from accomplishing your goals. You can also identify little successes and celebrate key milestones if you have your goals written down.

Saves You More Time

A well-written and clearly defined goal reduces the number of times spent on guesswork. Once you have your goals written out, you can see the bigger picture better. That way, you can reduce the waste of resources and achieve better time management.

Guidelines for Writing Down Your Goals

So, when it is time to write your goals down, what should you do? Do you scribble down any thought that comes into your head and then refer to it in pursuing your goals? Or, are there laid down principles, values, aspirations, or structures to follow? For instance, here are some guidelines to follow:

- Identify what your work or life goals are.
- Write the goals down using the SMART Goal principles.
- Identify the reasons you want to achieve each goal.
- Make sure you don't have too many goals. In fact, there should be less than 10.
- Write down how you will go about achieving each goal.

"The trouble with not having a goal is that you can spend your life running up and down the field and never score." -Bill Copeland

To succeed with goal setting, you must always review your goals for consistencies. Also, working with an accountability partner will help you know when you've strayed away from it.

Create a Plan of Action

Writing down your goals without a clear plan on how to accomplish them is no different than wishful thinking. To succeed with your goal setting, you must devise a clear order on how you will attain that goal. Without a clear direction, you could become frustrated and stray from your goal.

Tips to Creating a Working Plan of Action

- Break down the goals into smaller tasks.
- Break each task into steps—daily, weekly, and monthly.
- Set a priority for achieving each task.
- Create a milestone for evaluation of success.
- Create a timeline for achieving each aspect of the goal.
- Be specific on what you intend to accomplish at each stage of the goal.
- Carry out regular reviews of your goals, timelines, and tasks to be sure you are in line.

"Shoot for the moon. Even if you miss you'll land among the stars." -Les Brown

To succeed in goal setting requires a concerted effort. You must take small doable steps daily.

Review Your Goals

Most people only take stock of their goals in the New Year. They make New Year's resolutions that they end up breaking within a week or two. The only way not to lose sight of your goals is to review them regularly. Reviewing your goals is like having a compass to serve as a guide. To increase personal efficiency, you need to review your goals often.

"If you don't know where you are going, you will probably end up somewhere else." -Lawrence J. Peters

Why You Must Review Your Goals Often

- It helps you identify the critical steps in your action plan to ensure consistency with the overall goal.
- Reviewing your goal keeps it fresh in your mind and helps motivate you to further action.

- As you implement your goals, a review of them will help you spot what needs re-adjustments to be efficient.
- You reduce the chances of going off course in implementing your goals.
- It helps you move faster and more consistently.
- You will eliminate the waste of resources when you review your goals. Efforts spent doing the wrong thing will be saved and further increase personal efficiency.
- It is a great way to strengthen your resolve.

"Life is 10% what happens to you and 90% how you react to it."
-Charles R. Swindoll

How to Effectively Review Your Life's Goals

Reviewing your goals will be easier to achieve if you have written them down. Only a person without a concrete destination in life will go through life without setting goals. However, to become a top performer in your industry, you must understand how to work your goals. If you already have your goals written the SMART way, then you can review your goals by doing the following:

- Pick a particular time each day to review your weekly goals. Make sure to commit to evaluating key performance index daily in line with your goals. Early hours of the morning work best for some people. It helps put one in top gear to face the day. Evening or bedtime works best for some, as they wake up having a clear idea of what their day will look like. However, we shall discuss more on this in the next chapter on the 5 A.M. Club.

- Evaluate your monthly goals at the end of each month to see how well you have fared.
- Summarize your daily, weekly, and monthly goals into three to ten steps. Putting your goals into smaller steps makes it simple to review them. It also helps you become familiar with the process without making it boring or cumbersome. You can

write the steps in your notebook, phone, board, or tools you work with daily.

- At the beginning of each week or month, review the activities of the past week. Take note of the daily, weekly, or monthly tasks completed. Look out for those still in the making and areas where things went wrong. Also, look at better and possible ways of resolving issues.
- Adjust your plans and review the steps to take for the days, weeks, and months ahead.

"If you want to reach a goal, you must 'see the reaching' in your mind." - Zig Ziglar

SMART Goal Setting Techniques

Clarity in goal setting is a major factor in increasing your efficiency. It also helps you to maintain focus. SMART goals go beyond writing a wishlist. They are a way of writing an actionable goal. A SMART goal takes into account the cost of achieving it. George T. Doran invented the SMART Goals method in 1981 for writing management goals and objectives. Key elements in the SMART goal include:

Specific

A SMART goal is one that is spelled out and identified. It is a clear statement about the expected results and the required actions to achieving them. We all have many things demanding our attention daily, but to increase personal or workplace efficiency, we must identify those tasks that will help advance our goals faster. For this reason, make a list of all of your goals and then select those that are critical to advancing your career.

For instance, will it be more likely for you to achieve 25 tasks or 5 daily? How about weekly? It would be best to prioritize each task and narrow-down to 5 to 25 in line with your goals. These five tasks should be the most important ones that will help you to achieve your mid to long-term goals.

Measurable

A SMART goal is one that can be measured. There should be a clear way to judge whether or not you have made progress toward your goal. When setting it, make sure you define how you are going to track success and the key factors you will use to show how you have worked toward achieving your goal.

Achievable

A goal is not a wish list meant for the fairy godmother. It must be something you can put resources together to achieve. For example, a person addicted to smoking cigarettes can overcome the habit. How? By staying away from it. He or she must also avoid friends or places with easy to access drugs or cigarettes. Therefore, to make your goals achievable, you must have the appropriate environment to support that goal. For instance, to cultivate the habit of reading, you could set a target of a number of books to read each month. Then, you take the next steps in selecting relevant themes or books. Lastly, you could pick a schedule for achieving the goal. From there, you place the selection of books for the month on your reading table, in your bag, or where you can easily reach them.

To make the goal achievable, it should be in smaller bits to start, so you avoid becoming overwhelmed. Again, you need to have the tools required to achieve your goals. If not, you have to work out a means to acquire those tools, either by training or seeking help from others.

Realistic

If you are making a wish, then it is okay even if it is a vague one. However, if you want to succeed in your personal or career goals, then it must be realistic. That means it must align with your personal or career goals in the long-term. You also must have access to the needed resources or know-how to get them.

Time-Bound

Every meaningful goal must have a start and end date. A goal without a timeline becomes challenging to measure the extent of success. Breaking down your goals into smaller bits with deadlines for each bit will make it easier to know when each aspect is not moving according to the plan.

Fixing specific timelines also sets the tone on the urgency of the goal. You can read more about how to write SMART Goals and get templates to guide you.

Chapter Summary

- Deciding what you want is the key to achieving your personal and career goals.
- Possessing the right line of thoughts and beliefs will help advance your course better, rather than self-limiting beliefs.
- You are in the best position to motivate yourself to achieve your goals in life.
- Your purpose serves as a compass to achieving your goals. Your purpose should drive your life's decisions and choices.
- One accurate way of finding your purpose is in taking action.
- Creating a mental picture helps make your life goals clearer and easier to accomplish.
- The image you see often can become your reality.
- Visual aids help motivate you toward attaining your goals.

- Writing down your goals increases the chances of accomplishing them faster.
- People who write their goals down focus better and are more likely to achieve them.
- A written goal must include a plan of action to accomplish it.
- A program of action makes it easier to measure growth and success.
- Reviewing your goals helps you to do a proper appraisal to identify issues, failures, achievements, and deviations.
- A SMART goal is one with an expected outcome and the action required to achieve it.

In the next chapter, you will learn about mastering your day so that you can achieve your life's goal. Join the 5 A.M. Club.

CHAPTER TWO:

Join The 5 A.M Club

Everyone has habits or habitual activities they indulge in. Some are good habits, others are negative habits. However, Robin Sharma says, "Winning starts at your beginning. And your first hours are where the great heroes are made. Own your mornings and you'll master your life." From discussions, highly productive and successful people wake up before 6 A.M. to start their day. Apple CEO Tim Cook, AOL CEO Tim Armstrong, Investor Kevin O'Leary, the CEO of Xerox, Ursula Burns, Twitter, and Square CEO Jack Dorsey, GE CEO Jeff Immelt, all have one thing in common—they all wake up between 3:30 A.M. and 6 A.M. to connect with their day.

For nearly a decade now, I've woken up before 5 A.M. to start my day. And waking up early has had a phenomenal impact on my day and overall life. Habits are things you do often. You do not need any prompting to carry out habitual acts. Why is it important to develop positive habits? Any habit can be learned, negative or positive. Imbibing positive habits will have a lifelong impact on your goals. That's what Robin Sharma's 5 A.M. Club is about. You rise in life to the degree you allow yourself to.

I noticed that I had become very busy and had no time to read, but knew that reading was an important part of my life and a learning tool. When I did a reappraisal of my life's goal, I had to admit this truth. And that's exactly what we all need to do often: reappraise our goals.

What is that single activity or skill you could learn that will have a positive impact on your life or finances?

Using Robin Sharma's 20/20/20 rule, I had to work out a way to help me read so I could increase my productivity. The rules state twenty minutes of exercise, twenty minutes of planning and twenty minutes of studying. Well, I plan my day at night before getting into bed. It works better for me as I get up feeling organized, knowing my activities for the new day. I already had a regular schedule for 30 minutes of exercise each morning. Also, it helps to start with exercise, because, once I get into an activity, my day starts fully and I can get distracted. Because of this, I restructured the 20/20/20 for studying, breaking it into 20/20/20 in the morning.

To help me succeed in this challenge, I placed the books for reading in the morning on my reading table. Also, I made sure my alarm clock was set one hour earlier to accommodate the new reading routine for 4:30 A.M. The first day, it was not so pleasant. When the alarm came on, I literally hit the snooze button. By the second ring of the alarm, ten minutes later, I had to drag myself out of bed if I was going to succeed. It takes discipline and a firm decision to excel at any goal.

Day 1 was a total mess as I felt useless and as if I should go back to bed. I barely made it through the first morning as my eyes were heavy, my body felt numb, and I just kept yawning over and over again. Day 2, yes I got out of bed with the first ring of the alarm. I grabbed a cup of coffee and made it to my study. Day 2 was no better than day 1. I slept late, trying to prepare materials for my meeting for the new day. By morning I felt like I should skip day 2, but I still pushed myself to it.

It was after I did my usual daily reflection and planning before retiring for the night that I realized what was amiss. Now, I wake up one hour earlier than I used to and that has taken some time out of my six to seven hours of sleep routine. Since my new wake up time was

5 A.M, I had to push my sleep time to 11 p.m. to strike a balance. Most days, I have to get into bed by 10:30 or 11 P.M.

By day 3, I wasn't so tired like I was day 1 and 2. That improved the quality of the time I spent reading. It also helped me to achieve my goal faster. The power of habit. If you can sustain the desired trait for at least 30 to 40 days, your body will adjust to it.

Robin Sharma's 5 A.M. Club Secrets

Robin Sharma is a renowned Canadian speaker, writer, and success coach with parents from Indian and Kenyan. In his early twenties, Sharma had to deal with the issues most diversity immigrants faced. He desired very much to excel and was willing to put in the extra effort to succeed.

After graduating from law school and becoming a successful lawyer, Sharma wanted more from life. That led to his studying the lives of other successful men and women to understand what makes them tick underneath. The success strategies of these great personalities gave birth to Sharma's books: *Megaliving in 1994*, *The Monk Who Sold His Ferrari* and his most recent, the *5 A.M. Club*.

Robin Sharma's 5 A.M Club

Robin Sharma has led a simple, but disciplined life based on experiences and training gathered over the decades. That's what gave rise to the 5 A.M. Club. Sharma's personal discipline learned in his 20s helped project him to success and avoid the mistakes made by so many people. Today, he speaks to thousands of people at conferences and other events.

Sharma says that if you can form the habit of rising on or before 5 A.M. every morning to implement the 20/20/20 formula, you can increase your personal productivity. He calls it the 'Victory hour.' If you can judiciously follow the 20/20/20 rule over time, you will become smarter, agile, more self-confident, and experience a boost in creativity.

Sharma's Victory Hour 20/20/20 Formula

To increase personal productivity here is how to utilize your 'Victory Hour':

- Get out of bed by 5 A.M. (You can start by using the traditional alarm clock to help wake you up).
- Exercise and meditate for 20 minutes.
- Strategize and plan your day for 20 minutes.
- Read a book or online material to hone your skills or to learn something new in your field.

How Waking Up By 5 A.M. Can Increase Personal Productivity

Mental Alertness

Waking up early and working your way through the 5 A.M. club will help give you the needed boost to start the day. At such early hours of the day, most people are still asleep; therefore, you are not likely to face distractions. You can concentrate, feel at ease with yourself, and introspect about your goals.

Exercising every morning also has its own mental and physical health benefits for your body. The ability to manage your body weight will give you the feeling of being in charge. Daily exercises not only make you alert but put you in the right mood to face your day. Your body releases chemicals that help you to relax, de-stress, and possibly fight depression. See chapter seven for more details on habits to increase your physical and mental energy.

Expand Your Knowledge Base

Devoting your first few minutes of waking up daily to reading, I must say it is a powerful way to start the day. What one skill or knowledge do you need to acquire to help advance your career or personal goal?

Reading at least 20 minutes every day can impact your life greatly. People who read specific books for a few minutes daily have an increased chance of becoming leaders in their industry.

Reading, just like exercise, improves your cognitive abilities. It increases your learning power and develops your analytical and judgment skills. It is an excellent tool for boosting your intelligence and brainpower. Reading also improves your concentration level.

Feel Rejuvenated and Motivated

Starting your day in top spirit, you can achieve little successes such as exercise, reading, and more. This feeling helps to motivate you for bigger accomplishments all through the day. If you excel at little things, you get this 'I can do it' feeling. It increases your level of optimism and energy all day long. And before you realize it, you are conquering seemingly insurmountable problems.

"Motivation is what gets you started, habits are what keeps you going." - Jim Ryun

Increases Your Self-discipline

Self-discipline is one of the habits of highly successful people. Achieving anything meaningful in your personal or career life will not come cheaply. It takes tenacity, courage, and a strong push to achieve anything great. To wake up early during the cold winter takes resilience. To read daily takes practice and a strong will. To exercise daily for 30 minutes without skipping any day or stopping takes commitment.

To carry out daily tasks that will advance your career or personal growth takes discipline. Doing it at the right time and in the right manner takes even more discipline. Discipline requires both physical and mental strength.

"Watch your thoughts, they become your words; watch your words, they become your actions, watch your actions, they become your habits, watch your habits, they become your character, watch your character, it becomes your destiny." -Lao Tzu

10 Early Morning Rituals to Boost Personal and Work Productivity

What habits or traits do you think can help you achieve success in your career or personal life? You must learn the necessary skills for personal productivity. However, before you can become a top performer, here are some traits or habits highly successful people have:

They Get Adequate Sleep

The National Sleep Foundation says adult needs seven to nine hours of sleep daily for a healthy life. To be in the best frame of mind in the morning, you need adequate sleep. Being sleep deprived will reduce your concentration level at work. Therefore, to be at your optimum, you must have a regular sleep time.

Most high achievers get into bed early so they can feel energized and ready for the next day's tasks.

Get Out of Bed Early

Highly efficient people have specific sleeping and waking times. Some of them get out of bed as early as 3:45 A.M. to 4 A.M. Others start their day at either 5 or 6 A.M. At first, you might need the help of an alarm clock to get out of bed early, but with time, your body will adjust to this new routine. As if automated, you will wake up at about the same time daily.

Getting out of bed early each day gives you an excellent time for exercise, spiritual pursuits, mental development, and more.

Meditation Time

Highly efficient people understand the power of reflection. Meditation or reflection time helps you maximize the usage of your brainpower. If you do not know how to start, using a daily meditation app can help you establish a meditation routine. Daily meditation can also reduce stress, fight depression, help you relax, and deal with chronic pain.

Research by Wake Forest Baptist University shows that meditation can reduce pain by 40%. Meanwhile, taking morphine painkillers will achieve 25% pain reduction. According to NPR, meditation can reduce stress and blood pressure. It also increases a person's problem-solving skills, overall wellbeing, career, and personal relationships.

Research for the National Institute of Health and published by the U.S. National Library of Medicine reports that meditation can reduce cognition loss for the aged.

Avoid Coffee Straight From Bed

It's always tempting to gulp down your favorite brand of coffee first thing after waking up. More so, when the weather becomes freezing, the temptation doubles. However, highly successful people understand the importance of resisting the urge for a hot cup of caffeine first thing in the morning. On his way to the office each day, CEO of Twitter and Square, Jack Dorsey, says he stops at the coffee shop for his favorite coffee. However, he begins his day with exercise, then meditation before leaving for the office.

Scientific findings show that consuming caffeine first thing in the morning will block off the energy-boosting benefits. Therefore, your first java cup should come much later, say 9 A.M.

Take Delight In Workouts

I have addressed the importance of exercise and what it does to the body and psyche. Top performers across different industries have a clear understanding of how exercise can help them maintain optimal performance. Exercise helps rejuvenate the body, circulates blood faster, and keeps one mentally alert.

It does not have to be a rigorous activity and can be fun, light exercise. A brisk walk, swimming, dancing, and jogging. Any physical activity that helps your heart beat faster or blood to circulate will do.

They Organize Their Schedule for the Day

Yes, some powerful corporate individuals employ personal assistants to run their schedules, but highly successful people also check through and organize their schedules personally. Organizing your schedule helps to ensure your day goes as planned with fewer hiccups.

Once they prioritize the day's activities, it helps successful people to work in an orderly manner. They have a clear idea of what it is they want to achieve by the end of each day. Even when there are setbacks or interruptions, it becomes easier to track their progress.

Highly successful people organize their schedules to help them devote their most productive time of the day to their most critical task in line with their goals.

Healthy Eating Habits

Breakfast is one of the most important meals of the day. And high flyers understand the importance of eating breakfast for productivity's sake. Breakfast comes after the long fast from your last meal yesterday. Therefore, your body needs the meal to serve as fuel. You will feel a lot better eating and eating right to face the tasks of the day.

Sometimes, you get excited or do not feel the need to eat breakfast. So, you feel tempted to skip the first meal of the day. However, like Richard Branson, CEO of Virgin Group, says, you can eat something light to start the day. Fruits, whole grains, carbohydrates, proteins, and more should be ideal.

Dress Simply

Highly successful people tend to spend less time trying to figure out what to wear each day. They would rather invest the energy on more productive things than create mental stress from clothing. What most successful people do is to create a selection of simple clothing. They wear exciting color blends, sneakers, or easy footwear, as well as mix-and-match outfits. With such great combinations, it makes it easy for these CEOs and busy executives to pick their clothing daily. For instance, Facebook CEO Mark Zuckerberg told the Independent that he wears a particular collection of clothing to simplify his dressing and conserve his mental energy for the day's job.

Mark is popular for his jeans, gray t-shirt and sweatshirt. Other tech billionaires wear simple clothing too. Steve Jobs wore a turtleneck sweater and black jeans often. Snap CEO Evan Spiegel wears a white v-neck t-shirt with black jeans and white sneakers. Sundar Pichai, Google CEO prefers a simple track jacket, jeans and sneakers, Jack Dorsey wears his regular jeans, black round neck t-shirt, and sneakers. Looking smart doesn't have to cost very much or take all the time in the world. However, wear appropriate clothing and appear smart to boost your confidence.

Create a Work Pattern

How best to tackle the tasks of the day remains an issue in the front burner, eliciting varied opinions. While some people start the day by attending to smaller tasks like reading emails, letters, etc., others begin with the most challenging projects and then narrow them down. However, whichever works for you, ensure the first one hour of work is a productive one.

After prioritizing the tasks for the day, I start my work schedule with smaller jobs that do not require so much time to accomplish. However, these tasks can impact my bottom line for the day. Activities like checking my emails, letters, other messages, and more, usually come up when sorting the things I need to commence work. Once I have the documents and tools I need on my table, I launch into the more significant tasks of the day.

The more significant tasks might take another 3 to 5 hours or more to clear from my table. During work hours, I only read and respond to work-related emails at a specific time. However, during my social or casual breaks, I take out time to check emails and social media feeds when I need to take my mind off work for a few minutes.

Multitask

Although research shows that multitasking reduces efficiency levels at work, successful people exploit it in their routines. For instance, the New York Times reports that Microsoft Founder Bill Gates watches DVDs while exercising to continue learning. Personally, the restroom is a desirable place for reflecting or reading for me. It helps me to relax, reflect on past activities, and come up with great ideas on how to resolve some life issues. I not only empty my bowels but gain fresh insight into a task at hand.

Tips for Getting the Best From Sharma's 5 A.M. Club

- To get adequate sleep at night, try to switch off all of your technology gadgets, like your phones and tablets. I know this can prove difficult for some, but you need to have fewer distractions. Facebook CEO Sheryl Sandberg says switching off her phones at night is an excellent way to rest and avoid distractions.
- Make efforts to relax appropriately before bedtime so you can sleep with ease. For example, avoid eating heavy meals for one or two hours before bedtime.
- It helps if you have the right ambiance and lighting to sleep well at night. Therefore, avoid too much light in your room by switching off the bright lights. If you must leave the light on, then go for colored or warm lights.
- If you are new to waking up early, please take it slowly. Try waking up 15-30 minutes earlier than your usual time. After three days, you can increase your wake up time to between 45 minutes and one hour to achieve the 5 A.M. goal. This strategy will help reduce the strain on your body at first.
- Strive to maintain a routine with exercises. Instead of heavy sessions of one hour or more per day, make them light exercise sessions of maybe 30 minutes daily. The goal is not to wear you out or make it burdensome, but exciting.
- Take the liberty to wear whatever clothing your organization's culture permits, but always look for the best ways to combine colors and clothing to simplify your life.
- If your work schedule starts much later, the 8 A.M. club might be more appropriate for you instead of the 5 A.M. Club. Stick to what helps you increase personal productivity using Sharma's 20/20/20 formula.

Joining the 5 A.M. club gives you the time to take charge of your day. You have ample time to ruminate on issues and use the power of imagination to design or visualize your day. You can spend more time learning or doing research on the things you need to actualize your goals. That will help boost your energy to accomplish much.

Chapter Summary

This chapter looked at how your morning hours can affect personal productivity. Robin Sharma's 5 A.M. Club was used as a prototype to help you increase your performance. Take-homes from this chapter include:

- Highly successful people possess work habits that help them excel.
- Robin Sharma's 5 A.M. club breaks down what you should do during the first hour of waking up.
- Work out your days with Sharma's 20/20/20 formula.
- Exercise for the first twenty minutes, plan your day with another twenty minutes and study for the last twenty minutes.
- The study time allows you to learn a new skill or improve your skills in your career path.
- Studying for at least twenty minutes every day will help boost personal productivity.
- To excel at the 5 A.M. club, you need to balance your sleeping and waking times. Do not deny yourself adequate sleep because you need sufficient sleep to meet your goals. Instead, adjust your sleeping time to cover any shortfall in sleep time.
- Waking up quite early to start your day increases your mental alertness.
- The 5 A.M. club teaches you how to incorporate discipline into your day, which is something highly successful people do.
- Meditation is an integral part of your life and work schedule as it helps fine-tune your life, setting it up for progress.

In the next chapter, we shall be looking at how to create a personal Kanban to help you prioritize and organize tasks efficiently.

CHAPTER THREE

Create Your Personal Kanban to Prioritize and Organize Tasks

Life can sometimes become more complicated than you desire. Attending to customers, going through the motions of a 9 to 5 job, coping with the enormous bills at home, and more, all tend to make life hectic. We try to find answers about how to organize our priorities or how many tasks we can handle each day or week. We struggle with what tasks to take care of first and what other tasks to delegate.

Whether it is a small, medium, or large scale organization, prioritizing will always remain a veritable tool for success. Achieving personal productivity at work, academics, or with personal relationships requires the ability to organize tasks effectively. That's precisely why you need to understand how to create a personal Kanban for personal and workplace goals.

What Is Personal Kanban About?

The Personal Kanban is a model developed by Jim Benson and Tonianne DeMaria Barry. Kanban is a commonly used software by Agile IT experts to prioritize important tasks and engaging tasks, as well as to maximize time. It is an abridged and easy-to-use version of the Kanban methods designed to help improve your productivity. Personal Kanban allows individuals, either professionals or students, to become more efficient. Jim Benson's idea of personal Kanban is to simplify your life and take away the hassles of everyday living. Trying to take on too much can prove disastrous, and there is only so much an individual can handle alone. Hence, a lot of tasks get done shabbily or are left hanging for too long.

Jim and Tonianne's Kanban approach shows you how to prioritize your tasks by entering them into the system as *backlog* or *ready*. It makes it easier to determine the tasks that are actually of higher priority. With personal Kanban, you can track your work progress at the end of each week. You can identify the completed tasks and pending ones.

The personal Kanban involves a simple visualization of all of your responsibilities utilizing a whiteboard (or post-it notes) to indicate progression. To excel at prioritizing, you can create a structure for your tasks, creating three columns on the whiteboard. Each column will cover a specific category of tasks: *backlog* (which is ready), *doing*, and *done*.

To take control of your life, the personal Kanban is a powerful tool. Moreover, it works for every type of responsibility and goal-setting need to enhance workflow.

Why You Should Prioritize Tasks

Prioritization has to do with deciding on what activity is the most important to your goal so that you can attend to it first. It's the process of arranging tasks based on their order of relevance to your day-to-day goals or objectives.

More Value for Your Time

Time is a limited resource made available to everyone equally as 24 hours a day, 7 days a week, and 365 days in a year. Sometimes people spend their time on less valuable things. Not that those things are not essential, but they might not add as much value to your bottom line.

To increase your productivity, you need to spend more time doing things that are not only important, but also not as urgent. Learning to prioritize your time using the Kanban model will help you to get more value for the time you spend working.

Better Organized and Focused

Instead of doing things haphazardly, do a few things at a time, but in a better way. Personal Kanban teaches us to do the right work at the appropriate time. With a to-do list or a well-laid-out Kanban plan, you can organize your personal and work goals. It will help you to break down your weekly and monthly goals into smaller daily tasks.

Once you can achieve this structure, you become more focused on achieving your goals.

Increases Productivity and Profitability

With your personal Kanban, you should experience an improvement in your productivity. Increased productivity will result in a higher profit. Spending quality time on the things that produce a higher result in your career naturally leads to more profit and success.

Basic Principles of the Personal Kanban

The personal Kanban thrives on two basic principles, which are:

- Visualizing your work.
- Limiting your work progress.

Visualize Your Work

Visualizing your work is an excellent way to move concepts or other hectic, work-related activity into simple actions. Research has shown that the human brain responds faster and better to images or visuals than to words by at least 90%. Also, the human mind can process images 60,000 times faster than it can process text. Therefore, the Kanban works intrinsically as a visual task planning platform. It helps you visualize your tasks and simplify the task implementation process.

Limiting Your Work Progress

As a human, we sometimes try to act like superhumans with the ability to do more than we are capable of. We take on several tasks at the same time and end up with shoddy quality work. Recent research confirms that the human brain cannot carry out multiple tasks successfully at optimal levels. Hence, you will discover that some tasks get done better while others turn out badly.

When you limit your work progress, it doesn't mean denying yourself the opportunity to do more. Limiting your work progress makes it easier to focus on specific tasks and see them through to completion. Limited work progress makes it necessary to take on responsibilities that you can finish over time and stick through to the end. It takes away the problem of having several unfinished projects, breeding frustration.

Limiting work progress helps you give more value to your time in prioritizing each task before you. You learn to prioritize tasks and identify the most critical job to deal with each time.

The Personal Kanban mantra encourages you to start and finish a task before proceeding to the next. Your productivity will improve when not running several projects at the same time (multitasking).

It helps if you don't have to handle every job. Other strategies to get more done include delegation or outsourcing of tasks, instead of trying to do everything yourself. When you first get on the personal Kanban plan, your initial reaction will be a feeling of awkwardness. Most times, it feels like your life is under external control. If you are a person who gets personal satisfaction from juggling several activities, it will at first feel like you are under-performing. The impression that you are getting less work done is not accurate. Once you allow yourself to live within the WIP Limits (Work-In-Process), you will discover you have achieved far more over time. The results will be of exceptional quality and better for your corporate and personal goals. Even your clients and family will notice the improvement.

Negative Effects of Multitasking

I have been a victim of trying to multitask on several separate activities before. When I began my consulting career, I tried juggling the preparation of a business plan development task, seminar paper, and coordinating a social event. All the while I was making calls, sending emails, and trying to gather more facts for my business plan. I also had to make calls to caterers, media teams, event decorators, and more, so the event could go smoothly. Well, It all ended in a fiasco as I left out some vital aspects of the event. Only last-minute face-saving measures saved the day. As for my business plan, it wasn't ready for pitching at the appropriate time. And that's the reason you need to limit your work progress using the personal Kanban board. Some of the adverse effects of multitasking include:

Lowers Your IQ

Research conducted by the University of London shows that multitasking tends to lower your IQ by at least 17%. The effect of multitasking is similar to a person who has smoked marijuana or had a sleepless night. The individual ends up storing fewer details from the multitasked sessions.

Reduces Brain Efficiency

The American Psychological Association published an article in the Journal of Experimental Psychology on multitasking. It indicated that multitasking reduces the brain's ability to process issues faster. To process multiple tasks means shifting the brain's gear from one item to another, and that takes time. The brain has to make the shift by turning off one cognitive rule for another goal.

What's more, research at the University of Sussex states that multitasking can impair the brain.

How to Use the Personal Kanban Board

The personal Kanban board is comprised of 3 distinct columns that help you prioritize your tasks. The three columns contain the 'To Do,' 'Doing,' and 'Done' sections. The 'To Do' section is also known as the 'Option.'

Column 1: To-Do or Option

Under column one, write down every goal or task you have in mind to do. There are two strategies to adopt here. Write down 3-5 of your most critical tasks in the column. The second strategy involves writing down all of the assignments you intend on carrying out, no matter how many. When it's time to implement, you then decide the tasks to advance to the next column.

Things to include in column one can consist of work and personal goals. Workplace tasks include meeting with suppliers by Monday at 10 A.M., submitting a proposal to a specific client by noon, paying for insurance, drafting letters to prospective clients, replying to emails and inquiry, etc.. For personal tasks, you could include seeing your

SUPERCHARGE PRODUCTIVITY HABITS

physician by Wednesday at 2 P.M., taking your puppy out for a walk every evening, attending your kids' valedictorian ceremony on Friday by 10 A.M., etc..

With this in mind, you can create a custom plan for your 'To Do' column to cover workplace tasks and personal tasks. Personal responsibilities can include spiritual, financial, health, education, or social goals. When selecting a job to complete, focus on those that take you faster toward your long-term goals. Following the personal Kanban board will make you focus on the most important tasks instead of the most urgent ones for completion.

Column 2: Doing or In Progress

Each task should already have a timeline for execution. Once it is time to execute a particular job, you transfer that task from the 'To Do' to the 'In Progress' column. For instance, once you want to accomplish any item under your personal goal, such as seeing your doctor, you move it to 'In Progress' under column two. However, avoid adding too many items into the 'In Progress' column to avoid over-burdening yourself. If you somehow feel you have more than you can handle, please feel free to move some items back to the 'To Do' column once again. It is better to finish a smaller amount of tasks under column two before transferring more from column one.

Before this, however, you need to set up a WIP (Work-In-Progress) Limit. The WIP Limit refers to the maximum or allowed amount of tasks you should handle per time. These tasks should go to the 'In Progress' column two. Thus, you deliberately force yourself to focus all of your energy on accomplishing only those tasks.

And in most cases, those tasks make up what you can achieve with success. Remember, create standard WIP Limits and always stick to it.

Column 3: Done

Only a completed task should be included in the 'Doing' or 'Done' column. However, some jobs require a follow-up or can come up again in your list of tasks. At that point, you can re-introduce a task into column one before the 'Doing' list. That means, if you have seen your doctor this week, it should move to the 'Done' column, but if you have another appointment to see your doctor on a new date, then it can come under the 'To Do' column one again.

Every time a task successfully translates from column one, 'To Do' to column three, 'Done,' it evokes a feeling of fulfillment. That feeling helps to inspire you to get more tasks done. Following this process on the Kanban board will make the picture clearer and more exciting. Over time, you will discover an increase in your productivity level. The passion for getting more done will become stronger.

Creating Your Personal Kanban Board

You can create your personal Kanban board with ease. All you require is a whiteboard and Post-Its or stickies to begin making your board. Also, you can create a Microsoft Excel sheet or Word document containing the required columns and rows. Create a note with your preferred option with the three columns: 'To Do,' 'In Progress' (Doing), and 'Done.'

Besides using a whiteboard, you can make use of online task management tools like the free Trello tool or Asana. These tools allow you to create tasks and prioritize them.

Guidelines for Using the Personal Kanban

- Avoid overcrowding column one, 'To Do.' However, if it becomes necessary and due to the volume of tasks at hand, then include the tasks, by all means.

- Create a specific timeline for achieving each of these tasks so that you know when to move them to column two.
- Ensure that you do a scale of preference by placing the most critical job at the top of your 'To Do' column.
- It is also possible to have a separate column between columns one and two. Call this column 'Prioritized Tasks,' or column 1A. If you have too many tasks in column one, move the high-value tasks to 'Prioritized Tasks,' leaving the others for the general-purpose tasks. You can intermittently move tasks into column 1A before they get to the 'In Progress' stage.
- Regularly review and update your Kanban board. In line with your goal, the Kanban board should be reviewed daily or weekly to identify disparity or to update activities.
- If the tasks become more than your new schedule can cope with, then learn to outsource or delegate some tasks.

Simple Tips for Prioritizing Tasks

- Write down all of your tasks in a single location (the personal Kanban).
- Organize or prioritize your tasks using the personal Kanban. To effectively prioritize your tasks before writing them on the Personal Kanban, you can categorize them into the following:

Do — Tasks that require urgent attention.
Defer — Task that should be done later.
Delegate — Tasks that you need others to handle or outsource.
Delete — Tasks that might not offer much value or have stayed too long on the list.

The Eisenhower Matrix can help you to determine what should be in your To-Do list.

- Choose between planning the task for each day the evening before or early in the morning. If you revise the assignments for each day in the evening, then it will be easier to plan for the next day's tasks too.

- Be proactive about how you handle each day's job. Take the driver's seat by not reacting to activities, but by determining how each day's task should proceed.
- Create spare time for family, friends, and other non-work related activities. Relaxing and socializing can put you in a better frame of mind to get more tasks done productively.
- Be as flexible as things might need to be. Assignments that are not completed can be placed in the personal Kanban for another day.
- Pay more attention to those tasks that will have more effect on your long-term goals. Focus on the tasks that give you more results and not just the ones that are keeping you busy.
- You can have an accountability partner, someone who will hold you to your goals.

Chapter Summary

This chapter focused extensively on the following:

- Trying to cope with each day's activities can take its toll on your productivity, which is why you need to understand how to prioritize your life.
- Your personal and career goals can create a source of conflict; therefore, the personal Kanban can help prioritize your tasks better.
- The Personal Kanban is a productivity or task management system that allows individuals to prioritize each task for accomplishment.
- Prioritizing tasks helps you get more value out of limited time to make you more productive.
- The two basic principles of the Personal Kanban include visualizing your work and limiting your work progress.

- Visualizing your work involves creating a mental block by which your key performance can improve.
- Research shows that images have a 93% greater chance of making an impression on the human mind than text.
- Limiting your work progress is an attempt to say 'no' to taking on more tasks than you can on average complete in a day or week.
- WIP Limit refers to setting a specific number of tasks to accomplish without overburdening yourself or hindering your productivity level.
- Multitasking can result in less productivity.
- To use the Personal Kanban, you need to create three columns containing 'To Do,' 'In Progress' (or Doing), and 'Done.'
- The To-Do column should contain 3-5 (or more) tasks you need to accomplish in line with your goals.
- The In Progress or Doing column should list the jobs you are now ready to execute.
- The Done column should contain all of the completed assignments.
- It is best if you prioritize your tasks beginning with the most important, rather than the most urgent.
- Move each task from column one to the other as you make progress.
- The Personal Kanban should be made simple and not complicated.
- It helps if you have a whiteboard and Post-Its to create your Personal Kanban.
- Review the Personal Kanban regularly to update and improve it.

In the next chapter, you will learn the dangers of procrastination and how to overcome it.

CHAPTER FOUR:

How to Overcome Procrastination

Procrastination is a thief of time, like Edward Young rightly called it. In terms of productivity, procrastination is one major factor that hinders people from taking giant strides in life. It prevents people from making the right decisions at the right times or taking prompt actions toward achieving specific goals. In many ways, procrastination has kept a whole lot of individuals in the trap of working harder rather than smarter.

Opportunities tend to slip off the fingers when the time that should have gone into productive use slowly slips away.

Procrastination does not necessarily mean laziness, but a delay in carrying out a course. Based on research, Piers Steel states that nearly 95% of humans procrastinate to varying degrees. Many find themselves slaves to this habitual attitude and wish they could overcome procrastination. Even personal dreams and efforts end up a victim of procrastination. People run this cycle for years without any meaningful action toward one's desired goals.

Procrastination can hurt productivity. It often results in low self-esteem, depression, frustration, inadequacies, and guilt. Rather than beating yourself up, deliberate and concrete steps toward overcoming this trait should be the focal point. The fight against procrastination requires action. A procrastinator who wants to make headway in life must understand that the time to start is now. Overcoming procrastination is possible, but is a gradual process only achievable if you are willing to take the necessary steps.

The following steps will help you to overcome the scourge of procrastination:

Step 1: Admit It, You Do Procrastinate

The first step toward any self-actualizing pursuit is to identify that you have a problem that needs urgent attention or assistance. Telling yourself the truth makes the journey a rather short one. Putting off things indefinitely or getting distracted on a focal activity is not a healthy lifestyle for the highly successful. Here are some ways to check if procrastination has become your lifestyle:

Leaving Important Tasks Undone

Many people still fall victim to leaving the important stuff undone due to distraction and the inability to prioritize. People sometimes start a task with a lot of enthusiasm and then, due to pressure, distraction, challenges, and more, they abandon these tasks halfway. When something else comes up, they jump on that and forget what they were working on. If this act becomes habitual, then procrastination will become a lifestyle.

Abandoning High Priority Tasks for Something Less Critical

Some schools of thought believe dealing with the smaller tasks will give you the motivation to take on bigger assignments. Another school of thought believes the best part of your day should go to dealing with the most challenging tasks. However, some people take on smaller tasks but later push the bigger ones to oblivion. The danger here is that the high priority tasks end up not getting any attention.

Besides, pursuing the less critical tasks while precious time slips away can be counter-productive. And once you get accustomed to responding to urgent and pressing issues first, instead of learning how to deal with essential tasks, it becomes a habit that is hard to break.

Using Your Time for Others to Your Detriment

It's good to help and to try to solve work-related issues for others. However, allowing others to determine how your day goes is a recipe for failure.

Getting caught in the web of doing tasks for friends and family first could be a real time-waster out of your limited work hours. While it is not a bad thing to assist family, friends, and colleagues, it should not be to the detriment of your own work. Let all assistance go into your To-Do list so that it can fit into your program, rather than superseding your other tasks.

Waiting for the Right Time, Mood, or Condition

It is an illusion to assume that there is the right time, mood, or condition to get anything meaningful done. And too many people have become a victim of their own emotions and timing. Waiting for the right condition, or the 'perfect' time that never seems to come has plunged many into wasted years of not achieving anything tangible. Your mood could create an excuse for procrastination, stating the time is not right, or that all of the factors are not in place for smooth execution.

However, the truth is, there will never be a perfect time or the right mood to get anything done. Also, the conditions for accomplishing your goals might not always align. For this reason, you are in the best position to dictate to yourself what the right mood, time, and condition should be. As long as you want to, all excuses will give way to you.

"He that is good for making excuses is seldom good for anything else." – Benjamin Franklin.

"The trouble with excuses in that they become inevitably difficult to believe after they've been used a couple of times."
– Scott Spencer

Spending More Time on Less Important Activities

All tasks deserve your attention, but not all jobs require equal attention. Therefore, the ability to know the amount of time to devote to each task will determine your level of productivity. This is the formula used by top performers to excel. Reading and replying to emails is an important task, but might not require as much time as developing your seminar paper. For customer support staff, reading and responding to emails could carry more importance than writing the daily report during critical work hours. That means, for each person, specific tasks carry more significance than others. The ability to spend time appropriately on the right jobs will determine the extent of your productivity.

You No Longer Trust Yourself

When people get into the habit of breaking promises to themselves, trust becomes impossible. When there is a lack of confidence in one's ability, their productivity will begin to dwindle. It becomes impossible to find the motivation to do anything since they believe the tasks are not likely to see fruition, and so they give up.

Giving Up Easily

Giving up at the slightest challenge can become a good excuse to procrastinate. Once people face situations that look insurmountable, the tendency to quit becomes higher. Many times, the thought of going back becomes a great struggle. With too much time gone by, an overwhelming feeling begins to set in, leading to more procrastination.

Step 2: Find Out Why You Procrastinate and Deal With It

Everyone has what it takes to excel in implementing tasks, but most people lack the discipline and knowledge to make things work. The irony is that most people do not admit to themselves that one of their most significant problems is procrastination. Some of those who do know cannot explain the reason they procrastinate or lack the discipline to overcome it.

Writing yourself off is not the way to go; you have to work it out. However, you first need to identify the real cause of your procrastination. Here are some factors responsible for procrastination:

Lack of Interest

Once a person is not passionate about what they do, the tendency to procrastinate becomes higher. Delays or complete avoidance become the order of the day when you feel low about what you do. The only way out of such a logjam is to find your sparks.

For managers, assigning a task to somebody should follow specific criteria in order to succeed. Looking at a person's perspective on a task could go a long way in determining if they are the right person for the task. Here is what to do:

Decide On the Most Suitable Person for the Job

Delegating the responsibility to a person who is more likely to get it done is critical. Some people have a high tolerance level for particular tasks and assigning it to such people will result in bigger gains.

Break the Work Into Bits of Tasks

If one's tolerance level is low, breaking the job into smaller components will help. Try to concentrate on smaller chunks per time.

Schedule Time

Designating a particular time to get the task started is a good idea. Once you commence the duties, focus on completing those tasks before picking up another. Doing this will increase productivity and reduce having too many uncompleted tasks.

Lack of Motivation

The best way to go about the motivation factor is actually to start the task. Waiting for the right motivation might take a while and delay the job longer than is necessary. Once a project begins and you start seeing some level of success, the motivation level tends to increase. We will talk more about motivation in chapter eight.

Dealing with Personal Issues

Personal challenges can stand in the way of getting things done. When life's other challenges arise, the ability to handle them properly will determine whether or not it will harm your work. Therefore, the ability to manage your emotions in the face of challenges will determine the quality of work done.

However, in challenging situations, it is best to create a priority for managing tasks, as well as to break them into smaller chunks that you can handle. Focusing so much on your challenges will only result in a drop in productivity, but trying to look ahead will give you the energy to keep working.

Deficiency in Skills

People let their goals slide due to their tolerance level, focus, energy levels, or a lack of one skill or the other. Because of this, you must develop skills in the areas that will help you to advance your goals. Mentoring also provides an avenue to learn from those who have excelled in the same field as yours. Reading is another means to develop yourself or to learn from others within your area. The point is, if you must overcome the issue of procrastination, all activities that trigger procrastination need to go—and one way to fight procrastination is self-development.

Taking a look at the bigger picture, if procrastination is stealing your time, what will you do to stop it? Self-development can serve as a fortification against procrastination.

Fear

Fear is oppositional to faith and courage. People sometimes leave essential tasks undone due to the fear of the volume of the tasks. Unfortunately, delaying the job will only complicate issues as you run out of time.

There are too many fears in people's lives. There is the fear of failure, of the unknown, of negative feedback, and of rejection. For many, the fear of being evaluated or getting negative feedback denies them the zest to even start. Feedback is an integral part of measuring how productive you are and should not create a source of fear. See feedback as a tool to improve your productivity.

Whatever the form of fear is, this has hindered many from taking bold steps into starting new projects, moving to the next level in their personal and career life.

Feeling Anxious or Overwhelmed

Anxiety is a major cause of procrastination. Once a person is worried about certain things, they tend to procrastinate, and as the task delays, it leads to further anxiety over the non-completion of the task, while the cause of the tension remains.

As the events become more ugly, and task after task begins piling up, there is a tendency for you to feel overwhelmed. If you do not take prompt action to resolve the issues, seek assistance with the tasks, or complete tasks, depression can set in. Anxiety can create a crippling effect or mindset. However, with concerted effort, you can get things back on track.

Perceived Lack of Control

When people feel they are not in control of the circumstances of their lives, the tendency to procrastinate increases. Such people view external influences, such as the environment or other people, as being in control of their circumstances. Feeling helpless can cause depression or a feeling of worthlessness and cause the victim to delay tasks.

A sense of not being appreciated by a critical boss or parent can make one feel helpless. This feeling can slow down work progress or result in low quality work.

Step 3: Toughen-Up Against Procrastination: Strategies to Help

To overcome procrastination as a habit takes a conscious and deliberate effort. Research shows that it takes around 66 days to develop a new habit or to drop an existing one. Therefore, to achieve this goal, you must be able to unlearn and relearn. Unlearn the old way of doing things and relearn the new way to get things done. Changing habits doesn't happen overnight but requires a process involving persistence and patience.

How to Overcome Procrastination

You can overcome procrastination using the following strategies over time:

Learn to Forgive Past Procrastination

Don't be too harsh on yourself; let go of past procrastination. The inability to complete a specific task in the past or the non-attainment of a goal can be a severe mind stump. More often than not, people tend to allow past failures to stand in the way when trying to move ahead. However, holding onto the past will only increase the chance of a recurrence. If you must excel, then you have to find a way to let go of past failures.

The first thing to do is to realize it is just a weakness. As long as it is a habit, you can unlearn the same way you developed the habit of procrastinating.

Establish Your Goals

Get clearly defined goals and SMART goals in line with your personal and career objectives. Setting unrealistic goals can lead to further frustration, making your fight against procrastination difficult. To make your goals achievable, remember to write them down, as well as to set timelines for achieving them. There are several tools in this book to help you with setting realistic goals and seeing them come to pass, so keep reading to know more.

Commit to the Task

As stated earlier in this book, taking action is as necessary as setting goals. If you set goals and will not commit the needed time and resources to actualize them, then they will amount to nothing. You must make a concerted effort to develop skills, find out what you need, draw up a plan of action, and pursue the goals vigorously.

Focus On the End

Having a mindset of completion can help motivate you toward attaining your goals. You can focus on the outcome by visualizing what you want to achieve through that goal. But to succeed, you must have already drawn up a plan of action to achieve that goal. In this way, focusing on the end helps you to visualize achieving the goal.

In addition, focusing on a task will not remove the challenges that go with every job, but having a plan of action and a well-written goal will help keep you motivated and adjust your strategy as the need arises. To help you focus better, all distractions have to be dealt with to succeed.

Celebrate Small Successes

Promise yourself a reward for the completion of every milestone and give it to yourself. After all, you deserve it! It could be a treat to your favorite eatery at lunchtime. The excitement will boost your spirit when small successes are visible. If you do not celebrate yourself, who will?

Be Responsible for Someone

Asking someone to check up on you and your activities can be helpful. Knowing that you are answerable to someone else will boost your morale to complete tasks. Where a personal buddy is not readily available, applications like remote bliss can be a valuable tool.

Peer pressure provides an effective support system. Once friends and family are in the know about your goals, they are bound to keep asking about the progress.

Act On the Go

As soon as you receive new projects, place a priority on them by not allowing them to linger for so long without assigning them. By that, I mean work them into your To-Do list with a timeline and a plan of action. When you do that with each new task, you will feel more confident and in charge of your day as nothing gets past you. As a technique to avoid procrastination, never leave any tasks unattended.

Identify your most and least productive time, and schedule high and low priority tasks to fit these timings. Knowing when you are most productive will help you focus on the more important tasks on your To-Do list. Completing critical goals makes working on others less difficult or frustrating.

Rephrase Your Internal Thought Processes

What you say to yourself, over time, becomes what you believe. The phrases you use will either inspire or put a clog on the wheels of progress. Phrases like 'have to' or 'need to' suggest that one has no choice at all. Such comments alone can demotivate. Whereas phrases like 'I must' and 'I choose to' are pointers to the fact that you are in control.

Eliminate Distractions

Distractions are the greatest enemy to achieving your goals, and they can come in different forms: television, emails, social media, phone calls, as well as family and friends. Distractions can consume your most productive time, leaving you with unaccomplished dreams.

A good plan at minimizing or eliminating distractions will leave you with more time to concentrate on the task at hand. Even if the need arises, you can place your phone on mute and stay off technology tools that can distract you from your job.

Focus On Less Pleasant Tasks First

Deal with any tasks that can drain your energy first, while your energy levels are still high. Leaving energy-draining tasks until later might result in their being left undone. Other less draining jobs will not be so challenging to handle.

Change Your Environment

It might become necessary to have a different environment from the one you are already used to. Environments have a way of impacting your productivity. They can be a source of inspiration or a reason to procrastinate.

Certain conditions make a work environment unpleasant or productive, and they include:

- Hostility
- Poorly-arranged workstations
- Prejudice
- Shortage of work tools and supplies
- Faulty equipment
- Stuffy, damp, hot or cold environments

Procrastination can become second nature or habit. It takes a concerted effort, strong will, dedication, and a plan of action to deal with it. Overcoming your problem of procrastination will come with time, not overnight.

Action is key. Once you understand why you procrastinate and your areas of weakness, then you are on your way to dealing with them. Now, the time has come, will you delay (procrastinate) putting these plans to work?

Chapter Summary

- First, accept that you procrastinate and take concrete steps to overcome it.
- Get an understanding of the things people do that has made procrastination a lifestyle.
- From the list, identify why you are procrastinating and get to work immediately.
- Realize that procrastination is a shortcoming a lot of people have and forgive yourself.
- Choose the best anti-procrastination strategies that best suit you. Be sure they will work for you.
- Having a motivating mindset, focus on the end of the task rather than on the beginning.
- Don't work alone. Make yourself accountable to someone for checks and balances.
- Act as you go. Commit to the task and avoid a build-up that will encourage a relapse into procrastination. Just get into the action plan.
- As much as possible, keep distracting factors away from you. Develop a will not to indulge in them.
- Celebrate every successful milestone with a reward. A personal pat on the back can be highly motivating.
- By all means, change environments if need be. They have a way of putting you in high spirits for maximum output.
- What you perceive is what you believe. Mind the words you say to yourself. Change your internal dialogue to suit your new resolve.

In the next chapter, you will learn about the value of maximizing time and time management hacks.

CHAPTER FIVE

Hacks to Maximize Your Time Management

Time is a limited, but universal resource, and everyone has an equal share of 24 hours daily to accomplish much. However, not everyone makes the best use of their time. If not, how do you explain the fact that some people attain a higher degree of success than some others within the same 24 hour time frame? Does it mean highly successful people spend longer hours working than the less successful? The answer is: no! The simple fact is that some people have learned the art of managing their time more effectively. Others, however, might have more issues with time-wasters in their schedule. Therefore, how do you manage time to increase your productivity?

"Time isn't the main thing; it is the only thing." - Miles Davis

Explosive Time Management Tips for Increased Productivity

Here are time-tested, yet simple time management hacks to help you get on the road to greater efficiency:

Audit Time Spent

When you do a time audit, it will amaze you to discover where the bulk of your time goes. How much time do you spend on work and non-work related activities? How much time do you spend on tasks that will improve your bottom line and push you closer to your goals? How much time goes into checking and responding to emails, social media, and more? You might intend on spending only 30 minutes on emails and social media every morning, but end up spending over an hour.

Start by tracking your activities for a whole week to see areas of time wastage. One of the simplest ways to track your operations is by using time tracking applications like Toggl, RescueTime, or Calendar. At the end of the week, the app report will give you a better idea of how your time flies. Now, you can be in a better position to make the needed adjustments.

Time Each Task and Set Limits

Keeping the deadlines open is a recipe for getting nothing done on time or at all. Setting a timeline or restrictions for each task keeps you from procrastinating or delaying them. Creating buffers around your tasks makes it easier to manage a particular job. For a task that requires several days or weeks to accomplish, breaking them into smaller, manageable daily tasks can help. Each milestone achieved brings you closer to your overall goal.

I use buffers in helping to accomplish a task. When I have a speaking engagement, I like planning weeks ahead. Therefore, I usually create a timeline with buffers to help me complete the seminar paper on schedule. If, for any reason, the paper takes a longer time than scheduled, then it has to wait for another time slot. That's the only way to avoid eating into time for other activities.

However, make sure the timelines are not bogus, but something you can achieve in reality. You can get someone to hold you accountable by letting them know what you want to achieve and the timeframe assigned to achieve it. Your accountability buddy can help ensure you stay on track for success.

"It takes as much energy to wish as it takes to plan."
- Eleanor Roosevelt

Plan Ahead

"Measure twice, cut once" is a popular proverb in the building construction or carpentry world. It focuses on engineers or carpenters getting things right on the first attempt. And that's how valuable planning ahead is to your goals.

Having a plan of action will save you the stress of wandering or focusing on the less critical tasks. Some tasks are more vital to your success than others. Without adequate planning, you can end up achieving very little.

Best Time to Create a Plan or To-Do List:

Start the Night Before

At the end of each day's work can be the perfect time to make plans for the next day's activities. As little as 15-30 minutes is what you need to create a To-Do list of the most important assignments for tomorrow.

The exciting thing about planning ahead the evening before is that it helps you eliminate likely distractions. Doing your plan ahead of tomorrow puts your mind in top gear and readiness for tomorrow's activities. This can also help to motivate you and get you excited about work. It also increases your focus and channels your energy toward your most productive tasks for the day.

Start First Thing In the Morning

While some people prefer planning their day the night before, others do so first thing in the morning. You can make a list of 3 or 5 of your most urgent and important activities for the day. Then, set a timeline on your most productive time to achieve them.

However, always do a review or double-check your plans to avoid errors or mistakes. Any mix up with your schedule or activities can result in wasting more time trying to remedy the situation.

Say No to Multitasking

Multitasking or task hopping is a productivity killer. The erroneous belief that juggling several tasks at the same time will help you get more done is not true. Research confirms that carrying on several tasks at a time can have a negative toll on the human brain. Multitasking can also result in lower quality work. More so, you end up spending a longer time multitasking as your mind tries to make the shift between two tasks.

For this reason, the solution is single-tasking. Make it a habit to start and finish tasks before moving on to the other. You can set timelines, milestones, and timers to put you on the right track, one task at a time. Intentionally develop your mindset to focus on one task.

Protect Your 'In the Zone' Time

What time of the day are you most productive? The best time to schedule a demanding task is at the time you are more alert mentally. You can schedule that time into your calendar or To-Do list.

Protecting your 'in the zone' time is the same as understanding your patterns. We all have habits, but the idea is to pick up healthy habits that help increase personal productivity. Each person has a time of the day they are most productive. The best time to get certain tasks done should be at the time you get your burst of energy. For instance, if you think best in the morning, after working out, after lunchtime, or late at night, then create a schedule around that time. However, it will depend on the type of goal you wish to achieve: personal or workplace.

Science proposes four hours of work a day as all you need. Sounds absurd? Well, it doesn't necessarily mean you only get to execute tasks for four hours and play for twenty hours. It says to focus on the most critical tasks using your most productive hours of four hours in a day. The rest of the hours could go to resolving less demanding tasks.

Keep Meetings on Task

Staff meetings constitute an integral part of strategic planning, re-appraisal, and continuous work assessment. However, to make staff meetings fruitful and productive, they must be streamlined and follow laid down procedures. Allowing a meeting to run without a To-Do list or Agenda might end without concrete decisions being reached. You must provide clear directions for any meeting and set timelines and objectives for each item on the list.

Each meeting must start and end on time. Also, some organizations make it a habit to call meetings too often. You can resolve some issues without meeting with everyone. With the aid of technology, some tools make it easier to disseminate information and get feedback without calling frequent meetings. Tools like Trello, Zoom, Slack, and Asana allow groups to discuss and share ideas without stretching work time. Another strategy could involve scheduling regular weekly or monthly meetings and reports, instead of impromptu meetings.

Create Email Handling Time

Emails can be a major source of distraction, and you must be deliberate about how to handle your messages. As much as important messages can come in, you do not want emails directing how your work flows daily. The problem with responding to emails as they come in is that you become more reactive than in charge of your day. The solution is to have a time scheduled for reading and responding to emails.

To help concentrate on the most productive tasks, I usually have specific times for responding to emails. Usually, two to three times a day is ideal for email handling, but never around your productive time.

One strategy I use is to select the email messages to open, read, and respond to at specific times. When responding, make sure the responses do not exceed five sentences to save time.

Turn Off Notifications

Notifications are quite helpful in keeping you up to date with email and social media messages. They can, however, also serve as a major source of distraction and make you lose focus on important tasks. Important notifications can come from your email or social media feeds, but to manage them properly, only enable those notifications that will help you advance your tasks and goals. Even at that, it still may not be necessary to enable notifications on your PC and all of your smart devices. Such acts only increase the chances for distraction.

Alternatively, you can disable notifications when working on your most demanding tasks. When you complete the tasks, push notification can be enabled again.

Watch Your Social Media Usage

Facebook, Twitter, Instagram, SnapChat, and more is an interesting sport that serves different purposes for people. However, staying on social media for too long can be distracting. Therefore, you need to limit the amount of time spent there deliberately. However, some businesses use it as part of their business tool. If you are a social media manager, run ads, have an eCommerce store, or monitor customer support, create a concrete plan for social media usage.

Whatever your social media needs, have a to-do plan that incorporates it and creates timelines for it. Arrange its usage in a way that allows you to do more productive activities. If it is more of a social tool, then keep it social and civil.

Buffer Up! Cut Yourself Some Slack

Cut yourself some slack by incorporating buffer times into your schedule. You are a human, and your brain needs time to cool off. The human brain, by default, is not a twenty hour fully operational machine. Certain mental and physical functions of the brain need rest so that they can maintain peak performance. Hence, research shows that the brain works critically on average 90-minute per time before a decline. After this time, your brain needs some form of distraction to remain motivated and focused.

It's not a sign of diligence or hard work to remain on your desk all day. Fortunately, other non-critical tasks or activities do crop up in the course of your day, and that may be the best time to attend to them. However, moving from one mentally demanding task or meeting to another isn't a brilliant idea or a productive way to live either. Rather, help your body refuel by meditating, taking a walk, or simply daydreaming. It will help clear your mind.

Besides work, having a buffer time can give you ample time to get to the next meeting early. Your schedule should have such buffers as much as it allows you to get through one activity to the other. It should also allow you time to unwind and rejuvenate. Schedule your activities like this: a big chunk of a task, with bite-sized buffers. About 25 to 30 minutes of buffer-time should be ideal.

Be Fair to Yourself

You are the most vital aspect of your work schedule or task. Without you, there would be no task accomplished; therefore, take good care of yourself. If you fall ill, burn out, or lose your life, someone else will take your place. Yes, your legacy will live on, but your family and friends will have to face the pain of your sudden departure. Even if you do not lose your life, developing health complications will only slow down your productivity and make it impossible for you to pursue your lofty ideas and goals.

Take out time to relax, have fun, exercise regularly, eat healthily, and to spend time with family and friends. Sometimes, it pays to do what pleases you. Be selfish! Take a vacation. In the end, use the motivation and experience to get your brilliant ideas or tasks done.

I have a spacious office with a work table, a small conference room, and a living room. When I go through demanding tasks, sometimes I unwind for a few minutes by relocating to the living room. I can lay on the sofa, allow some distraction by seeing a program on television, listen to music, or a sitcom. I do anything other than work. And when I'm back at my desk, I'm all fired up, ready to go!

Use the 80/20 Rule or Pareto Principle

The 80/20 law states that 80% of your results or successes come from 20% of the effort put into them. So, does that mean you only need to spend 20% of your time working? Or, should you come into work just one day a week, after all, that's 20%. No!

The Pareto principle means you should pay more attention to the critical things that help you achieve success. If you spend more time on the things that give you more results, then you may see your productivity shoot up. So, what happens to the less critical or smaller stuff? Let it go!

You can also apply the Pareto principle to any aspect of your life. Marketers also apply the 80/20 rule. For marketing, 80% of marketing profits come from 20% of the customers. In human resources and employee relations, 80% of the most productive tasks come from 20% of the employees. For self-development and time management, 80% of your successes come from 20% of your efforts or actions.

For this reason, applying the 80/20 principle, you can scale up productivity in the areas that affect your bottom line. It will help you know how to assign tasks to employees and how to help them improve. It can also help you understand what areas to spend more time on and which to improve. For marketing, the Pareto principle can help you streamline your customer base to focus on serving the performing customers. Then, you can work out a strategy on how to convert the non-performing prospects or customers.

10 Bad Habits that Destroy Your Productivity

- Spending too much time on a single task, even when it can take less time.
- Sleeping through the morning hours instead of planning your day.
- Browsing the web without any clear cut plan.
- Not planning or prioritizing your day.
- Working for long stretches of hours, peering into your PC screen without taking a non-work related break.
- Maintaining unhealthy eating habits, like skipping meals or having the wrong diet.
- Waiting for years for the perfect time to start pursuing your goals.
- Making excuses for not pursuing or accomplishing your dreams.
- Only working on urgent tasks and leaving the important or non-urgent tasks undone.

- Leaving tasks until the last minute before executing them.

Chapter Summary

In chapter five, we have looked at the following concepts:

- Time is limited, but everyone has an equal amount of 24 hours daily.
- Successful people share the same number of hours as the less successful, but the differences lie in how the successful manage their time.
- Successful people create a schedule to help manage time effectively.
- Always break down tasks into smaller achievable pieces.
- Draw out your plans ahead, either in the evening before the close of work or morning before the start of work.
- Multitasking is not a sign of efficiency, but only helps in producing lower quality work.
- Avoid spending productive time on social media or emails as it can derail you from achieving your goals.
- Give yourself some non-work related breaks.
- Always buffer up your schedule, so you have short breaks of 25 minutes within each significant task.
- Practice the Pareto principle, or 80/20 rule that says 80% of your success will come from 20% of the effort you invest in it.
- Excessive sleep in the morning hours, spending too much time on a single task, and more, are some of the negative habits affecting your productivity level.

In the next chapter, you will learn about the three pillars of productivity you require to become a top performer.

CHAPTER SIX:

The 3 Pillars of Productivity You Need to Unlock Your Full Potential

You have what it takes to be more productive and enjoy unlimited success. However, it will require a strong desire, decision, action, and a few productivity hacks to succeed. The TEA is a productivity framework that has the potential to move you closer to your goals. It will help you to manage your time, energy, and attention more effectively to overcome the challenges on your way to fulfilling your dreams.

A survey published in the New York Times showed that 81% of Americans have thoughts of writing a book. The study found out that if these people had pursued their dreams, at least 200 million books would have been written. However, only 80,000 people get around to writing and publishing their work annually. The above figure accounts for 0.4% of those who wish to publish their work. The remaining 81% only talk about their dream of writing a book.

What, in essence, actually stops most people from attaining their full potential in life? The simplest way to answer this question is with the TEA framework. The other answer is that those who excel at their craft make taking action on their goals a matter of habit, rather than something on their wish list. They commit to their goals, set a plan of action, and refuse to allow any excuse to stop them from achieving them. Successful people are die-hard doers and not procrastinators.

You will become more productive when you learn how best to manage your time, attention, and energy. So, what is the TEA framework?

TEA: Three Obstacles Framework to Increased Productivity

Obstacles and challenges are real. These three simple categories explain the barriers people face in their pursuit:

- Time
- Energy
- Attention

The TEA framework is a powerful tool that helps individuals self-diagnose the hindrances to attaining their true potential. Once they are able to identify these challenges, then they can better focus on their most important tasks. Usually, such tasks are the ones that will have a massive impact on their bottom line.

Category 1: Energy & Attention, But No Time

Time is an essential factor for success, and anyone who must attain success must know how to manipulate time in their favor. However, those within this category possess the energy, desire, and passion to help them succeed. They believe they do not have enough time to get things done correctly. Thus, they develop the mentality of one who is stuck or trapped. This feeling of inadequacy will cause those under this category to execute tasks haphazardly, delay tasks, or outright abandon their responsibilities. When you develop this type of mindset, here is how it reflects:

- There is so much to do and so little time to get things done.
- It would have been nice if time would extend beyond 24 hours.

- It appears that time always seems to run faster than ever.

The best way to describe people with no time, but more energy and attention is...overwhelmed. When you get to the point of feeling overwhelmed, if you do not tread with care, everything begins to scatter like a pack of cards. It is at this point when productivity starts to diminish.

Sometimes, it is not that you do not have enough time to get tasks done. It might be a case of not having a well-planned schedule or To-Do list. At other times, it could be that the person has procrastinated on the task until time has run out. Also, some people take on more responsibilities than they can handle. Instead of delegating part of the functions, they try to manage the situation themselves until things go awry. At other times, the jobs might, in reality, be bigger than the person can accomplish in the designated time frame. In this situation, the person requires a more realistic and flexible schedule to start and finish the task.

Other scenarios include an employee who gets to work quite early in the morning and does not return from work until late at night. Again, a supplier who makes too many trips daily, trying to deliver goods to clients at distant locations. A working-class mom with a 9 to 5 job, kids to cater to, and a degree to complete will most times feel overwhelmed. One thing is a common feature with all those mentioned above. They all have the energy to get things done and pay attention to their craft, but always feel overwhelmed due to limited time.

3 Components of Effective Time Management

Time does not exist in a vacuum but can be quantified. The quality of each second you use depends on whether or not it drives you closer to your goals. Therefore, time works best in the following situations:

1. Systems

Life is a combination of dependent and interdependent structures or systems. Each of these systems impact on the other in unique ways. Your ability to understand and manipulate or utilize these systems in accomplishing your goals will determine your level of success. For instance, technology can either help advance your course or serve as a distraction, depending on how you use it. The government and its agencies help create an enabling environment for businesses or individuals to thrive. However, if you get caught on the wrong side of the law, it can become your worst nightmare.

An organizational structure with the chains of command can help navigate business operations for success. When an organization or individual builds systems around their business operations, they increase their chances for success.

2. Strategies

A strategy is a tool used by highly successful people in enhancing their performance. It is a game plan, a compass, or a road map to getting to where you want to in your personal or business life. To win the battle of life, you need a strategy. Your strategy determines the kind of result you get from a given task or situation.

To succeed at anything, you must be willing to change your approach if the current one becomes a stumbling block to your progress. If checking your emails only distracts you from your critical tasks, then it may be a wise decision to restrict email viewing to a specific time.

3. People

Systems and strategies make it easier to accomplish your goals efficiently, but working with people is a different ball game. To excel, you must incorporate systems and strategies. How you go about relating with people will determine whether or not a strategy will work or fail.

Systems revolve around people as they will be the ones to implement them. To succeed in working with people, you require effective communication, teamwork, and the ability to delegate. You should be able to outsource, set expectations, provide an action plan, and give room for creativity. People work more effectively when they feel involved in a system, own the process, and can relate to it.

Strategies for Expanding Your Time

So, what can a person with motivation, but no time do? It's not likely you will be able to expand time, but these simple strategies can help you create ample time to get things done:

1. Schedule Daily Tasks on Your Calendar

Create a daily plan of all the tasks you need to accomplish, with a specific time for each. Have a calendar like the Personal Kanban board, Google Calendar, or Outlook to help you schedule. In creating a daily plan, remember to add buffer time to it. Also, break the responsibilities into smaller, manageable tasks. Do not overcrowd your table, but include time for family and friends in your program.

Follow through on your plans and avoid leaving things until the last minute.

2. Responsibilities

The fact is that you can only do as much as a single person can. Since you are not superhuman, you must rely on others to get things done from time to time. You need to learn the art of delegation and outsourcing where necessary.

3. Free Up Your Schedule

Some tasks on your To-Do list have been there for ages without any action being taken on them, but they are taking up valuable space for handling other meaningful tasks. When you free up your schedule, it gives you more space to complete critical tasks, while you allow others to handle the remaining ones. You might be an excellent worker, smart, and organized. However, if you spend the bulk of your time on the less essential tasks, you may be efficient, but not productive (effective) enough.

4. Create a System for Scheduling Time

Creating workable systems with timelines to get all tasks executed will help you spend quality time on essential jobs. You want to get more done, but that cannot possibly happen without assigning tasks to others. You must learn how to use what (time) you've got.

Effective time management goes beyond filling your day with work. It involves working in a simple, systematic, and timely manner, but also to know when to stop working. To excel at what you do, you must create a system or routine that works well and learn to stick to it.

Category 2: Possessing Time and Attention, But No Energy

When an individual lacks the energy to accomplish tasks, they begin to feel frustrated. They have the time and attention to complete the task but require steam or energy. A lack of energy can result in demotivation, procrastination, and more. Thus, such people end up not following through with their primary tasks. A burnt-out person sometimes says, 'I'm tired, weak, or exhausted and don't feel like doing anything.' Other times they say, 'I don't feel up to it.'

Scenarios of people with time and attention without energy include:

- A professor with groundbreaking research ideas, but who can't seem to put the pieces together to go public.
- The overall best marketing salesman (three years in a row) in your department who can't meet your marketing expectations anymore.

- Any employee who you can't seem to trust with handling bigger tasks.

"The key that unlocks energy is desire. It's also the key to a long and interesting life. If we expect to create any drive, any real force within ourselves, we have to get excited." -Earl Nightingale

You may have all the degrees in the world, purchase all the tools for working, but without the zest or energy, you are moving nowhere. When a person loses steam or becomes exhausted, even with adequate time and attention, they might find it near impossible to deliver efficiently still. It will take some adjustments to increase their productivity when energy levels drop.

Simple Strategies to Get an Energy Boost After a Decline

Public speaker Tony Swartz says, we all have the same number of hours per day, but each person's level of energy, quality, and quantity, depends on us.

The following ideas will help you boost your energy levels:

- Give yourself enough sleep instead of staying up late at night watching a movie. It will help you rejuvenate or regain your energy. Time remains 24 hours a day and has not once reduced or increased in human history. Your energy, on the other hand, does fluctuate. Energy levels can peak or drop fast, depending on cause and effect.
- Successful people understand the importance of conserving their energy. Expending all your energy on a task without taking time out to rest can lead to burnouts or low-quality work. Even if you assume you can still push yourself to work, you will end up with low quality work and become unmotivated.
- Read books that will help motivate you and give directions on how to stimulate growth. Reading suitable materials can help boost your energy levels by inspiring you or helping you to

see what you do wrong. This book is an important go-to resource for discovering how to boost your energy. We shall discuss more on how to increase your energy in the next chapter.

- Take out time to exercise as it will help energize your body. Exercise can serve as a motivator.
- Break down big tasks into smaller, manageable ones and restrict yourself to a single task instead of multitasking.
- Take breaks from work often.
- Eating the right food combination can help increase your energy levels.

To remain productive, you must use your time wisely and channel your energy to completing the right tasks. Real progress doesn't come from trying to do so much, but in ensuring the little tasks you do turn out for the best.

Category 3: Time and Energy, But No Attention

Possessing a low attention span usually results in the feeling of being overwhelmed by any tasks one executes. Having a vibrant ability to pay attention goes beyond focusing on finishing tasks. The ability to focus or pay closer attention is what shapes life's major decisions and feats. Here are examples of statements made by people having issues with maintaining focus:

- Where do I start?
- There is so much to do, I don't even know where to start.
- Wow! How time flies!
- With a longer day, I could get more tasks done.

Sustained attention helps you achieve success on each job over time. Once you can single-task and not lose focus, then you are on your way to more significant achievements. Healthy attention requires the utilization of your time and energy toward achieving defined tasks successfully. The inability to focus or pay attention to what's important and not urgent will make all the difference.

Example of People With High Energy and Time, But No Attention

- A university professor who spends his time chatting with students instead of lecturing or conducting field research for seminar presentations.
- A person with a plan to set up a Non-Governmental Organization to cater to the needs of displaced persons, but ends up only talking without taking action.
- A music composer who spends most of his time writing songs without selling any or releasing a song to the public.

Simple Strategies to Increase Your Attention Level

A person with available time and the energy to do the work, but who cannot pay attention is said to be distracted. This is what you can do to boost attention level:

- Prepare your work station for the day's job by clearing your desk out.
- Before leaving for home today, create a plan or to-do list for tomorrow's task.
- Use the Personal Kanban board to help create a mental picture of what you want to achieve by the next day. It will help motivate and prepare your mind to single-task.
- Turn on 'Do Not Disturb' to minimize distractions once you intend on commencing a crucial task.
- Use the Pareto principle or 80/20 rule to focus your attention on the 20% of the efforts that help you succeed. Remember, 20% of the work effort produces 80% of the results you see.
- Focus — To increase your focus, you must work out ways of avoiding distractions.

- Goals — Find out what one skill you need to learn or one activity that can drive you closer to your goal. Create a plan of action and get to work implementing it.
- Mindset — Habits and belief systems can affect your productivity levels. Identify those traits that do not help you achieve your goals.

Chapter Summary

In this chapter, we discussed the following:

- Increasing your productivity does not happen by accident. It takes dedication, planning, and the TEA principles to excel.
- Time, Energy, and Attention are the three pillars to improved productivity.
- There are ten times more dreamers, or people who only talk about their goals, than there are those who take action on them.
- Highly productive people are die-hard doers, not dreamers or procrastinators.
- The TEA framework is a powerful tool to help you diagnose what hinders you from attaining your true potential.
- Some people have high energy, pay close attention, but have no time.
- If people with no time but energy and attention can learn to prioritize and manage their time effectively, they will become more productive.
- People who believe they do not have time, act like they are stuck or trapped. The best way to describe them is overwhelmed.
- Building systems, evolving strategies, and working effectively with people are the three great solutions to improving time efficiency.

- To use time effectively, you must organize, delegate, and unclog your schedule.
- Another category of people have time and pay attention, but do not have energy.
- People who have the time to carry out tasks and focus, but no energy to implement them, they get frustrated.
- The lack of energy can cause a loss of steam and lead to demotivation or procrastination.
- Adequate sleep, reading the right books, exercise, eating healthy, taking breaks from work, and breaking down tasks into smaller chunks will help regain your energy.
- Another category of people have time and energy to work, but no attention to detail.
- Possessing a low attention span can create a feeling of being overwhelmed.
- Focus and uninterrupted attention will help you excel in each task.
- Starting and finishing a task successfully will lead to effectiveness and efficiency.
- Systems and strategies are the building blocks of successful time management, but you require people to piece the puzzle together.
- It will help if you have a functional team to excel at any task.
- Communication, clear direction, and effective leadership are the tools for success and increased productivity.
- To help increase your attention level, remove things that cause distractions, like social media and email. Use 'Do Not Disturb' to remove distractions.
- Always work with a schedule and plan your next day's activities before leaving the office.
- Productivity is not about getting as much done as possible, but on finishing each job efficiently and effectively.

In the next chapter, you will learn about habits to increase your physical and mental energy.

CHAPTER SEVEN:

Habits to Increase Your Physical and Mental Energy

Your energy is the principal vehicle for bringing your dreams to reality. If given the opportunity, we all want to achieve our goals. Achieving one's goal is an integral part of human existence, but how many people truly achieve their life goals? How many have what it takes, even the physical and mental alertness required to see their goals to fruition? Many times people lack the will power, zest, or motivation to actualize their dreams. These deficiencies directly relate to each person's lack of physical and mental energy required to propel people into action.

The mind is one of the greatest tools each person possesses. To fully activate energies like confidence, happiness, focus, motivation, increased willpower, and productivity, the mind has to be in top gear. Your thought pattern affects your output and can sometimes determine how others see you. When you think happy thoughts, you become more content over time. When you are confident, it begins to reflect on your outward appearance.

If you must succeed in any endeavor, you need high mental energy, and often people discover, over time, that they lose steam and cannot get anything done anymore. What they lack is the required mental and physical energy to pursue their dreams. However, every ability evolves into a habit when people take the time necessary to study and acquire these habits. Mental and physical alertness is a function of certain habits people develop. If you see a person with low motivation, a lack of confidence, low physical and mental energy, sometimes it has to do with their habits. There are energy killing and energy-boosting habits, and the ones you subscribe to will determine how productive you can become.

"The first requisite for success is the ability to apply your physical and mental energies to one problem incessantly without growing weary." -Charles Caleb Colton

You need to inject new energies continuously into your life to remain balanced in your personal and career pursuits. But to make these new energies part of your DNA requires following a process, developing positive habits, and taking action always.

With that in mind, here are proven habits to set you on the right pedestal:

10 High-Powered Physical and Mental Energy Hacks

Tackle What You Dread the Most

Doing what you fear first gives you the confidence and energy to deal with other less critical jobs for the rest of your day. The first success provides motivation and an opportunity to exhale. Once you achieve success with the first task, it reduces the chance of procrastinating on other less critical tasks.

Visualize Before Bed

The thoughts you take to bed are essential in setting your mood for the next day. Nothing matters more than your state of mind just before you get into bed to sleep. It places you in the right frame of mind when you wake up. By visualizing possibilities before bed, you draw a direct connection between pleasure and waking up.

A positive mindset gives you all the energy you need to begin the day. It adds to the quality of your day and boosts your confidence level. This high energy can affect every other activity you get involved in over the course of the day.

However, visualizing works best when you have an action plan for each day and utilize your evening before to plan the next day's activities. This plan serves as a motivator.

Unclog Your Mind

It's true the never-ending things on the to-do list can leave a person feeling overwhelmed and the mind clogged. Also, with technology, the fast-paced world, deadlines, tons of email messages, appointments, and more, managing your day can become even more difficult.

To keep the mind free and mentally alert, delegate some tasks where necessary. Delegating to someone else relieves the stress level and reduces the volume of activity to worry about. Other activities, such as taking down notes, keeping a calendar, and setting reminders will help simplify your life.

Having a to-do list transfers work pressure from your mind to your schedule. It is a strategy that will help you unclog your mind and increase your mental energy. Also, it helps you focus more on a task without anxiety or a cluttered mind.

Getting the Right Amount of Sleep

Having the right amount of sleep per day has a direct correlation with your ability to function at optimal capacity. Sleep has a way of affecting the mental and physical state of an individual. The more sleep a person gets, the more mentally alert they are, and vice versa.

Also, it helps to know your sweet spot, which is the right amount and the right kind of sleep you need. For some, too much sleep makes them groggy and exhausted. While some people might do well on six to seven hours of sleep, others might need eight hours or more to function fully.

Another point of note is the quality of sleep. Before retiring for the night, you might need to turn off all devices that interrupt your sleep. Comfortable environments and the right kind of bedding can serve as a motivator for enhanced sleep. Other things that can boost the quality of sleep include:

- Taking a warm bath to relax the muscles.
- Reading a book in bed.
- Avoid screens two hours before bedtime.
- No caffeine after 3 P.M..

Spend a Good Chunk of Your Day Pursuing Your "Heart Project"

Heart projects are those specific things you pursue that center on your ultimate passion and goals. When you focus your energy on your passions and goals, it never seems like a task, but a hobby. Your heart project gives a new meaning to your life, making you very excited and revitalized.

Your passions give you something to always look forward to. They give you a reason to wake up daily and to hit the road with infectious enthusiasm.

Have a Sense of Gratitude

Starting the day with the right mental attitude gives a positive disposition to life. A good reminder of the things that are working in your life can help you approach the day in top gear. Try practicing being grateful always to enjoy greater mental energy. Be grateful for the things people take for granted, such as good health, a job, and the fact that you can earn a living salary. Be thankful for the relationships you have and all the seemingly small things that are currently working for you.

Remember that challenges are a part of life and tend to make you stronger. So, whatever challenge comes your way, look at things from the positive side. Everything cannot go down for you at the same time. A lifestyle of gratitude takes away boredom and reminds you of the most important things in life. Practice the act of writing down the things that are working in your life and focus more on them.

Have a Positive Outlook on Life

Being positive and optimistic about life is a great approach to boosting mental energy. You can replace a depressive feeling with positive thoughts to experience an energy boost. The state of your mental energy is a great determinant of your productivity levels. A negative disposition only causes a decline in your mental energy. Think positive thoughts and take advantage of opportunities as they present themselves.

Eat the Right Foods

The food we eat has a way of not only affecting our physical energy, but our mental energy as well. The saying 'you are what you eat' simply means you can draw energy from eating energy-giving foods by eating right. Food has a way of cramping our mental energy. For instance, carbohydrates turn sugar into fat in the body. This invariably weighs you down and leaves you feeling full and tired.

Eating unhealthy food leaves you with no nutritional value. Such foods decrease the overall wellbeing of the body and make you tired. A tired body automatically affects the mental state.

Adopt a plan to make helpful eating choices a lifestyle. Choose a diet that enhances mental alertness. Eating more calories earlier in the day than at night time will have a positive impact on your energy. Obesity is not one of the things you will want to add to your list of worries.

Healthy foods are rich in fiber, fruits and vegetables, protein, and other essential minerals that should be part of your diet to improve your energy. Also, water acts like magic to the body and it pays to stay hydrated all day long. However, drink water to stay hydrated, but do not allow water drinking to interfere with your work.

Get Inspired Through Exercise

Exercise is great for the brain, not only for weight control, but also to lower blood pressure. It can also help with depression and anxiety. Exercise boosts one's mood by kicking up your endorphin level, which is the 'feel-good' chemical in the body.

When involved in exercise, the heart rate increases and invariably decreases the stress level in the brain.

More benefits of exercise include:

- Better sleep
- Increase in self-esteem and self-confidence
- Brain boost

Stay Active but Enjoy It While on It

Sticking to exercise routines can be a near-impossible task for some people. However, besides the traditional jogging and brisk walk forms of exercise, you can find an enjoyable active method to keep your body functioning. Also, engaging in sports and hobbies is an excellent way to keep the body energized and the mind active.

Engaging Activities Include:

- Working out with friends
- Going for short walks
- Running
- Hiking
- Biking

- Dancing
- Skating

Surround Yourself With Happy People

Most people are naturally sociable, others are not, but relationships are an integral part of human existence. High energy, happy people carry the virus with them and if you stick long enough around them, you will become infected with happiness. They make you happy and full of energy.

Your relationships, therefore, will increase or decrease your energy level as you choose your associations. Ensure that you stay with people you enjoy being with.

Having a social network that aligns with your goals and needs can provide a kind of support group. Support groups can help increase your self-worth and reduce stress levels. Social gatherings are particularly useful for introverts who find interacting a little challenging. It allows them to express themselves, have fun, and laugh to serve as a boost.

Let Your Mind Travel in Meditation

Meditation involves deep thinking or using the power of imagination to recreate your world from what it is to what or where you desire it to be. Meditation helps you tap into the abilities of your mind to predict a better future through mental visualization. Successful people make use of meditation to find answers to even thorny issues.

The ultimate goal of meditation is inner peace and relaxation. Studies have shown that meditation (no matter how brief) is an excellent tool for reducing stress. Stress can have a toll on your physical or mental energy, and meditation can provide stress relief. Taking a couple of minutes daily to engage in mindful meditation will help ease most forms of stress and anxiety. Meditation is a useful tool in the fight for mental health and for fighting mental disorders.

Rejuvenate Your Body and Mind in a Yoga Session

Yoga has provided intrinsic value to humanity over the ages. It is a physical and mental exercise that helps rejuvenate the body and motivate the mind. Yoga combines postures, meditation, relaxation, and breathing techniques. There are a lot of benefits associated with yoga practice in the development of your physical and mental energy.

Yoga Benefits:

- Improves muscle strength – This protects against back pain and arthritis.
- Increases blood flow – Yoga releases energy in your body cells and aids blood circulation.
- Increases heart rate – Since Yoga involves physical exercise it causes rapid heart beating.
- Drops blood pressure and blood sugar.
- Makes focusing easier – Studies have shown that yoga practice improves coordination, memory, and IQ levels.
- Improves sleep.
- Reduces the fluctuation of the mind.

Get Into the Play Mood More Often

The saying that 'all work and no play makes Jack a dull boy' refers to the mental and physical state of wellbeing. Any activity that is fun and gives us joy or a childlike spark could be termed as play. Being busy with no time for fun activities or hobbies can have its toll on our energies. Play is different for every individual based on needs, interests, and wants. It doesn't necessarily have to be on your to-do list, but an activity you find fascinating. The fun activity could range from cooking, dancing, listening to music, going to the cinema, to field and track events — any hobby.

Create Routines

Creating energy-boosting habits as a part of your work or personal routine can help keep your energy levels high. Also, you can seek out small activities to boost energy fast while at work. Routines in sleeping habits, eating times, exercise, Yoga, a grateful attitude, and work activities can be very beneficial. Once you can master routines and it becomes a part of your life, then your productivity will go up.

Address Issues Head-On

Leaving issues on the front burner or unattended for long can have its toll on your energy levels, causing stress. Mental stress can drain your energy as much, if not more, than physical strain. Once you are mentally stressed, the first thing to do is to identify the triggers. The next thing to do is to begin devising strategies to tackle stress. Tackle them head-on and gain more energy for success.

Learning to increase your energy should be rather interesting. The use of substances should not be an option. Taking action is a vital aspect of finding your energy. Once you can make these practices a habit, they eventually become a lifestyle and more natural to achieve.

Chapter Summary

- Increasing your physical and mental energy requires deliberate actions that require incorporating them into your lifestyle.
- You need to inject fresh energy into your life regularly to enjoy a balanced flow of energy.
- Taking care of the tasks you dread the most will give you the energy and confidence to do more.
- Organize your thoughts by visualizing the job before you go to bed.
- Free your mind of overwhelming feelings and too many tasks.

- Sleep is important. Get enough of it.
- Your heart project is in the area of your passion and should be pursued with enthusiasm.
- Have an attitude of gratitude always.
- 'You are what you eat.' In other words, eat the right food with the proper nutritional value for your body.
- Engage in inspiring active or physical activities that you enjoy and your energy levels will go up.
- Socialize more by surrounding yourself with happy people.
- Happy people carry infectious energy.
- Meditation is a powerful energy booster.
- Practice yoga to improve your energy levels.
- You need to play more. The right type of play creates an exhilarating feeling.
- Get into regular habits that condition the mind for good.
- Take the bull by the horns when dealing with problems.

In the next chapter, you will learn how to get yourself motivated within a few minutes using science-backed tricks.

CHAPTER EIGHT

Motivation in Minutes: Science-Backed Tricks

What keeps one going amid differing circumstances and challenges in life? When an idea does not seem to work, or one faces setbacks or failures, what gives you the courage to keep trying? Even when it isn't convenient, what causes you to rise early in the morning to meditate, study, do your routine exercises, or head to work?

The truth is that no genuine success can ever occur without motivation. Motivation is the driving force, just as fuel aids a vehicle's movement. Motivation is what gives wind to your sail, the driving force that keeps you going when everything else seems not to work. However, being motivated or staying motivated is not as easy as it looks. It tasks your physical and mental energy. When that happens, how do you remain motivated?

Here are some scientifically proven ways to get you focused and motivated for increased productivity within minutes:

Boost Your Confidence With a High-Power Pose

The Required Length of Time: 2 Minutes

Your body language is a central factor in how others perceive you. It also affects your internal body chemistry. The way you carry yourself and perform certain activities, your posture, movements, and more send positive or negative vibes to others. Amy Cuddy from Harvard says that "our nonverbals govern how other people think and feel about us."

Research from Princeton, Harvard, and other institutions point to how body language can affect interactions in the workplace. Using the right words can help pass the right message. However, body language can influence the meanings you read into any message.

Therefore, just as body language affects a message, so does it affect your motivation level. Professor Amy Cuddy of Harvard School of Business, speaking on body language, says that the power pose provides another channel for communicating non-verbally. The way you carry your body can say a lot about you as well as affect your productivity levels. Your body language, postures, and carriage can tell a lot about you.

What's a Power Pose?

There are two known kinds of power poses, which are the high and low power pose. High power pose deals with positioning your body in an open instead of a slouched or hunched position, even if seating or standing. In a high power pose, you keep your chest and arms spread open and avoid staying in a slouched position.

Hence, researchers identify that maintaining a high-power pose can increase your testosterone levels, a hormone responsible for a confidence boost. The high-power posture, also in the process, reduces cortisol levels, which are responsible for increasing stress in the body.

However, in a lower power-pose, the individual slouches in a position that makes you appear small or bunched up.

Therefore, to give yourself the needed mental boost, try out simple high power poses and see the effect on your productivity levels. Always consciously stand or sit in a high power pose manner. A study at Princeton shows that body language carries more expressions than just facial.

Remember to actively, not passively, communicate and align your entire body facing the other person when talking with them. Smile often, as research also confirms that smiling can boost your confidence level too.

Give Yourself a Fresh Start

The Required Length of Time: 3-5 Minutes

Most people make resolutions, particularly at the beginning of the year, and this helps serve as a source of motivation. By making resolutions, you give yourself a chance to start anew. It can also create a burst of energy to accomplish more tasks, according to a study conducted by the Wharton School of Business.

A publication by the Institute of Operations Research and Management Science identified that the use of salient temporal landmarks helps people in attaining their goals. They develop the willpower to tackle any task when they decide to make a fresh start. Such fresh starts occur during temporal landmarks like their birthdays, a new week, a month or year, holidays, a new semester, or session. Using Google search, the team identified some areas requiring a fresh start to include dieting, visiting the gym, and committing to achieving goals.

To make a fresh start, using landmarks, people can move on from past imperfections to pursue bigger goals that will impact their lives. In other words, the decision to make a fresh start could serve as a source of motivation leading to a change in behavior and increased productivity.

How Do You Get a Fresh Start in Life

Everyone has past and recurrent events in their lives. Some of these events can push one closer or farther from achieving their goals. However, a critical look at those events or occurrences can turn into a fresh start. You can set a negative or positive situation into an avenue for a fresh start. For example, a recent loss of a job, break up, graduation, or relocation to a new community can serve as motivation to start that business you have been saving for or longing to set up.

Temporal landmarks help you disconnect from past failures and make a concrete plan on how to advance your goals. To help inspire you to succeed, you need to take the next step, which is to write down your goals. Create a plan of action or to-do list to channel your new-found energy in achieving your goals. Also, having a fresh start does not have to be limited to the beginning of the year, but at any time you discover the need to re-define a situation or occurrence.

Indulge Yourself a Little With a Treat of Chocolates

The Required Length of Time: 1 Minute

Eating chocolates might appear bad for your teeth or too sugary for you. However, chocolate can have powerful motivational benefits. Chocolate contains dopamine-releasing properties with chemical reactions known to produce these chocolate effects on your brain:

- Dopamine causes an increase in the heart rate leading to higher motivation.
- Eating chocolate releases serotonin and phenylethylamine into your bloodstream. Serotonin is a neuro-transmitter and can help calm your nerves, while phenylethylamine promotes stimulation. White chocolate contains more of the two properties and offers more value. Dark chocolate contains antioxidants that help slow down cognitive decline and increase your concentration level.

- Chocolate works as a mild form of antidepressant. When you consume chocolate, it causes a chemical reaction in the brain that stimulates a feeling of bliss, a 'feel-good sensation,' and motivation.

Build Your Brain Power With Healthy Foods

Eating healthy will have a direct impact on your overall health. Your health is the only guarantee of enjoying wealth when you finally become successful. However, to successfully set, pursue, and achieve your goals you need your health.

Certain classes of food only help to slow down your mental and physical development as well as to make you ill. Your body needs the right amount of nutrients to rebuild or repair worn tissues. When you give it the right food, it can not only provide the energy to do work, but also boosts your brain development.

What Foods Can Boost Your Brainpower?

There are a lot of foods that, once eaten, can serve as fuel for the body in helping you reach your goals. Examples of motivating foods include foods rich in protein, healthy fats and oils, fruits and vegetables, nuts and seeds, whole grains and more.

Foods rich in Vitamin B serve as a stimulant and can help increase your energy levels, motivation, and brainpower. For instance, Vitamin B contains dopamine responsible for giving you a motivated feeling. You can get a good dosage of Vitamin B in turkey, salmon, tofu, bananas, spinach, hazelnuts, walnuts, and avocado pear. However, foods with high cholesterol and fatty foods are not so healthy or helpful for brain development.

Fish like salmon, containing oils and Omega 3 fatty acids can aid speedy brain development. It can also protect against memory loss and dementia. Besides chocolates, nuts and seeds also slow down cognitive decline. Other fruits and vegetables that contain dopamine properties include spirulina, blueberries, etc.. Studies show that avocado pear contains properties that fight the free radicals responsible for cell damage, reduce the progress of Alzheimer's disease and dementia. Avocado pear is an excellent food for building muscle function and learning development.

Spend Time in Nature

Nature has a unique way of connecting with the human sweet spot. It can motivate you even in the worst of situations and the most unlikely circumstances. It's so easy to get trapped in the madness of earning a living and pursuing set goals that you forget to enjoy even the little you've earned. You sometimes forget to take time out to enjoy even the gifts of nature.

"In the depth of winter, I finally learned that there was in me an invincible summer" -Albert Camus

One of the best ways to get motivated in minutes is to allow nature to slip through your being. Spending more time in nature will not only help you to unwind, but also inspire you to crack hard-nut work issues. So, what can you do?

Take a walk

Walking acts like medicine to the body and the human psyche. Instead of driving or possibly take a taxi, bus, or train, can you take a walk home? Or at least stop a few meters from the nearest bus stop and walk the remaining way home. Several things normally occur when you take a walk. It gives you time to reflect on the activities of the day, weeks, and months. You can also meditate on nutty issues at work, and because it is a different environment, you don't feel choked.

You can also take a walk on the beach. Walk on your bare feet, the waves to the left, trees to the right, music from a distance, other fun-seekers running around, screams, and excitement in the air. Just sipping in the cool summer wind can do much magic to your soul. As you ponder on the issues of life, your goals, work, and personal life, it won't take long to get a burst of energy coming in.

Go On a Vacation

A trip to some of those places you have always dreamed of can create the needed motivation you seek. There are dozens of exciting and exotic locations, natural reserves, game reserves, and waterparks to explore. Besides the wonderful sites to see, merely being in the green will give you a usual volume of motivation and energy.

Research from the University of Essex shows that colors communicate tones, moods, and feelings to people. The color green is said in two different studies to serve as a motivator, while sparks of green can boost your creativity levels. Hence, surrounding your office or room with a touch of green should do wonders for your energy.

For example, Andrew is a guy who likes creating his to-do list for the next day when he is getting ready for bed. He looks through the activities of the day, successes, failures, uncompleted tasks, and more, and then schedules them into the next day's activities. Once Andrew completes this task, he lays on his bed and then tries to visualize... *What will tomorrow look like?* he asks himself. *What do I want to achieve for tomorrow? What problems do I have to surmount in my work and personal life tomorrow to achieve my goals?* After some time, he puts out the reading lamp and rests for the night. When morning comes, Andrew is pumped up, excited about the day's activities and can't wait to hit the ground running

Research confirms that people respond differently to situations, and that helps to motivate them. Science identifies that there are two types of motivation, intrinsic (internal) and extrinsic (external). For instance, when you clean your home just when you are expecting some friends to come to visit, that's external motivation. Extrinsic motivation depends on something external or from your environment to stimulate a course of action. Belle Cooper, says extrinsic motivation can be summed up using conditional statements, such as 'if,' followed by a reward. For example, 'if you can hit a target of five sales consistently in the next three months, you will qualify for Regional Marketing Manager.' That's an external incentive for getting a task done. Rewards tend to narrow the thinking processes to succeed.

However, researchers at Princeton identify that such a reward system for external motivation, over time, leads to poor performance. Tasks involving innovation and creativity produce higher performance when there is internal motivation. For instance, staying after close to work on your skills in order to improve upon something is intrinsic motivation. Intrinsic motivation is part of what promotes creative works. Your goal is the motivating factor.

Elements of Intrinsic Motivation

Dan Pink talked about the three elements of intrinsic motivation:

- Autonomy
- Mastery
- Purpose

Autonomy

Autonomy deals with making choices. When you have a sense of ownership or feel you are in control of your choices, it gives you intrinsic motivation. Such a person can look at all possibilities creatively to get the task done. As such, having areas within your control on a job will give you some level of motivation about it. For example, your boss gives you a project to execute. If you have room to make some decisions on the structure, progress, and delivery date of the tasks, it becomes easier to feel motivated than if you only have to do as instructed. So, seeking ways to increase your autonomy on a task will naturally lead to motivation as you can own the process.

Mastery

When you love what you do it helps you get better at it, even without external motivation. You will be willing to develop yourself to get better at your task when it matters to you, not just to the company, and when areas requiring your skills come up, you will feel excited and motivated to use your skills.

Purpose

When you feel like a project or task is something bigger than your personal interests, then your focus is on purpose. Motivation becomes intrinsic when the individual's focus in on the benefit, such as how a task will add to society or benefit the company's customers. You become motivated when you see the actual value a project will add to customers and others.

Chapter Summary

In this chapter, we have discussed the following ideas extensively:

- Challenges are some of the hallmarks of pursuing any worthwhile goal in life. People somehow find the motivation to pursue their dreams despite their obstacles.
- Motivation is what causes someone to rise early each day to pursue a dream, even after setbacks and failures.
- Motivation comes from internal (intrinsic) and external (extrinsic) sources.
- High power poses help inspire you to keep working.
- Your body language says a lot about you and can affect your motivation levels.
- Seating or standing in a slouching or hunched position is a low power pose, and it can affect your motivation at work or in an interview.

- Seating or standing in an open or upright position with squared shoulders facing ahead is called high power pose. It can help boost your energy levels and increase motivation in the space of two minutes.
- Making a fresh start in life can serve as a motivator.
- People make weekly, monthly, and yearly resolutions. Other resolutions come during their birthdays, after a loss of a job, or a breakup. This temporal landmark system serves as motivation to either stop or start doing certain things.
- Indulge yourself a little by eating white, brown, or dark chocolate as it contains dopamine, which is one of the feel-good ingredients for motivation.
- Eating foods rich in protein, oils, omega 3 fatty acids, seeds, and nuts, etc. can help boost your energy levels and motivation.
- Staying locked up indoors or all week in the office is enough to kill motivation. Taking a trip with mother nature can stir up something in you. Take a walk, go to the beach, and let these things inspire you.
- You can get motivated or feel a sense of autonomy when you feel like you can own the process or have played a significant role in the decision-making process of a task.
- Mastering the process of getting things done within your organization can serve as a substantial boost for you. Once you enjoy doing what you do, if need be, you can study more to hone your skills.
- It can work with a purpose, such as for the overall good or benefit of others, it tends to serve as a drive to continue on a mission. Knowing how much value or impact you have on customers and humanity can create motivation.

In the next chapter, you will learn about the secret to increased efficiency and focus using the Pomodoro method.

CHAPTER NINE:

The Pomodoro Method — The Secret to Increased Efficiency and Focus

There are so many tasks to accomplish every day, and it seems like there is never enough time. You have tight deadlines, but no time to get everything done. Now, it may have gotten so bad you constantly have to take work home so that you can meet your target deadlines. During some weeks, everything goes smoothly, and you hit your target. On others, it's a struggle. And it's all adding up, making you more and more frustrated. You are beginning to lose steam. So, what do you do in such situations?

A lot of people struggle with maintaining focus at work. Sometimes, people sit all day at their desks but still end up achieving little due to lack of concentration, fatigue, or the lack of motivation. The secret ingredient you need is the Pomodoro method for better focus and efficiency.

When I first heard about the Pomodoro technique, my interest peaked immediately. Being a life coach, however, it took some time before I could find time in my schedule to study the Pomodoro technique and to give it a shot for myself. I had heard a lot about the value of the method and was eager to try it out and, to say the least, the result on my productivity level was phenomenal. If you are struggling with maintaining your focus and efficiency at work, this is just the right tool to try: the Pomodoro method.

What Is the Pomodoro Method?

The Pomodoro method is a time management tool to help increase your efficiency and focus at work. There is hardly ever enough time to get everything done. With this in mind, the Pomodoro technique teaches you to work with the available time on your hands. Instead of racing against time, Pomodoro encourages you to streamline by structuring your time into 25 minute and 5 minute segments.

In other words, you break your workday into smaller chunks of 25 minutes and 5 minutes. The 25 minutes go into accomplishing parts of your tasks, while the 5 minutes are for short breaks. This is known as the Pomodoro method. However, after about four intervals, or Pomodoros, then you can extend the break to 15 to 20 minutes.

What's the Value in the Pomodoro Technique?

The Pomodoro design helps you focus on what is most important daily. Sometimes, we carry on work with the impression that we have enough time to get the day's job done. Then, we allow distractions to get in our way. An urgent email comes in from a friend, and then you think, 'Message from John... Okay, let me quickly reply to the email...", and you suspend your current task at hand. Before you know it, you're caught up in other distracting tasks, and half of the day goes by without accomplishing much. Once the deadline is just two days away, then you're in a frenzy, trying to squeeze everything in so you can deliver on time.

The Pomodoro technique provides an immediate sense of urgency about your work. It helps you focus even if it is only for 25 minutes on your most important tasks. After 25 minutes, you can allow yourself some distractions before getting back to work on the same tasks. The argument is that, once you have the discipline to follow through on this formula, at the end of each day, you will have increased your productivity astronomically. So, instead of squandering time on distractions, you focus your time on your key tasks.

If you invest in intervals of 25 minutes for tasks, with 5 minutes for breaks, for 12 times in a single day, you will have worked for 300 minutes by the end of the day. If you add up 5 minutes times 12, that's 60 minutes, which results in at least 7 hours of work in a day. You still have at least one hour for a break, assuming you work 8 hours per day or a 9 to 5 job.

The Pomodoro technique helps increase your productivity by cutting down on distractions and getting more tasks done. The forced breaks take away the daily fatigue or burnt-out feeling at the end of work. In addition, it's unhealthy to spend endless hours cranking at your desk, hoping to get more tasks done. Forcing yourself to work with the Pomodoro method helps you to achieve more while keeping your energy levels high.

From an evolutionary biology point of view, the human brain should not work under so much undue pressure at a stretch. Although the brain can withstand the stress (after all, it can handle extremely complex pressures), over the years, the effect of the strain will likely show on your health. The human brain helps you survive any situation, but cannot stay focused on one task for so long without a drop in concentration. Therefore, using a simple technique, such as Pomodoros, your brain can enjoy an energy boost, constant alertness, and an increase in the quality of work produced.

Strategies to Make the Pomodoro Technique Work for You

Not everyone has the same work schedule or nature of work. Because of this, you can tailor the Pomodoro technique to suit your unique circumstances. For instance, a person in marketing, engineering fieldwork, or a writer or journalist, will have a different working environment.

Initially, using such incessant breaks will appear awkward and unnatural. I must confess, it is a cumbersome experience when you start, micro-managing tasks with a timer. In fact, at first, I had several shifts from 25 to 45 minutes so that I could cater to some urgent issues. At other times, I had to attend to a prospective client with large accounts and altered the setup. Also, I had meetings with clients during the day, training sessions, and all of that to deal with. Under such circumstances, I had to turn off the Pomodoro timer to get other things done.

However, to help achieve my goal, I had incorporated the Pomodoro technique with the personal Kanban board. On days where I had to work more from the office or at the desk, I used more of the Pomodoro method. It helped me to get things organized faster and more efficiently. On such days when I have meetings with staff or personal coaching sessions with clients, I suspended the Pomodoros, as I can't make others leave with the 25 minutes to 5 minutes schedule. Still, incorporating the Pomodoro technique this way, I experienced an exponential increase in productivity levels. It helped me single task better and got more done faster.

Here is how the Pomodoro method can work for you:

Work With a Stopwatch or Timer App

Since you must create a timestamp, a stopwatch or app will serve as the best way to set the 25-minute intervals. There's no way to discipline yourself to the Pomodoro method without a timer. Checking the time manually will result in more disappointment than success. Besides, once you get caught up with work, you are bound to forget your timing.

You can download the Pomodoro Timer app from the iTunes store for Apple users. Or try ClearFocus for Android users.

Single Task, Not Multitasking

It should be clear by now the dangers and disadvantages of multitasking. To increase your productivity, try to single-task by assigning only one task to a 25-minute interval. If you need more than a single 25 minutes to get that task done, then use as many 25 minute intervals as possible, but be sure not to spend more time than a single task should take normally.

Be Committed

As much as you want to be flexible, it will help if you stick to the Pomodoro technique to get the maximum benefits. It's often tempting to skip the breaks and to keep working, especially when there are tight deadlines to meet. However, you must stick to your breaks, just as you stick to the task intervals.

Set Daily Goals

Like we already talked about, set daily goals in line with the tasks for that day. Each day's task should be specific to 25 minutes of work time and 5-minute breaks. Use as many as 25 minutes and 5-minute breaks as the day's activities will allow. Extend the breaks from 5 minutes to 15 minutes after the first four intervals of 5-minute breaks.

Stay Focused on Work

There are bound to be interruptions and other urgent or emergency issues. However, you must make it a habit to concentrate on your work for every 25 minutes and use the 5 minutes breaks as designated. The moment you allow interruptions to come into your day, others will use the excuse to disturb you. You will end up achieving little if there is too much interference.

Delay Email Reading and Social Media Distractions

Just because emails form a part of your work activities, does not mean you can allow email interruptions. Do not check your emails when taking care of a specific 25-minute task or during the 5-minute breaks. The 5-minute breaks are for non-work related activities that allow you some time to rejuvenate. If you spend 5 minutes on any work at all, that means you did not give your brain any time off.

There should be a specific time in your daily schedule for handling emails. You can have email reading come up two to three times in a regular work schedule. This will help in avoiding email or social media interruptions during crucial work time.

Enjoy Your Breaks

Since the 5-minute break intervals are not for working, what should you do with them? Five minutes is not a lot of time. Use your breaks to concentrate on non-work related activities. That's the only way you will be physically and mentally alert after the break. The reason the break is not more than 5 minutes is so that your body does not adjust to the resting period and get out of the work mode.

To use the 5 minutes effectively, you can get up from your work station and take a walk or grab a cup of coffee. Walking helps relieve body tension, as well as to loosen your muscles. Taking a deep breath to fill your lungs with oxygen offers a lot of benefits to your brain and the body. The oxygen released into the brain serves as a boost that can help you maintain focus. A more relaxed body makes it easy to work more efficiently and invariably get more quality tasks done daily.

In a nutshell, I started out testing the Pomodoro technique and ended up advocating this method to my clients. From personal experience, I concluded that the Pomodoro method might not fit into everyone's work schedule or lifestyle. One could, however, adopt the formula in resolving different work-related situations. The benefit for me is that using the Pomodoro technique on office and desk-related tasks helps me to be more productive.

Other Time-Tested Strategies to Improve Focus and Efficiency

Define Your Goal Clearly

If you must reduce distractions and focus your energy, then you need to state your goals clearly by writing them down. The value of a clearly stated goal is that it forces you to focus or concentrate on what truly matters to your work. If you do not have your goals stated, it will be more challenging to utilize the Pomodoro method. It will be best if you have defined goals to plan the structure of 25 minutes and 5-minute breaks.

Also, stating your goals makes it possible to build mental blocks. You can visualize the process to get tasks done and possibly see what it will look like once completed. When stating your goals, remember to write down what you intend to achieve through that goal and why. These last points help to motivate you toward pursuing the goals.

Take Your Time

It sometimes appears as if you are not hardworking when you take things slowly, but it's not true. Success is not a one-meter dash or a journey; it's a destination. Success is where you want to be, and everyone goes at their own pace. Working at a defined pace gives you the feeling of being in control and not overwhelmed. When working on tasks that require a lot of mental energy, working simply is a discipline that you must learn. Working at a defined pace allows you to pay attention to critical details, and that's how you should structure your tasks into the Pomodoro technique. At such a pace, you will be racing for quality content and not against time.

Can You Do It Now?

Some tasks appear hectic, and you may be tempted to leave them for later. However, you end up not doing them at all or waiting until it becomes urgent and important. When you leave a task until the last minute, it adds more mental pressure to your brain. Research shows that at least 15% of adults procrastinate what they need to do. Procrastination can drain you of motivation and give you the feeling that there is so much to do and so little time to get things done. This feeling can hurt the quality of your work. Procrastination can, over time, become a habit that results in low self-esteem. However, you can keep this in check by giving yourself strict deadlines, breaking the tasks into bite-sized chunks, and planning in advance.

A strategy that can help against procrastination is using the two-minute rule. With it, any job that only requires about two minutes to complete, you do immediately. Do not allow such tasks to add to the list of unfinished jobs. Some of these activities include sending an email or clearing out your desk. However, make sure everything is planned in your to-do list.

Join the 5 a.m. Club

Remember Robin Sharma's 5 A.M. Club? You can go back to chapter two to read more about it. However, rising early in the morning to plan your day, and getting into shape will make it easier to get the best out of the Pomodoro method. Using the 20/20/20 formula can help you to plan your day, get enough exercise, and meditate on what will help you succeed today. This should help you to relax and become more productive, giving you the needed boost to take charge of your day.

Conducive Environment

An unfriendly work environment kills motivation and can cause loss of concentration. Make your work environment less hostile, more inviting, and comfortable. Things such as the color of the office, furniture, and curtains can set the mood for work. Color communicates sadness, happiness, and excitement. Usually, brighter colors like green work best for motivation. The same goes for lighting. A poorly lit environment can cause a strain on the eyes. Lighting can also set the mood for a lively or melancholic atmosphere.

Take note of the sitting arrangement in the office, as a clumsy sitting arrangement can also affect focus. An overcrowded office will cause distraction and inconvenience. Ventilation and access to utilities, such as the restroom, etc. help you to concentrate better. Music can also help improve concentration. Music can encourage pleasant emotions and thoughts. It can also stimulate the mind, as well as help you to relax. Music can also help to channel your thoughts and overcome other subconscious distractions. However, the choice of music will determine the value you get. Music with lyrics, however, may give you too much to think about and further create a distraction. As such, instrumental music often improves concentration more effectively.

Delegate Tasks

We shall discuss more on delegation in the next chapter. However, delegation helps share the responsibility and increases your capacity to do more. It can also help you to become more efficient, while improving the quality of your work. Delegation also enhances creativity and flexibility, as more hands may mean better ideas on how to achieve a task.

The intrinsic value in the Pomodoro method is the ability to get more done in as little time as possible, while maintaining your concentration level. Therefore, schedule work time and break time accordingly. To excel at any innovative idea, including the Pomodoro method, will take cooperation and discipline. No one can help you achieve success if you don't give it a shot.

Chapter Summary

- The feeling of 'so many tasks and so little time to get them done' can result in a drop in concentration.
- The Pomodoro method is a time management tool that helps you focus your energy on accomplishing the critical tasks, increasing concentration and productivity.
- The technique works by splitting your work time into 25 minutes of serious and focused work and 5-minute breaks.
- With carefully planned tasks, you can attain at least 25 minutes of work with 5-minute breaks, 8 to 12 times in a day.
- The Pomodoro technique helps you break the day's tasks into smaller manageable bits of 25 minutes to help you concentrate better.
- It enables you to reduce distractions or to not focus on less important tasks during critical work hours.
- The use of a Pomodoro timer or stopwatch, as well as mono-tasking instead of multitasking, is a powerful Pomodoro strategy to improve productivity.
- Set daily goals and follow through to increase productivity.
- Your 5-minute breaks should only be used to relax and not to focus on work.
- To succeed with the Pomodoro method, you must commit to a plan, avoid procrastinating, and delegate where necessary.

In the next chapter, you will learn about how to delegate effectively to get more tasks done and to increase productivity.

CHAPTER TEN:

How to Delegate Tasks

Some schools of thought state that 'if you want something done right, you do it yourself.` However, even though it makes sense to get things done yourself, the big question is, how much can a single person really achieve alone? When emperor Napoleon Bonaparte established the above statement, probably what he had in mind was the need to create structures and strategies at management levels so that execution of tasks would go smoothly. I came to this conclusion because Napoleon was a great French leader and Emperor. He rose to power during the French Revolution in the 1770s and championed the conquest of significant portions of Europe. If he meant the execution of tasks without the help of others, I doubt that the great Emperor would have been victorious at war as he had to work with his cabinet, generals, and a large troop of soldiers to succeed.

Delegation is a useful management tool for the success of personal and corporate goals. However, it's easy to delegate too little or too much to any given task. To strike a balance, knowing how to delegate is crucial.

As a critical skill, it is expedient that managers learn to delegate or outsource projects or tasks. Delegation saves a lot of time, reduces the workload, and allocates enough time for more important responsibilities. When you assign jobs to qualified or experienced subordinates (freelance or in-house), it enhances productivity. Investing in training for in-house personnel is valuable as well.

What Is Delegation?

A delegation is an act of conferring authority or power on others to act on your behalf to carry out tasks. When delegating, you assign responsibilities to subordinates with specific terms of reference for the execution of such tasks. Meanwhile, while the responsibility lies on the staff to carry out the job, the superior must ensure proper communication, understanding, and adherence to standards and deadlines. This is the ability to recognize and convert the talents of team members for managerial goals. A high level of productivity is a reward for delegation. The workflow becomes smoother and less stressful when you delegate.

Reasons Managers Don't Delegate

Loss of Authority

Some managers find it difficult to delegate because they feel they are relegating their authority to someone else. Most people see delegation as a sign of weakness or think that the other person will do a shoddy job. However, letting others take up responsibility does not evoke fragility, but your ability to trust others. It also helps you see how well you can duplicate your strength in others by communicating effectively or through training. Delegation is a tool used by highly effective managers.

No One Does It Better

Another myth or misconception about delegation is that no other person can do better than you, but the truth is, delegation, most times, it brings creativity and different points of view to a project.

Delays in the Delivery of the Task

Again, some people hold the view that delegating a job will result in delays. It's true, you do need to bring subordinates up to speed before they can execute a task adequately, but how much can a manager achieve alone? Some of these issues can be resolved with proper staff training. Working alone limits your capacity to executive more jobs. There is so little a single person can achieve, but together, a team will get more done. Delegation not only helps to duplicate the effort and save time, but it also increases the quality of the work delivered.

Why Managers Delegate

The bulk always stops at the manager's table. This phenomenon creates some level of panic and dissuades people from delegating. However, the question for most leaders is: how should I delegate? When you delegate, you do not lose, but share your authority so that you can get more done.

A business has several important aspects to its functions. Marketing, sales, production, distribution, coordination of staff, and more, make up what managers face daily. The only way to successfully execute these roles is to allow others to work with you, while you focus on the strategy of the business. No business can excel where the manager buries himself in the daily operations of each unit. The manager needs to entrust unto faithful stewards parts of his or her powers while concentrating on strategies for expanding the business. Managers can focus on the bigger picture when they learn to delegate.

Increased Capacity

When a manager becomes overwhelmed beyond his ability, devising a system for sharing the work is the smartest thing to do. Why spend three months scrambling between six tasks when you could assign two teams or four individuals to carry on with it? The fear of losing quality or missing deadlines will, over time, result in lower quality work and more issues with deadlines. When the management team doesn't delegate, they experience more burn-outs than are necessary.

More Reasons to Delegate Tasks:

- The decision-making process and chain of command becomes more visible and operational with delegation. It also helps create a stronger and improved pool of talents amongst the team. Through assigning powers, others can develop better communication skills, sufficient motivation, supervision/guidance, and leadership traits.

- Delegation makes the superior-subordinate relationship more meaningful and recognizable. The authority or power can easily flow from the top to the bottom in an organization. With this recognized hierarchy, results are quite achievable.

- Delegation to both subordinates and superiors can bring about the expansion of the organization. This invariably will lead to creating more managerial roles and possibly the need for more outlets. It is an essential factor for an organization looking forward to horizontal or virtual growth; this is a plus.

- Effective delegation can help subordinates flourish and own the process. Subordinates no longer feel like just a number, but are more at the center of events. They are motivated to work because they have this feeling of importance in what they do. Every cadre of management can receive some form of job satisfaction, which further leads to stability and healthy relationships.

- Delegation of responsibility keeps you abreast of your work and puts the manager in the position of a distribution system or powerhouse rather than as a reservoir. The more you allow teams to develop, the more confident they will become. The more confidence other team members have, the more efficient and productive they will be. In the end, it will result in an improvement in the quality of work done in the organization.

- Delegation provides managerial training for subordinates. It is a vital tool for effective planning, development, and for encouraging promotion. It allows everyone to gain experience and grow on the job.

Simple Hacks to Delegating

For delegation to work effectively, it must be systematic and procedural, with timelines, checks, and balances. It doesn't just involve assigning duties and responsibility, but works best if you have a mastery of delegation methods. Delegation is a skill that requires training. Reading books, such as this one, can provide insight into delegation. Here are some simple steps to delegation:

Determine the Duties You Want to Delegate

The first step in delegation is to decide what jobs and responsibilities you wish to assign to members of the team. Break tasks into smaller units as a way of ensuring a good understanding of the objective. For instance, little jobs like flight bookings, scheduling meetings, or responding to emails should form part of the job responsibilities of an assistant. Some of such logistics might appear not to take much time, but there are more productive uses of your time.

Decide on the job in the list that suits you best and those that would be done better by someone else. You might not be skilled in certain areas, and doing the task takes a lot of time. Delegating such a responsibility to a person better equipped than you is ideal, provided they have a clear understanding of your instructions. There are some tasks that require your attention personally, but to help you plan, you can assign tasks based on the job description, roles in the office, or designation. Where you have senior, mid-level managers, and junior staff, you can assign tasks based on the level of authority and attention required. You can also use individual strengths and skills to decide what job to attach to other employees.

Consider Time Constraints

Delegating gives you more time to focus on the bigger picture. It enables you to focus on the intricacies of the business and the strategies required for reaching the company's goal. In assigning tasks, not all members of your team can deliver jobs as quickly as you might expect them to. This action might have to do with their wiring or strength in specific areas. Therefore, as a manager or team lead, you need to understand the depth of team members in deciding who takes on what.

Remember, the purpose of delegation is a smooth workflow. You don't want to miss a deadline or become overworked. Irrespective of the fact that you are better at managing tasks, time might not be on your side. The time-sensitive project should go to fast and capable hands on the team.

Determine Who You Will Delegate Each Task To

It is essential to know the strengths and weaknesses of everyone on the team. This will help you determine what responsibility to delegate to each personnel. From the list of prepared tasks, match each person with a job based on their strength.

Critically looking at their skill set or personality makeup can give you a clue as to who should handle a task. To delegate a job that requires teamwork to a single person, because he is a highflyer, might not always turn out right. Giving the role of team lead to a person who doesn't like teamwork sometimes might de-motivate or slow work progress. In some situations, solo-players learn to become team players and great leaders once they get the opportunity. Also, some other people do better when they work in a team than when working solo. It is your duty as a manager to spot and harness the values in personnel.

Sometimes, for flexible tasks, allowing people to select what project to execute might also help in achieving more significant successes at work. When people can own a project, they feel better motivated to work. Most times, people select projects that they love or have a passion for and will likely achieve outstanding results.

Be Fair in Your Delegation

When assigning tasks, express confidence in your subordinate's abilities, but delegate objectively. Set a timeline from the outset of the project to avoid badgering them while they make progress. Incessant interference can put the team on edge or come off as a lack of confidence in their ability. Allow the unit to tackle problems on their own. After all, what's the point in delegating responsibility if you are going to micromanage them?

From the outset, be clear about your expectations, and be detailed with instructions. Specify the goals, vision, and milestones you want them to achieve. If they miss out on something vital, explain it to them again. Make them understand that you trust them and want to see them grow. Once they feel you are counting on them, they are more likely to deliver.

In the words of Jeffrey Pfeffer, the Thomas D. Dee II Professor of Organizational Behavior at Stanford University's Graduate School of Business, teaching your subordinates how to think and ask the right questions could be your most important task as a leader.

Avoid comparing team members with each other, as each person has unique traits and qualities. They do not all have the same speed, ability, or IQ level. Everyone operates on a different plane. Take that into consideration. Some subordinates may require motivation and a favorable disposition from you, while others may not need motivation.

Take time to study their temperament, as it goes a long way in the delegation process.

Tips for Delegating Tasks

Delegate Promptly

Learn to delegate assignments early enough to avoid unnecessary pressure. Give reasonable timelines for the execution of projects. Time constraints and the eagerness to beat deadlines can result in low-quality performance or errors with the project. As a manager, recognizing a project meant for delegation is a skill to learn. It will help you save time on not attending to the tasks or waiting to delegate.

Years of Experience and Qualification Can Help You Decide How to Delegate

In assigning tasks, individual skills, talents and personality, years of experience, expertise, academic qualification, and professional experience can help. People with various backgrounds can add more value to a project than relying on your capabilities or expertise alone.

Be Explicit With Context and Direction

Don't just hand over the task and expect them to figure it out. An adequately given guideline containing the functions and expectations will go a long way. It is always advisable for the team to work with documented terms of reference, by which they can hold each other accountable. Ensure that the team lead communicates their plans (a report) back to you to be sure they have everything correct before they forge ahead. Ambiguity in instruction might lead to erroneous execution of projects, waste of resources, and time.

Make Them Fully Responsible

All chains of command should be fully understood to help the team work efficiently. Some projects might require access to funds, logistics, and other resources. Always let the team know who they can speak with to get these things. Make sure the team can have access to the communication channel in case of issues. If you aren't there, assign someone to receive reports and to take action for urgent matters. In all you do, let the team do their groundwork and take the initiative for their daily operations without interference.

Create a Feedback Channel

As an addendum to the process, allowing open communication in the course of the project promotes increased productivity. Create time for the team and appreciate the efforts of subordinates by putting a feedback mechanism in place to make delegation an easy tool in the future. Feedback helps you know how each person feels about the projects, the team, and other issues. It will help you glean useful information to make the work process better for the future. Also, if there is any vital information that was left out or overlooked for any reason, feedback can help capture such details. Some people do not express their views better in a team. Using feedback forms, surveys, and more, you can learn one or two truths from reserved team members. When it is time to criticize a person's work or operational process, do so constructively and without prejudice. Criticism should help correct and be used to take the right course, rather than to condemn. Therefore, criticism should focus on activities, not individuals.

Ensure you get a response on how comfortable it was to execute the task. You can also assess your performance as a manager in terms of assigning tasks, clarity of giving out instruction, ability to provide support for the team, and more. Armed with a comprehensive feedback system, you can also get useful plans and strategies for delegating projects.

Show Personal Interest in the Progress of the Work

Try not to be intrusive, but to request updates and give your perspective where necessary. In a case where performance appears below standard, don't take back the task. Provide as much support as you can and ensure they have a better understanding.

No individual has a monopoly on knowledge; therefore, even your subordinates should have the freedom to share ideas with you. You sometimes gain better perspectives from those you least expect. As each person strives to become better in their skills, you must invest in learning resources to lead or delegate better.

Effective delegation works better when you can help other team members grow on the job, develop the right skills, and take charge in turns. Delegation is about authority, responsibility, and accountability. Leaders must learn to use delegation to everyone's advantage, employee motivation, growth, and development.

Chapter Summary

- Delegation is a skill everyone needs to learn, particularly managers.
- The ability to delegate will determine how much success an organization or individual can enjoy. Delegation is utilizing several people's efforts to get tasks done, instead of allowing one person to get everything done.
- It saves time and allocates enough time for other responsibilities.
- Delegation reduces the workload of managers and allows them to make essential inputs.
- Putting aside all misconceptions about delegation will enable you to forge ahead.
- Delegation does not mean relegating your authority to others.

- When managers delegate, they multiply their effort, dividing it amongst their subordinates.
- It gives enough room to plan and strategize on more critical goals.
- The decision-making skills of the managers will improve the more they delegate.
- Delegation quickly results in business expansion and growth.
- It allows subordinates to identify and hone their skills.
- Delegation should follow a well-structured process.
- Decide on the duties to be delegated, determine who gets what, and put time factor into consideration.
- Give delegates ample opportunity to figure things out for themselves.
- Avoid micromanaging the team; it is the opposite of delegation.
- Providing an effective feedback mechanism in place will ensure things work better for the team, as well as to help you gain insight into challenges and successes in the group.
- When there is open communication, the workflow becomes smooth.

FINAL WORDS

It's been an exciting adventure, taking you through some of the most valuable productivity hacks available today. If you have come this far, taking your time to go through this book, then I dare say you mean business. If you put to practice most of what you have learned here, the difference in your productivity level should be evident in a matter of weeks. Also, within the space of 365 days, there should be an exponential growth in your achievements.

However, just to jostle your mind a bit, within the space of ten chapters, this book has looked at ten critical areas that will shape your future. By now, you can clearly outline the problems or issues confronting you in terms of your productivity. There are three key issues we addressed in this book that have to do with your productivity. First, the ability to draw up a workable plan that will help you to achieve your goals in life; second, the ability to focus your energy—it is best if you focus on critical things that will enhance your success in life—and third, your ability to stop the habits that can kill your productivity and develop the habits that will see you accomplish the life you have always dreamed of.

Having identified these three key issues, *Supercharge Productivity Habits* has provided the following time-tested solutions, or hacks, to help you become more efficient, productive, and a top performer in your industry. Central to your success are these three abridged solutions this book recommends:

The Need for a Workable Plan

It helps to have a plan to achieve your goals. That's one fact that this book has established. Having a plan in your head is no plan at all, as you cannot measure input and output effectively. To make your plan work effectively, you must first have a clear understanding of what you want out of life.

Your purpose will help you develop a workable plan of action. Focus your goals around your purpose. You are likely to be more successful and passionate in the areas in line with your purpose. Also, it will help if you have the right beliefs, develop the right habits, and shun negative beliefs. In addition, when setting goals, they should be SMART—Specific, Measurable, Achievable, Realistic, and Time-bound.

Focus Your Energy on Being Productive by Using Tools That Enhance Your Efficiency

Your success rating will depend on so many factors, but the first thing to consider is that you must act now. Procrastination is one of the major obstacles stopping people from pursuing and achieving their goals.

Robin Sharma's 5 A.M. Club provides an excellent tool for enhancing your productivity. Using the early hours of the morning, plan your day using his 20/20/20 principle. That means you spend the first 20 minutes exercising or meditating. The second 20 minutes should be used as a strategy session to plan your day. Then, the last 20 minutes should go into developing skills in an area that will help you achieve your one big goal.

Another exceptional tool this book looked at was the Personal Kanban planner and whiteboard. The Personal Kanban works by helping you to prioritize your tasks to focus on what's most important.

It is made up of three columns. The first column is To-Do or Options, where you list all of your goals and tasks. The second column is Doing or the In-Progress column, where you place the tasks you want to work on now. The third column is the Done column, where you place the tasks you have completed. Having these details on your Personal Kanban whiteboard will help you to focus your energy on meaningful goals, pursue them, and complete more tasks at a faster rate.

With the Personal Kanban, you visualize your work when planning. Visualizing helps you see how the tasks can play out and helps to spur interest and excitement to start and finish them. The second principle of Personal Kanban is limiting your work progress. It involves starting and finishing a task before moving on to another one.

The TEA principle of Time, Energy, and Attention can help you fulfill your potential. However, some people only have two of these three attributes, hence they are not productive.

When you have energy, attention, and no time, you feel overwhelmed. People such as this have lots of energy and also pay attention to the most important tasks, but may feel out of time to complete them due to poor planning or procrastination.

Other people know how to manage their time and can pay attention, but lack the energy to get tasks completed. In cases such as these, a lack of energy often leads to frustration. However, eating right, sleeping well, exercising, and breaking tasks into smaller chunks, will help them to do better.

The third category of people have enough time and energy, but have a problem paying attention. These people are easily confused and overwhelmed. Whatever you do, you need the right dose of motivation to achieve success. Using science-backed tricks, like the high power pose, can help you to keep your motivation levels up.

To help increase your efficiency and focus further, the Pomodoro method can come in handy. Instead of spending 3 to 4 hours working at different tasks with little results, you can focus on a single task for 25 minutes and then take a 5-minute break. Doing this in intervals of 25 minutes and 5 minutes all through the workday can help you to get more done.

Kill the Habits That Can Kill Your Productivity

In the course of this book, I have identified several productivity killers and what you should replace them with.

- Replace multitasking with mono or single-tasking.
- Replace procrastination with action, doing it now (two-minute principle).
- Instead of working alone or trying to get things done alone, delegating tasks to others will help you to get more done faster and more efficiently.

So, What Next?

Take this book as a personal guide or companion. The truths learned here can last you a lifetime. One of the best ways to keep improving in what you have learned is to have *Supercharge Productivity Habits* as a reference book.

Put What You've Learned Into Practice

The investment in resources and time outlined in this book can only pay off once you take action with what you have learned. With the aid of tools like the Personal Kanban whiteboard, Robin Sharma's 20/20/20 rule, the 80/20 or Pareto principle, the TEA strategy for productivity, and the Pomodoro method, you are sure to become a top performer. All you have to do is put them to work.

Get an Accountability Buddy

One of the best ways to help yourself achieve your goals faster is to have someone to hold you accountable for setting them. Let your accountability partner know what goals you have decided to achieve and have them hold you up to it.

Build Teams

If you are a team lead, manager, or chief executive, the best way to increase your overall productivity is when other members of your team have access to the tools that help you. With this in mind, to help you rise faster, create a learning session with other members or staff to implement some of the strategies you have learned.

My Final Gift to You

If there is only one thing you can take away from this book, then I want it to be this fact: to be a top performer in any discipline, you must commit to a clearly defined plan of action. That action must be backed by the right beliefs, laced with discipline, and achieved one step at a time.

Success does not come from trying to do everything but in ensuring that the one thing you do, you do it right.

RESOURCES

15 Ways to Boost Mental Energy Levels. (n.d.). Retrieved December 19, 2019, from https://www.faisonopc.com/office-supply-blog/boost-mental-energy-levels

10016 Therapists, Psychologists, Counseling - Therapist 10016 - Psychologist 10016. (n.d.). Retrieved December 19, 2019, from https://www.psychologytoday.com/us/therapists/10016?profid=318497&search=hershenson&ref=2&sid=1488894923.8327_24335&name=hershenson&tr=ResultsRow

admin. (2019, April 16). SMART Goals: Tips for Goal Setting. Retrieved December 19, 2019, from https://www.performancecoachuniversity.com/smart-goals-tips-for-goal-setting/

Alexander, L. (n.d.). How to Write a SMART Goal [+ Free SMART Goal Template]. Retrieved December 19, 2019, from https://blog.hubspot.com/marketing/how-to-write-a-smart-goal-template

American Psychology Association. (2010, April 5). Psychology of Procrastination: Why People Put Off Important Tasks Until the Last Minute. Retrieved December 19, 2019, from https://www.apa.org/news/press/releases/2010/04/procrastination

Baer, D. (2016, May 29). Why You Need To Unplug Every 90 Minutes. Retrieved December 19, 2019, from https://www.fastcompany.com/3013188/why-you-need-to-unplug-every-90-minutes

Benefits of Exercise. (n.d.-a). Retrieved December 19, 2019, from https://medlineplus.gov/benefitsofexercise.html

Benefits of Exercise. (n.d.-b). Retrieved December 19, 2019, from https://medlineplus.gov/benefitsofexercise.html

Benefits of Exercise. (n.d.-c). Retrieved December 19, 2019, from https://medlineplus.gov/benefitsofexercise.html

Benefits of Exercise. (n.d.-d). Retrieved December 19, 2019, from https://medlineplus.gov/benefitsofexercise.html

Berkeley University of California. (2019, August 13). The Impact of Ventilation on Productivity. Retrieved December 19, 2019, from https://cbe.berkeley.edu/research/impact-ventilation-productivity/

Bradberry, T. (2015, January 20). Multitasking Damages Your Brain And Career, New Studies Suggest. Retrieved December 19, 2019, from https://www.forbes.com/sites/travisbradberry/2014/10/08/multitasking-damages-your-brain-and-career-new-studies-suggest/#3dfdd3f956ee

Brain scans reveal "gray matter" differences in media multitaskers. (2014, September 24). Retrieved December 19, 2019, from https://www.eurekalert.org/pub_releases/2014-09/uos-bsr092314.php

Branson, R. (2010, September 17). Richard Branson On the Business of Life. Retrieved December 19, 2019, from https://www.americanexpress.com/en-us/business/trends-and-insights/articles/on-the-business-of-life-1/?linknav=us-openforum-search-article-link2

Cambridge Dictionary. (2019, December 18). prioritize definition: 1. to decide which of a group of things are the most important so that you can deal with them.... Learn more. Retrieved December 19, 2019, from https://dictionary.cambridge.org/dictionary/english/prioritize

Chu, M. (2018, May 17). Research Shows Listening to Music Increases Productivity (and Some Types of Music Are Super Effective). Retrieved December 19, 2019, from https://www.inc.com/melissa-chu/research-shows-listening-to-music-increases-produc.html

Clear, J. (2013, June 6). How to Stop Procrastinating and Stick to Good Habits by Using the "2-Minute Rule." Retrieved December 19, 2019, from https://www.lifehack.org/articles/productivity/how-stop-procrastinating-and-stick-good-habits-using-the-2-minute-rule.html

Conti, G. (2019, October 23). How to Delegate Tasks Effectively (and Why It's Important). Retrieved December 19, 2019, from https://www.meistertask.com/blog/delegate-tasks-effectively/

Corliss, J. (2019, August 5). Mindfulness meditation may ease anxiety, mental stress. Retrieved December 19, 2019, from https://www.health.harvard.edu/blog/mindfulness-meditation-may-ease-anxiety-mental-stress-201401086967

Coscarelli, J. (2012, March 2). 63 Minutes With Jack Dorsey. Retrieved December 19, 2019, from http://nymag.com/news/intelligencer/encounter/jack-dorsey-2012-3/

Cuddy, A. (n.d.). Your body language may shape who you are. Retrieved December 19, 2019, from https://www.ted.com/talks/amy_cuddy_your_body_language_may_shape_who_you_are

Darius Foroux. (2019, October 29). The Pomodoro Method: Take Strategic Breaks To Improve Productivity. Retrieved December 19, 2019, from https://dariusforoux.com/takebreaks-pomodoro/

Depression. (n.d.). Retrieved December 19, 2019, from https://medlineplus.gov/depression.html

Don't read my lips! Body language trumps the face for conveying intense emotions. (2013, January 15). Retrieved December 19, 2019, from https://www.princeton.edu/news/2013/01/15/dont-read-my-lips-body-language-trumps-face-conveying-intense-emotions?section=science

Dowling, T. (2017, November 25). What time do top CEOs wake up? Retrieved December 19, 2019, from https://www.theguardian.com/money/2013/apr/01/what-time-ceos-start-day

Economy, P. (2018, May 17). This Is the Way You Need to Write Down Your Goals for Faster Success. Retrieved December 19, 2019, from https://www.inc.com/peter-economy/this-is-way-you-need-to-write-down-your-goals-for-faster-success.html

Facebook COO Sheryl Sandberg talks personal tech. (2011, October 3). Retrieved December 19, 2019, from https://usatoday30.usatoday.com/tech/columnist/talkingyourtech/story/2011-10-03/talking-your-tech-sheryl-sandberg-facebook/50641034/1

Foods for change and motivation | Jean Hailes. (n.d.). Retrieved December 19, 2019, from https://jeanhailes.org.au/news/foods-for-change-and-motivation

Golemanova, R. (2019, October 15). 4 Easy Steps To More Successful Delegation. Retrieved December 19, 2019, from https://blog.hubstaff.com/delegate-tasks/

Grimsley, S. (2015, December 18). Delegation in Management: Definition & Explanation. Retrieved December 19, 2019, from https://study.com/academy/lesson/delegation-in-management-definition-lesson-quiz.html

Hartmans, A. (2018, May 7). How to dress like a tech billionaire for $200 or less. Retrieved December 19, 2019, from https://www.businessinsider.com/clothes-worn-by-tech-billionaires-2018-5?IR=T

Harvard Health Publishing. (2019, August 1). How much sleep do we really need? Retrieved December 19, 2019, from https://www.health.harvard.edu/staying-healthy/how-much-sleep-do-we-really-need

Hess, A. (2018, May 17). 10 highly successful people who wake up before 6 a.m. Retrieved December 19, 2019, from https://www.cnbc.com/2018/05/17/10-highly-successful-people-who-wake-up-before-6-a-m.html

How Lighting Affects the Productivity of Your Workers - Blog | MBA@UNC. (2017, September 11). Retrieved December 19, 2019, from https://onlinemba.unc.edu/blog/how-lighting-affects-productivity/

Introducing the Eisenhower Matrix. (n.d.). Retrieved December 19, 2019, from https://www.eisenhower.me/eisenhower-matrix/

Jack Dorsey LIVE Chat on. (2015, December 22). Retrieved December 19, 2019, from https://www.producthunt.com/live/jack-dorsey#comment-202183

Knapp, A. (2011, August 9). Meditation Leads to Greater Pain Relief Than Morphine. Retrieved December 19, 2019, from https://www.forbes.com/sites/alexknapp/2011/04/07/meditation-leads-to-greater-pain-relief-than-morphine/

Kosner, A. W. (2014, January 6). Why The Best Time To Drink Coffee Is Not First Thing In The Morning. Retrieved December 19, 2019, from https://www.forbes.com/sites/anthonykosner/2014/01/05/why-the-best-time-to-drink-coffee-is-not-first-thing-in-the-morning/#ba25f357a717

Laliberte, M. (n.d.). How to Be More Productive In Your First Hour of Work. Retrieved December 19, 2019, from https://www.rd.com/advice/work-career/productive-first-hour-work/1/

Lung Institute. (2017, January 27). Oxygen Levels and Brain Function. Retrieved December 19, 2019, from https://lunginstitute.com/blog/oxygen-levels-brain-function/

Manson, M. (2019, December 17). 7 Strange Questions That Help You Find Your Life... Retrieved December 19, 2019, from https://markmanson.net/life-purpose#footnote-2

Martin, G. (n.d.). "Procrastination is the thief of time" - the meaning and origin of this phrase. Retrieved December 19, 2019, from https://www.phrases.org.uk/meanings/procrastination-is-the-thief-of-time.html

McCall MD, T. (2017, April 12). 38 Health Benefits of Yoga. Retrieved December 19, 2019, from https://www.yogajournal.com/lifestyle/count-yoga-38-ways-yoga-keeps-fit

Murphy, M. (2018, April 15). Neuroscience Explains Why You Need To Write Down Your Goals If You Actually Want To Achieve Them. Retrieved December 19, 2019, from https://www.forbes.com/sites/markmurphy/2018/04/15/neuroscience-explains-why-you-need-to-write-down-your-goals-if-you-actually-want-to-achieve-them/#5c06091e7905

NPR Choice page. (2008, August 21). Retrieved December 19, 2019, from https://choice.npr.org/index.html?origin=https://www.npr.org/2008/08/21/93796200/to-lower-blood-pressure-open-up-and-say-om

Pardon Our Interruption. (n.d.). Retrieved December 19, 2019, from https://www.apa.org/research/action/multitask

Pink, D. (n.d.). The puzzle of motivation. Retrieved December 19, 2019, from https://www.ted.com/talks/dan_pink_the_puzzle_of_motivation?

Pochepan, J. (2019, February 19). This Aspect of Office Design Subtly Influences Employee Behavior. Retrieved December 19, 2019, from https://www.inc.com/jeff-pochepan/use-psychology-of-color-to-influence-your-work-day.html

pubmeddev. (n.d.). A pilot study of yogic meditation for family dementia caregivers with depressive symptoms: effects on mental health, cognition, and telomerase acti... - PubMed - NCBI. Retrieved December 19, 2019, from https://www.ncbi.nlm.nih.gov/pubmed/22407663

Rampton, J. (2017, August 18). 15 Scientifically Proven Ways to Work Smarter, Not Just More. Retrieved December 19, 2019, from https://www.entrepreneur.com/article/298941

Robin Sharma | Official Website of the #1 Bestselling Author. (n.d.). Retrieved December 19, 2019, from https://www.robinsharma.com/

Schmitz, M. (2018, December 21). The 3 Pillars of Productivity You Need To Unlock Your Full Potential. Retrieved December 19, 2019, from http://www.asianefficiency.com/productivity/tea-framework/

Shandrow, K. L. (2015, March 9). How the Color of Your Office Impacts Productivity (Infographic). Retrieved December 19, 2019, from https://www.entrepreneur.com/article/243749

S.J. Scott. (2019, December 5). How to Get More Energy: 20 Tips to Boost Your Energy and Get More Done. Retrieved December 19, 2019, from https://www.developgoodhabits.com/get-more-energy/

Soojung-Kim Pang, A. (2017, May 9). Why you should work 4 hours a day, according to science. Retrieved December 19, 2019, from https://theweek.com/articles/696644/why-should-work-4-hours-day-according-science

Sorkin, A. R. (2014, September 6). So Bill Gates Has This Idea for a History Class ... Retrieved December 19, 2019, from https://www.nytimes.com/2014/09/07/magazine/so-bill-gates-has-this-idea-for-a-history-class.html?_r=0

Tadeo, M. (2014, November 8). Mark Zuckerberg on why he wears that same T-shirt every day. Retrieved December 19, 2019, from https://www.independent.co.uk/news/business/news/mark-zuckerberg-i-dont-like-spending-time-on-frivolous-decisions-such-as-clothes-or-what-to-make-for-9846827.html

The Bionic Manager - September 19, 2005. (2005, September 19). Retrieved December 19, 2019, from https://money.cnn.com/magazines/fortune/fortune_archive/2005/09/19/8272899/index.htm

To Multitask or Not to Multitask. (2018, July 17). Retrieved December 19, 2019, from https://appliedpsychologydegree.usc.edu/blog/to-multitask-or-not-to-multitask/

Valentine, M. (2019, September 25). 7 Habits to Increase Your Physical and Mental Energy. Retrieved December 19, 2019, from https://www.goalcast.com/2018/12/19/habits-increase-physical-mental-energy/

Walden University. (2019, May 16). 5 Mental Benefits of Exercise | Walden University. Retrieved December 19, 2019, from https://www.waldenu.edu/online-bachelors-programs/bs-in-psychology/resource/five-mental-benefits-of-exercise

Wang, D. (2018, September 7). 5 Surprising Tips To Increase Your Motivation Immediately. Retrieved December 19, 2019, from https://open.buffer.com/increase-your-motivation-tips/

Wertz, J. (2019, July 1). Open-Plan Work Spaces Lower Productivity And Employee Morale. Retrieved December 19, 2019, from https://www.forbes.com/sites/jiawertz/2019/06/30/open-plan-work-spaces-lower-productivity-employee-morale/#5d2f826761cd

What Is SMART and How Do I Write SMART Goals? (2019, July 3). Retrieved December 19, 2019, from https://www.thoughtco.com/how-do-i-write-smart-goals-31493

Why People Procrastinate: The Psychology and Causes of Procrastination. (n.d.). Retrieved December 19, 2019, from https://solvingprocrastination.com/why-people-procrastinate/

Wikipedia contributors. (2019, November 4). A picture is worth a thousand words. Retrieved December 19, 2019, from https://en.wikipedia.org/wiki/A_picture_is_worth_a_thousand_words#cite_note-1

Wong, K. (2016, December 9). The Case for Silence While You Work or Study. Retrieved December 19, 2019, from https://lifehacker.com/the-case-for-silence-while-you-work-or-study-1789847745

Proven Speed Reading Techniques

Read More Than 300 Pages in 1 Hour.
A Guide for Beginners on
How to Read Faster with Comprehension
(Includes Advanced Learning Exercises)

John R. Torrance, Productivity Coach

TABLE OF CONTENTS

INTRODUCTION

How often do you find yourself scrolling through your newsfeed, whether on Facebook or some other news app, and see an article you want to read, but think to yourself: 'I don't have time to read that'? Perhaps you find your reading list piling ever higher with books you haven't read and don't intend to read any time soon. We live in an ever more digitized world with more and more pertinent or interesting information pouring out of everywhere by the second. Our time holds more value than ever. For these reasons, choosing how to spend it becomes a critical decision. Everyone prioritizes their time differently. Some place work-related reading at the top, while others choose politics or other current events. Others still use reading as a way to think about nothing else for a while, a blissful distraction if you will.

Whatever your goal, this book will teach you a secret. You can do all of this, even beyond your current reading goal, with the power of speed reading. Now, you may say that you already read quickly, but let me ask you a couple of things. How often do you find yourself reading something and jumping back a paragraph because you seem to have forgotten every word you just read? Maybe you get hung up on a word or phrase because you do not quite know what it means? Sometimes you might even read to the end of a page or chapter and cannot fully remember what the point was, correct? Speed reading presents a solution to each of these hang-ups and more. By giving you specific pointers to address each concern, there should be no more roadblocks on the journey to speed reading success.

I struggled with reading for a long time. My busy day would enlarge my to-be-read pile, and I'd never get through it all. I nearly gave up, overwhelmed by the reading I wanted to do compared to the time I felt I had. As a productivity coach, however, I needed to press on, and keeping my characteristic look-out for new solutions to boost my efficiency, I stumbled across speed reading. Once I found these easy and effective techniques, I tried and tested them before adopting them in my own reading. My productivity skyrocketed, and I never looked back. Except in particular circumstances, I always speedread, and the amount of reading I did before pales in comparison to the amount I do now.

Writing this book would have taken far more time than it did without the help of speed reading. The hours and hours I spent at the library, surfing the internet, or wracking my brain coming up with ideas or points to include would have taken substantially longer without the ability to read at 1,500 words per minute. Whole books about speed reading became accessible where they previously would not have been. With so many experts on speed reading, each with extensive and well-documented reasons, practices, techniques, and their own tips and tricks, it could have taken months to compose this document. I am proud to say that it took only a couple of weeks. They were busy weeks, do not get me wrong, but I cannot help but praise speed reading for keeping it from taking longer.

So what? You may say, looking for a more tangible or understandable benefit than simply just being able to read faster. Speed reading has numerous other benefits beyond mere consumption of words. Reading faster helps you learn faster, making the time barrier to developing new skills substantially less than before.

Not only will speed reading accelerate your information intake, it might rocket-boost your career as well. The more you read, the more you know, and the more you can share with other people, empowering you in whatever setting you find yourself, work, friends, parties, or anything else.

In addition, speed reading can transform unused hours at the end of the workday into productivity. Taking advantage of this bonus time, you can take an online course for another degree or certification that could advance your job prospects and increase earnings. Your confidence will grow with your understanding of a given topic, thanks to the expansion of your fundamental knowledge. You will also remember a lot more, which may seem strange considering how quickly you will read the information. But with that much more information to take in, naturally, your memory will evolve, particularly as your skills continue to improve.

Do not just take my word for it. Experts back up these claims. Nothing replaces firsthand experience, but the topic of speed reading has naturally enchanted researchers, who spend a great deal of their lives reading.

Some debate whether speed reading inhibits reading accuracy and represents a trade-off. However, scientific studies, such as the one conducted by the University of Michigan Library, concluded that retention improves with the ability to read things faster. A 2016 article in the academic journal *Psychological Science in the Public Interest* analyzed the credibility of speed reading and concluded that speed reading is not a magic bullet. However, *So Much to Read, So Little Time* conceded that there is a substantial improvement in overall speed and effectiveness with key speed reading strategies, only with a trade-off of decreased comprehension.

Luckily, this book has strategies to combat small sacrifices, making them virtual nonfactors. We will hear about tactics from other experts in the speed reading sub-field as well with methods from names such as Scott Young, Jim Kwik, and Evelyn Wood highlighted throughout. If that is not enough, the Internet is littered with experts on anything and everything related to speed reading or otherwise. You will hear from several of them, including Ron Cole, Jordan Harry, Jim Kwik, and Tim Ferriss, as they testify to the benefits of speed reading. With my own experiences and the backing of peer-reviewed research, this book will serve as a primer to the speed reading neonate.

How much exactly will these tips and tricks help? For reference, the average person reads about 200-300 words per minute. Does this seem good to you? Before you come up with your opinion, what if I told you that you could read 1,500 words per minute or more? Most speed reading experts cap the upper limits of their word processing speed at 500-600 words per minute, calling it the most you can realistically read without a serious sacrifice to retention. However, world speed reading champions, like Anne Jones can routinely read at upwards of 3,000 words per minute. Jones set the record at 4,700 words per minute with a retention rate of 67 percent. I cannot make you a world record holder in the shadow of Anne Jones, but you will get closer to her rate than the limited rates of other experts. I can promise that with the information and exercises contained in this book, you can count 1,500 words per minute as a baseline. With ample time and practice, you may even exceed that expectation. Who knows, you could possibly be the next world champion speed reader. Just do not let that be your realistic expectation.

Here is the progression of the next ten chapters.

Chapter one will detail the benefits of speed reading. They are numerous and far reaching, anything from increasing your reading output to expanding your memory and comprehension. This chapter will lay the groundwork for your expectations as far as what you will get out of this book. If you do not like what you read here, you can put the book down, but I doubt that will be the case.

Chapter two tackles three misconceptions about speed reading. I am not entirely certain how they developed, but they seem to have taken on a sizable following in popular culture. Speed reading seems like a superpower, especially for literal superheroes in fiction that claim to read 10,000 words per minute. It is ludicrous. The second involves subvocalization and the falsehood that you need to get rid of it to read fast. Also not true. Lastly, reading automatically helps you read faster. Again, not true. This chapter will dispel these myths

Chapter three charges you to embrace whatever level at which you currently read. By breaking down where you stand now, you can honestly develop things you want to work on throughout the book. Bearing in mind how you read and what kind of reader you are lets you move forward with making yourself a better one.

Chapter four introduces you to a basic tenet of speed reading, calculating your speed. By following the formula you can set a quantitative baseline for your reading. Remember this technique down the line. It will come in handy as you try to measure your reading speed and its progression.

Chapter five launches you headfirst into improving your reading speed, by giving you the tips and tricks you need to start out. It involves goal setting, first and foremost, to moderate your expectations for your improvement, ensuring that you find the right balance of ambition and realism. It includes skimming, the most well-known speed reading technique. Other tactics, such as stopping subvocalization, reading phrases, meta-guiding, Rapid Serial Visual Presentation, will build your speed reading foundation.

Chapter six will calm any fears you may have about sacrificing comprehension for speed, something opponents of speed reading will use to base their arguments. Reading comprehension goes beyond just taking in the words and understanding them. It extends to visualization, expanding your vocabulary, and other active reading strategies. Speed reading can lead to a small sacrifice in retention, but the practices in this chapter will help you mitigate those losses substantially. Reading quickly doesn't necessarily impair your comprehension.

Chapter seven will acknowledge that the underlying basis for getting better at reading lies in simply doing it more. You will develop familiarity with the things you read, as well as routines and habits that will lend themselves to your continued reading. The crucial first step in becoming a master speed reader is establishing a strong base.

Chapter eight deals with the problem of keeping track of your reading and giving you structure to document your habits. It recommends tried and true methods while conceding that times have changed and new ones exist that can help you just as much as the old ones. It matters much less how you keep track of your reading than the fact that you do. It helps you maintain focus on your goals and makes you feel good about your progress, regardless of the rate at which it comes. The best way to keep track of that? Time your reading using the formula in chapter four every so often. That will give you verifiable data to follow and let you analyze it however you want.

Chapter nine takes a deep dive into one of the most popular and successful speed reading tactics. Skimming and scanning sound like cheap cop-outs due to the connotations they have taken on, but, in reality, they help you identify and acquire the most important parts of the reading. We will not give away too much in the introduction, but they require a much more active and engaged reading style that you may have previously assumed.

Lastly, **chapter ten** will give you the inside scoop on the most advanced reading techniques, straight from the experts like yours truly. At first glance, they may seem identical to methods in chapter five, but it would be more appropriate to refer to them as extensions of the methods in chapter five. The chapter discusses one of the first speed reading experts, Evelyn Wood, from whom you can learn about one of the more bizarre things to happen on a college campus in the 1960s.

Think of the smartest people you know, whether from popular culture or from your workplace or family life. Do you envy them for the sheer amount of things they know? Do you wish that you could do and say the things they do? Do you want to show off your newfound knowledge to get even, perhaps finally claiming victory at your weekly trivia? Speed reading can be the weapon that keeps you in the intellectual arms race of sorts. If you keep reading this book, you too can unlock the superpower of knowledge and give yourself an edge in whichever form you want it to manifest. All it takes is small tweaks to your current practices and habits, the ones I mention in this book. With them, you will be able to exponentially improve your daily information consumption.

However you want to think about it, whether in terms of words per minute gained, improved comprehension, or time saved, speed reading techniques will make you a better reader. They will do all of those things and more, transforming your reading time from the chore it could have been previously to something you enjoy doing because of the feeling you get or the skills or knowledge you obtain. In purchasing this book you have taken the first step to capitalizing on the promise of considerable potential.

CHAPTER ONE:

How Will Increasing Your Reading Speed Help You?

Let us begin with a thought experiment. Think about all of the required reading you have to do on a given day. Include all of the emails, texts, social media scrollings, news articles, briefings, or any other reading you may do on that day. How much time would you save if you could do it in a third of the time you take now? Or even more ambitiously, what if it took only a fifth of the time it does now? It seems almost too good to be true, does it not? Not quite a superpower out of a Marvel or DC Comic book, but certainly something to strive for. This ability would alter the course of many of our lives.

Quickly reading and comprehending books, articles, and other materials with retention of quality would enable us to round out our perspectives and broaden the scope of our understanding. Armed with this newfound capacity to know things, personal success in whichever form you choose would come more easily. Career paths would move quicker with promotions or raises following your increased productivity in the workplace. Businesses would operate more quickly and effectively. You might even be able to make more lasting first impressions after demonstrating how knowledgeable you are. This book will help you in these ways and more.

In what should not surprise anyone at all, this book will make you a speed reader. With the tips and tricks in this book, you will read more in less time. Your improvement could manifest itself in a doubling or tripling of your current reading speed. You will learn to skim, overstepping information of lesser significance to land only on crucial information.

We will dive into it in more detail later, but there is a misconception about skimming. Some view it as just quickly passing over all of the information on the page without fully engaging with it. This could not be more false. Skimming does involve reading a lot of information quickly, but the process is much more active than that. Skimming relies on a thorough preview of whatever you decide to read, picking out key words, phrases, and ideas to pay attention to while you read. Your eyes pick up on these valuable points, allowing you to skip over anything you may not deem important enough, such as examples. This way your brain is primed to pick up the same important information in less time.

Many people consider speed reading a hack of sorts, something that improves your life so much that it seems like cheating. Few people, though, recognize how exactly it can help, other than reading fast. The lifestyle website *Life Hack* posted an article entitled "10 Reasons Why You Should Learn Speed Reading", and gave some broad and specific examples of just that. Ranging from empowerment to enhanced problem-solving skills, the article offers plenty of justification for the skill. It says that as an empowering skill, speed reading boosts your comfort level wherever you may be, since it allows you to read up on more topics and therefore sound smarter when you talk. Particularly at parties, it gives you more to talk about and makes your opinions smarter, since they are based on more facts and less on speculation. It can make you smarter in a more tangible sense as well since you can turn your newfound ability to consume higher quantities of information and translate that information to certifications or degrees. Think you do not have time for that master's degree or program you keep putting off? Speed reading could be the difference in the equation and make you more money as a result.

Speed Reading Improves Confidence

In addition to more comfortable and better educated, speed reading can make you more confident, particularly in the workplace. If you spend your time and newfound reading capabilities brushing up on anything and everything related to your job, you will get better at it. And the comfort you exude at parties will factor in discussions with your boss as well. In that situation, and any where you may encounter resistance from an argumentative standpoint, you will calmly and easily respond with something you remember from your speed reading.

Speed Reading Augments Memory

Speaking of which, you will remember a lot more after learning to speed read. It makes sense since your reading ability and comprehension is a function of how well you can remember what you read. While there's definitely a requisite amount of memory capability you need in order to read in general, reading more, especially faster, helps train your brain. Reading will facilitate more connections between information and memory in your brain, making it easier to quickly conjure up useful facts or knowledge. How nice would it be to remember something you are supposed to do, whatever it may be, without the jump-out-of-bed panic that often accompanies poor memory? Not only that, your augmented memory can make you more creative, as well.

Speed Reading Quickens Learning

Of course, the most obvious benefit of speed reading is that it enables you to learn more quickly. Spending less time per read means you can read more. Reading more means learning more. Part and parcel with that is sophistication. You are smarter, more comfortable and confident, better educated, and can retain more, that helps your brain tremendously in creating new synapses, or connections between brain cells. The more neural pathways your brain can utilize and the stronger they are, the better you will get at the sheer act of thinking.

Speed Reading Hones Focus and Decreases Stress

Related to that, the act of thinking, particularly with the kind of focus that speed reading requires, can induce meditative qualities. Think about when you are in the zone, in any application, be it sports, work, art, quite literally anything. That feeling when all else drops away and you can focus your entire attention on one task? Speed reading tends to induce that. Not only will this help you focus, but it also has serious stress-relieving qualities as well. This leads to an overall improvement in emotional well-being. Given the relaxing nature of reading, it reduces stress and takes your mind off of worries and other intrusive thoughts that neither benefit nor increase your health. The material absorbs you when you read faster, promoting focus on the information you are reading more than anything else. As an act of active meditation, you achieve the same meditative state as a Buddhist monk.

Speed Reading Opens Up Career Opportunities

Naturally, a decrease in stress allows you to focus on more important things, such as your career. Do you think Bill Gates or his ilk let stress stop them from becoming some of the greatest innovators to live? The ability to limit stress, whether as a result of saved time from speed reading or something else, presents a significant quality of life boost. The clarity of mind that it affords enhances problem-solving capabilities, for example. The best ideas are often instincts, according to this logic, and speed reading helps develop those instincts.

Speed Reading Increases Logic and Problem Solving Skills

Of course, a critical component of problem solving is logic. Your ability to think logically also increases with speed reading. Just think shortly on the goals of speed reading. You've got to understand swaths of information quickly. In order to do as much, you must logically sort information into two pools: important and unimportant. Doing so as quickly as speed reading requires will undoubtedly improve your ability to think and process logically.

A Couple Misconceptions About Speed Reading

You will find yourself laser-focused on whatever you read. Most people have the ability to read at 200 words per minute, with some logging higher counts at about 300 words per minute. Many readers have a misconception that in order to focus more on what you are reading, you need to slow down and digest every word. This is false for two reasons.

First, traditional reading styles and the methods through which they are taught lack efficiency.

Second, people read slowly due to a lack of focus. Think about it. How many distractions do you have when you sit down to read a book? The most salient distraction is probably in your pocket as you read this. When your phone buzzes, it's almost as if the world around it pauses for a moment, does it not? It could be anything: a text, a Facebook notification, a like on your Instagram photos, updates to your Twitter feed, an email from your boss, or simply a dank meme. Whatever it is, our highly connected lives limit the capacity for quiet. You can scarcely catch a moment of uninterrupted time. However, the focus required to speed read makes this point moot. You haven't got the time to be distracted.

And again, we circle back to some of the main benefits of speed reading. If focus is improved, so too are comprehension, memory, and retention of information. The brain is like a muscle. If we train our brains in this way, they will grow stronger and perform better. Speed reading challenges our brains to perform at a higher level. When you train your brain to be able to take in information faster, other areas of your brain will also improve.

What Do the Detractors Say?

A quick google search will yield all sorts of articles and testimonies about how speed reading isn't all it's cracked up to be. Opponents will argue that reading at such high speeds reduces comprehension. Some contend that the human eye and brain cannot coordinate to process words and sentences quickly enough to make much more than 600 words per minute attainable. These studies are well funded and founded, your brain doesn't in fact operate quickly enough for traditional reading methods to function at that speed.

How Can That Be?

So doesn't that make this book a waste of time? No. The techniques contained in this book will teach you how to account for the fact that traditional reading methods don't suffice for 1,500 words per minute reading speeds. There are many studies, similar in authenticity and integrity to opposing ones, that confirm the legitimacy of reading at high speeds. It dates to 1950 when the University of Nebraska conducted a study of 150 business students about speed reading. Don Clifton, chair of the psychology department, divided the students into two groups, one called Gifted with a 350 words per minute average reading speed. The other so-called Normal group clocked in at 90 words per minute. Each group was given the same speed reading course, to varied reactions from faculty, worried that it would corrupt the Gifted students. The Normal group showed significant improvement, increasing to 150 words per minute. That 66 percent increase paled in comparison to the Gifted group, which shot up to 2,900 words per minute, an increase of 828 percent.

You'll notice the extremely high reading speed as well as the percentage increase and that this book offers something lower. Maybe you'll discredit that study as evidence. That's okay because there are plenty more. Take, for instance, the University of Utah study conducted by Leann Larsen, entitled *Does Speed Reading Improve College Student's Retention Level and Comprehension?*. Basing her analysis on three articles that this book will discuss later, she hypothesized that students who learn to speed read gain comprehension of more material and retainment of the information better compared to the students who do not. John Macalister of the Victoria University of Wellington in New Zealand concluded that speed reading does in fact increase student's reading speeds, even when the text is authentic, or new to them. *Speed reading courses and their effect on reading authentic texts: A preliminary investigation* focuses less on retention, but acknowledges that retention was a critical component to the study and was maintained even with high speeds.

Speed Reading Makes Reading More Enjoyable Overall

Naturally, we enjoy doing things we are good at, and with improved reading skills, reading will transform from something we feel obligated to do into something we enjoy. When we enjoy doing things, we put more effort and energy into getting better at them, whether we realize it or not. This book will engage you with advanced learning techniques. Want to learn a new language? Speed reading helps you discover and navigate the grammatical and vocabulary nuances of whichever language you choose. Want to incorporate a new business skill into your work? Similarly, speed reading makes refresher or augmenting courses much more accessible. You can even increase your value to an employer.

Speed Reading Helps Eliminate Bad Habits

Lastly, think about how many bad habits you have formed. It takes conscious and dedicated efforts to unlearn them and replace them, and even more practice and discipline to keep up the new habits without developing more bad ones. Speed reading presents an opportunity to discover and replace bad habits you may have. These stem from your elementary education. Everyone had a teacher that they did not particularly like or realized in hindsight failed at his or her job. How would you like them to have a profound impact on your past, present, and future? I can't imagine anyone would, especially if they were not popular.

This book makes these examples as well as many others realistic. To take the most advantage of these tips and tricks, I recommend you have the following materials handy when doing exercises in this book: Pencil or pen, highlighter, paper, calculator, watch or stopwatch, and, of course, your book or reading material.

More Than That, Speed Reading Makes You a Better Reader

Before you dismiss this as obvious and move on, let me explain. Of course, it will make your reading faster. Beyond that, though, speed reading, in the form of the techniques included in this book, will give you tactics that you can use to make your reading more efficient. For the purposes of this book, I want you to use them at high speeds. However, you can still use them at any speed you like. Paul Nation wrote an article about just this, with an emphasis on language fluency. Somewhat elemental, *Reading Faster* noted that recognizing letters leads to faster processing of words, and so too recognizing words faster processing of sentences and ideas. Continuing this building block, he analyzed how simple sentences turn into complex sentences. This increases not only speaking and writing but reading too. Nation brought up two core techniques which this book will address in the coming chapters, skimming and scanning. He differentiated skimming as reading a text quickly, aiming for acquiring the big picture of what it is about, at the expense of some details. Scanning, on the other hand, requires the reader to seek out specific information, in the form of names or numbers. Nation acknowledges the merits of each but concedes that skimming offers more benefit than scanning, for ease of use, in the pursuit of language fluency. As a summarization, Nation posits that skimming represents the next building block in the development of language fluency and results in a more proficient ability to read it, along with the other functions of writing and speaking.

Chapter Summary

- You can cut the amount of time you currently spend reading substantially.
- You can fill that time with more reading, multiplying the amount of effective reading time in your day.
- More than just time spent and amount of reading, speed reading comes with other benefits and byproducts, like career advancement and skill development.
- Speed reading combats ineffective traditional reading styles and discredits the assumption that slower reading is more focused and effective.
- Speed reading promotes focus because it requires and facilitates a concerted effort to consume and retain information as quickly and accurately as possible.
- Speed reading challenges the brain and strengthens it, and, in the same way as a bicep or other muscle exercise, also supports and strengthens other parts of the brain.

- Speed reading will help you enjoy reading and make you better at it.
- Speed reading reveals the opportunity to learn new skills at a faster pace.

The next chapter will debunk myths you may have been taught about reading faster. With the support of evidence, chapter two will alleviate your reservations and misconceptions about speed reading with thorough research.

CHAPTER TWO

3 Myths You Were Taught About Reading Faster

While there are many misconceptions about speed reading, some exceed the scope of myth. This chapter will dispel 3 popularized myths about speed reading to further convince you that speed reading is real, effective, and can benefit you tremendously. They exaggerate what speed reading is, looks like, and does for you. Without further ado, here are the 3 biggest myths about reading faster.

Myth #1: You can read 10,000 words per minute

Let us put this one into mathematical perspective. 10,000 words with Times New Roman at 12 pt font size, the same as this text here, with single spacing, is 20 pages, and with double spacing is 40 pages. With 500 words and 250 words on each page respectively. Also, 10,000 words per minute reduces to 166 ⅓ words per second, making the rate about a page or half a page per second. Scientific studies show that the brain typically processes images, not words, in about 100 milliseconds. In a 2014 study conducted by Massachusetts Institute of Technology, neuroscientists found that the eye needs as little as 13 milliseconds to process concepts as shown in images. Applying both of these calculations, that amounts to 16 ⅓ words per 100 millisecond and 2 ⅙ words per 13 milliseconds. Those speeds are quite literally lightning-fast and frankly unattainable, particularly when considering the difficulty of picking words out of a sentence, paragraph, or page.

Think about it like this. This book is roughly 30,000 words. Do you think you could realistically read a third of this book in a minute? It's absurd. That's not what speed reading is about.

These processes, unlike the processing of images displayed in the MIT study, require the movement and refocusing of the eye, substantially lengthening the time required to read and comprehend the information. The assertion that the human brain can read at 10,000 words makes for great imagery in movies or TV. Superheroes like Superman, The Flash, and Quicksilver might be able to do it. But there is a reason that this is, for the most part, fiction. Only superhumans possess this ability. 10,000 words per minute is simply impossible, as Calvin of *Calvin and Hobbes* famously says, "reading is easy if you do not sweat comprehension."

Myth #2: Subvocalization Impedes Speed Reading

For those of you who may be unfamiliar, subvocalization is the voice you hear in your head while you read. Some speed reading experts contend that the elimination of subvocalization is the key to speed reading. Scott Young, however, admits that while this does enhance your ability to process words more quickly, the tradeoff involves a marked decrease in comprehension. So how then, if you do not eliminate subvocalization, can you possibly hope to read faster? With subvocalization critical to reading comprehension, the fastest readers quite simply are better at it and do it faster. As a testament to the efficacy of this practice, NASA constructed a system to register these impulses in order to browse the web or control a spacecraft. In exactly the same process that subvocalization will help you learn a new language, it facilitates your reading comprehension.

Myth #3: Reading Is the Same as Practicing Speed Reading

One might think that the simple act of reading enables us to read faster. However, like any practice, if we do not correctly implement the techniques or methods intentionally, we develop bad habits that we often do not recognize. In the name of full or over-comprehension, we can reread sentences or paragraphs, or get fixated on words or phrases we are unfamiliar with. Furthermore, unless you actively stretch your normal reading speed, you are not practicing speed reading.

But wait, you may say, those best-selling, page-turning novels I read beg to differ! Your point would be valid so long as you account for the fact that these books are intended to be read quickly. They rely on simple concepts, comprehension, and vivid imagery to advance the plot and thematic points they write about. Also, how often do you read a book like that, or any other for that matter, and remember the whole thing? Practicing speed reading requires a little sacrifice of retention at first. Continued, mindful practice will in time improve your retention as well, but expecting speed and comprehension to improve simultaneously is perhaps overly optimistic. As such, when you are reading, do so for the purpose of enjoyment. To improve your speed reading, dedicate specific time to improve the speed at which you read.

Chapter Summary

- Because of the somewhat mysterious and seemingly unattainable nature, speed reading myths exist and tend to further mystify it or make it seem more inaccessible.
- These myths exist because speed reading appears too good to be true.

- The first one is hyperbole, that people can read as many as 10,000 words per minute.
- The second myth is that you must eliminate subvocalization, the inner voice in your head when you read, in order to achieve realistic levels of speed reading.
- Lastly, people do not naturally improve their speed reading just by reading normally.

Now that we have established the benefits of speed reading and discredited falsehoods about it, let us start to talk about your expectations for your own reading and speed reading. You may have visions of yourself blazing through all manner of reading. First, though, we need to find a baseline. This next chapter will figure out where you are now with your speed reading.

CHAPTER THREE:

Embrace Your Level of Reading

Just like any other skill, beginning to learn speed reading requires honesty about your current abilities. You would never walk into a gym or weight lifting class and start trying to bench press 300 or more pounds on your first try. If you were an aspiring actor or actress, you would never step onto a set for a movie for which you hadn't rehearsed lines. If you're an artist, you'd never find your first painting in a museum next to a Picasso. You get the point.

In the same way, you need to acknowledge and embrace the fact that you may be a beginner speed reader. You'll undoubtedly have goals to strive for on day one, but you need to let go of the idea of being a master at day 1. If you, as you do right now, read at about 200 words per minute, it will take more than the amount of work you can put in in one day to build up and maintain a reading speed of 1,500 words per minute. With that bit of tough love behind us, we all start somewhere, and wherever that place may be, it is okay, especially since by purchasing this book you have chosen to improve. Nonetheless, like anything else in life, in order to know where you are going, you have to know where to start. Set lofty goals or expectations for yourself, but understand that it is not easy and may not come as quickly as you would like. In that case, do not be hard on yourself, just keep working.

Let us analyze a bit more where you are right now. How would you describe yourself as a reader? What things do you like to read most? What things can you not stand reading? What things would you like to read more? Are there certain things you would like to get through faster when you read? Are there things you want to better understand when you read them? Most importantly but not quite as obviously, examine the explanations for your answers. Why do you say or do these things?

Fun fact, did you know that reading is not a natural human biological function? That is right, unlike things we often associate with reading, like seeing, hearing, feeling, or even language, our brains do not naturally know how to read. Instead, humans acquired reading as a skill and developed it culturally. Dr. Yuval Noah Harari explains the evolution of reading and writing from its foundation as an accounting for grain storages and purchases in his book *Sapiens: A Brief History of Humankind.* By co-opting other developed cognitive strategies such as image recognition and linguistic parsing, language first incorporated things that could be touched, seen, heard, smelled, or tasted. Concrete ideas such as these eventually allowed for abstract ideas to be communicated, such as religions, myths, fantasies, or legends. This created a sharp juxtaposition between the physical reality we all share and the imagined reality each of us inhabits ourselves.

It took many thousands of years, until roughly the Agricultural Revolution, before writing was invented and, with it, reading. A process we utilize on a daily basis and take for granted actually comes from a long and complicated history. Reading and writing are difficult and somewhat unnatural to humans. Otherwise, global literacy rates would be higher than the 86.31%, as the current figure cited by the World Bank stands. You might look at this percentage and exclaim, "Wow, that's pretty good." And it is. It's better than it has ever been in recorded history. Still, it demonstrates a critical fact: Reading is not an innate, instinctive skill.

Beyond the esoteric, meta-historical perspective, there are more tangible constraints to improving your speed reading. Feel free to blame any one or number of them if you get frustrated. Most broadly, not knowing the topic might have the greatest effect on your ability to read quickly. Abstract and difficult to understand topics will almost assuredly slow your pace as you grapple with the content at hand. Secondly, not knowing the words will also slow you down. The more words you do not know, the more you will have to scratch your head trying to figure out what it means before your stubbornness frustrates you into consulting a dictionary. Lastly, not knowing the sounds will impede your reading progress. This bit isn't particularly common in your native language, but it does happen every once in a while. Loan words from other languages have the potential to stump you while you read, in the same way that learning other languages would. Conversely, the more about the topic, words, and sounds you know, the more your speed reading will increase.

Chapter Summary

- Before you can access where you want to go, you need to know where you are now, speed reading is no different than anything else that way.
- Think about yourself as a reader. That is the best way to determine your stepping off point when wanting to speed read better.
- Understand that reading is not something you should take for granted and is actually foreign to the human biological default hardware settings. Your ancestors developed it in a complicated process millennia ago.
- More relevantly, there are constraints to your reading. Not knowing the topic, words, or sounds in the reading can impede your progress.
- On the flip side, increased knowledge of the topic, words, and sounds will make your reading easier.

Now we have established an abstract baseline of sorts, based on your own descriptions of yourself as a reader and the understanding that reading is difficult and complicated. In the next chapter, you will undertake a more quantitative assessment of your fundamental skills as a reader by calculating your reading speed. This will turn your abstract goal of wanting to generally read faster into a recognizable goal of exactly how much faster you want to read compared to your current reading speed.

CHAPTER FOUR

How to Calculate Your Reading Speed

If you are trying to increase your reading speed, then you need to keep track of what it is. This calculation was developed for students taking the LSAT, the standardized test for those who wish to get into law school. Follow the instructions to get a good estimate of your effective reading speed.

The Formula

Estimate the number of words on a page by counting the number of words in two lines and dividing by two. So if there are 37 words in two lines, then the word count per line is 18.5.

Count the number of lines on the page page. Multiply by the number of words per line. So, if there are 50 lines on a page, 50 x 18.5 = 925 words on a page.

If you want to be even more accurate, you can simply use software to check the number of words on a particular eBook page.

Read a page. Count how long it takes in seconds.

Divide the words per page by the seconds it took you to read the page. Multiply by 60 to get the words per minute. For the purpose of this exercise let us say it took you four minutes and 30 seconds to read the page. That amounts to 270 seconds. 925 divided by 270 is equal to 3.425. That times 60 is about 205 words per minute.

Let's repeat that formula and simplify here. Determine the words per line (WPL). Next, determine the lines per page (LPP). Multiply WPL by LPP to get the words per page (WPP). Now get your stopwatch. Start it. Read the page. Convert the time to seconds. Divide the WPP by the seconds. Multiply by 60 to get your words per minute (WPM).

One more time, the formula is as follows:

WPM = WPP (LPP x WPL) / Seconds x 60

Now you can calculate your own WPM (reading speed), but before you do so, take a couple of steps to ensure you're focused:

- Find a quiet spot to read alone
- Eliminate distractions (TVs, cell phones, browser tabs, etc.)
- Make sure you're comfortable
- Have your stopwatch and book at the ready

Got all that? Now calculate your own reading speed and write the figure somewhere so you can track your progress as you read this book.

Periodically, measure the speed at which you read. Ideally, you should use the same book, or at least the same author, to standardize the test. Otherwise, you would get an inaccurate estimate of your reading speed. Reading the same book will ensure that you are not reading faster or slower due to the difficulty of the book to read. It can also be a book you have already read. In fact, that may be better than a book you have not read because, at least in theory, you should know all of the words in the book.

After conducting the test and calculating your own reading speed, see where you stand below. These figures were taken from a study sponsored by Staples to market for an e-book and were cited in a

Forbes magazine article. Use this information only as a benchmark to evaluate where you are. Do not get discouraged if the result is not what you want, because by reading this far into the book, you have demonstrated a good commitment to improving your reading speed. With time and practice, your speed should see a considerable increase.

- The average reading speed of an adult is 300 words per minute.
- A typical third-grade student reads at a rate of 150 wpm (words per minute).
- Eighth grade students can usually achieve speeds of 250 wpm.
- Your average college student will hit about 450 wpm.
- An average "high-level executive" takes in about 575 wpm for their super important corporate job.
- Given the high level of education required of their job (usually a doctoral degree), an average college professor reads at 675 wpm so that they can get through all of the immeasurable amounts of work their students produce and still meet grading deadlines.
- Speed readers can reach limits of 1,500 wpm or more, particularly with the help of speed reading books such as this.
- We already mentioned her, but Anne Jones is worth mentioning again. As a World speed reading champion, she reaches an astounding 4,700 wpm.

Chapter Summary

- Calculating your reading speed is easy. Following the formula, you can determine reading speed in five minutes or less.
- Estimate the words per page by counting the words in two lines and then dividing by two.
- Count the number of lines per page then multiply by words per line.

- Alternatively, for those reading electronic books, highlight all the text on the page and check the word count using your e-reader or copy and paste the words into a word count checker.
- Read a page and count the number of seconds it takes.
- Divide the words per page by the seconds it took to get words per second.
- Multiply by 60 to get your words per minute.
- That formula can be represented as such: WPM = WPP (LPP x WPL) / Seconds x 60
- Regularly repeat the exercise to log your progress, using the same book, ideally.
- Use the information above as a reference for your speed reading level and a baseline to compare your progress to once you have practiced for some time.

Congratulations! You now know exactly where you stand as a speed reader. By this point in the book, you have heard a lot about the benefits of speed reading and some myths associated with it. You have established an idea of who you are as a reader and calculated your words per minute. You may be wondering when you will get to the good stuff, exactly how to improve your speed reading. Luckily, the next chapter will be the first that reveals tips and tricks about how to do just that.

CHAPTER FIVE:

How to Read Faster

Have a Goal

The first step to speed reading actually happens before you even really start to read a book, article, essay, or anything else you may choose. This involves setting a goal for what you read. Namely, what do you want to get out of whatever you are about to read? Do you want to learn about the latest in current events in a newspaper article? Or perhaps learn a new skill like you are right now? Maybe you picked up the latest bestseller that everyone is talking about and you want to check it out for yourself. The exact reason or goal does not matter nearly as much as the act of setting one. Having a goal in mind when you read helps you tremendously as you read. It keeps you focused on why you are reading. It helps you hunt down particular knowledge while you read, and alerts you when you need to slow down and focus for certain, crucial passages, maximizing your comprehension.

Do Something While You Read

What, like multi-task? Should I be trying to get chores done while I have a book in my hands? No, that's not what I'm suggesting. A lot of the struggles associated with general reading as well as speed reading come with a passive approach to it. By that I mean, you do nothing more than move your eyes over the words and try to comprehend them. In his book, *Breakthrough Rapid Reading*, Peter Kump hones in on this passivity, remedying this by prescribing active involvement with whatever it is you're doing, in this case reading. This maximizes your conscious concentration and reinforces your understanding of what you read. Quoting psychologist William James, he assesses that improving memory involves improving the habits we use to record facts. From this, Kump surmises that active reading and organization while throughout improves the ways in which you record or receive information. That's not enough though. Kump says that in order to make the information yours, you have to use it and apply it in some way. Whether that's repeating it or synthesizing it in conjunction with something else, you don't own it unless you do. This chapter will show you some ways you can apply this reasoning to your reading to take advantage of the benefits of active reading.

The Magic of Skimming

Modulating your reading speed helps readers get the most out of their reading while also increasing the speed at which they read. We call this technique skimming. By selectively reading information that you deem most important and glossing over unnecessary things, skimming can be incredibly effective once we determine the information we wish to obtain from a given text. Skimming can serve another purpose as well. Quickly reading the text over before you examine it closer helps your eye and your brain pick up on the information that interests you most. This familiarizes you with it in general before you commit to reading it in depth. A study found that this practice increases comprehension noticeably.

Think about the last time you studied for an exam. I realize it may have been quite some time ago for some, but bear with me nonetheless. When preparing for an exam or a big presentation, if you prefer, your time is limited. So naturally, you skip over any information that would not help you and begin with the most important. We quickly skimmed through the exam papers to figure out and understand the structure of it, what kind of questions would be on it, and which parts were worth the most points. From there we could maneuver the exam quicker and more efficiently because we knew where the biggest gains and losses were to be had. For instance, if an essay question was worth just as much as the multiple choice and short answer portions combined, we may start with the essay before getting to the fewer-points-per-question areas. In reading anything, generally, we find the most important information in the introduction and the conclusion. Taking this strategy, reading those parts while skimming anything in between would best serve us in terms of information retained.

Consider Replacements for Subvocalization

Here is where a modulation in subvocalization can help substantially. When skimming, we already sacrifice retention for speed because the information is not as important to us. Because we have already accepted this, we can stop subvocalizing as much to assist us in speeding through these sections. In instances such as this one, subvocalization is the primary factor, by far, in slowing down our reading. It grinds our reading speed down to about 300 words per minute. The pace of a snail, about a fifth of our potential! Your eyes and brain can process information at a much faster rate. Stopping that narrator in your head from slowing you down can double your effective reading speed pretty quickly.

Hold on a second there, you might say, it is much easier said than done. This is true, stopping subvocalization can be difficult, especially if you feel like you have to subvocalize to read effectively. It is definitely quite the trick, and it took me quite some time to kick this habit. Psychologically speaking, it is incredibly hard to stop habits. However, it is fairly easy to replace one habit with another. Rather than grinding your teeth and trying to stop subvocalizing, distract yourself somehow. Use your finger or a pencil to follow the words, listen to music or your favorite podcast, or chew gum while you read.

Learn to Group Words While Reading

Another difficult habit to overcome is reading each individual word one at a time. We were taught in school that in order to understand a whole sentence that we have to understand the meaning of each word. Even though the last time we last heard a lesson like that was potentially a very long time ago, we still hold its value as true. How often, though, do you read a sentence where you do not know more than one or two of the words? Even if you do, you can usually figure out what these unknown words mean through context clues. Using the same technique of reading a few words around one to figure out what it means, you can read a few words at a time to increase your reading speed.

You can do that because your eye spans about 1.5 inches, more than enough to read five words, maybe three or four if they are shorter. The better you get, the more you can increase this span, with up to nine words in it, working wonders for your reading speed. Again, this may seem easier said than done, but if you focus on every fifth word or so, the results may surprise you. This does take some training before you can fully take advantage of this skill. Like anything, time and practice improve it. I would caution you against using it for anything important, like a textbook, before you feel fully comfortable with it, though.

The article I mentioned earlier, "So Much to Read, So Little Time", addressed this phenomenon directly. It details how significantly acuity limits vision and constrains the reading process, inhibiting retention beyond the fovea, the center point of vision and the location where fixation occurs. This area constitutes up to 1 degree in any direction of the angle of vision away from it and provides the highest acuity compared to the parafovea 1 degree to 5 degrees away from the center of vision. The rest of the field of vision is the periphery and has little acuity. While the article contends that acuity decreases the further from the center of vision, some retention is still possible, as illustrated by the picture that follows. While the words blur more toward the ends of the sentences, they are still legible, and for the purposes of speed reading, can still be retained for higher speed reading rates. It is scientifically true that word recognition occurs most often and effectively in the fovea, but some does occur outside of it. For a deeper analysis of why that is, refer to the article for a description of how rods and cones in the eye work. Unfortunately, we do not have time for such a thing here.

As a part of his Backpack Series, Steven Frank wrote a book called *Speed Reading Secrets*. I highly recommend the read, even though this book represents an updated and more extensive version of it. Relevant to reading five or more words together at a time, he has an excellent exercise for developing that method for yourself. Placing three columns of words on the page, he prompts his reader to follow only the middle bolded words and see how many of the other words they can take in, even though the eyes of the reader are naturally drawn to the bolded words.

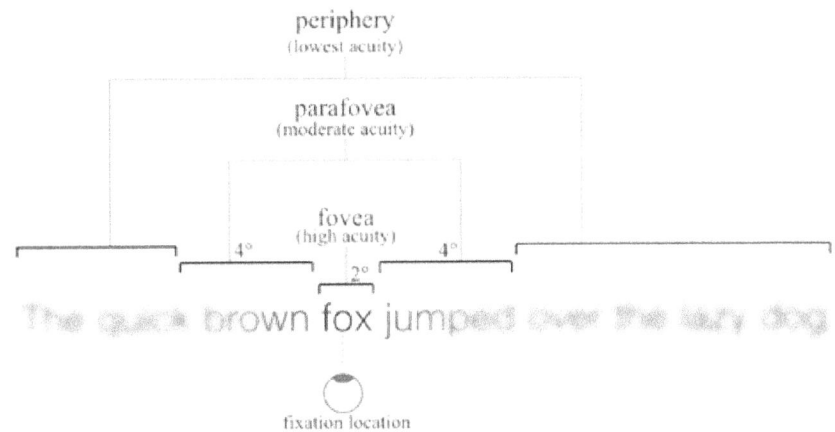

uncle	**penguin**	textbook
school	**light bulb**	jogging
alligator	**airplane**	adventure
umbrella	**soup**	fourteen
symbol	**friend**	bridge
literature	**envelope**	birthday
hungry	**skiing**	tennis
holiday	**shiny**	mathematics
bedroom	**clouds**	degree
green	**pencil**	nighttime
computer	**shoes**	dinner
graduation	**peanut**	candles
calendar	**elevator**	skate
ocean	**wallet**	hearing
sunshine	**brave**	music
mittens	**feather**	sister
history	**title**	doorway
words	**subway**	shampoo
prism	**movies**	occupation
sidewalk	**stomach**	princess

He then instructs his reader to try it again without the bolded words, just following the center column downward. The goal is to concentrate on just the middle section and see how many words the reader picks up anyway. Without the bolded word to take away the focus of your eye, your brain will process more words as your eye wanders more.

happiness	database	brakes
postage	capital	December
quantity	telephone	wristwatch
Boston	freedom	stapler
panther	pizza	motive
earthquake	socks	newspaper
maple	combination	squash
medicines	shoehorn	antenna
inflation	hammer	clothing

Spanish	detective	spectacle
knot	armchair	banister
postcard	temperature	modem
sticker	catalog	lawyer
bookstore	goggles	island
laundry	telephone	alarm
Monday	elevator	service
village	badge	guarantee
waterfall	note	evening
photograph	concert	plumber
ticket	locomotive	bubble
siren	octopus	professor

The relatively simple exercise demonstrates how easy this tactic can be. Frank points out that this technique translates even better to full sentences since they seek to convey a complete idea and the words flow together much better in that form. The words next to each other are not random, with no connection to each other. You do not actually need to read every word to get the idea of the sentence. As a final case and point, he puts a third column of words.

Once	you	train
your	eye	to
read	this	new
way,	you	find
that	it	is
not	so	difficult
to	do.	

Clark points out that sometimes one can divide sentences into clauses that match up nicely and can be used to read in groups. For instance, "before eating breakfast, he went jogging". Not all sentences are that conveniently cut up, though, and clauses vary in length. Some sentences get disjointed due to variation in word length. Dividing words and sentences on the page is still possible, though, just with diligent and somewhat creative application. Using the "Gettysburg

Address" as an example text, he shows how you can divide it into columns that work better, with three or four words per column.

Four score and	seven years ago	our fathers brought forth conceived in Liberty,
on this continent	a new nation,	that all men
dedicated	to the proposition	
are created equal.		

Now we are engaged	in a great civil war,	testing whether that nation, and so dedicated,
or any nation	so conceived	on a great battle-field
can long endure.	We are met	to dedicate a portion
of that war.	We have come	for those who here
of that field,	as a final resting place	might live.
gave their lives	that this nation	that we should
It is altogether fitting	fitting and proper	
do this.		

Ron Cole advocates for this style of reading as well, grouping two, three, four, and five words together to develop and practice this skill. In his book, *SuperReading for Success*, he outlines an innovative and unique reading method that he calls the Eye-Hop. He claims that simply more utilization of this method will correlate to an increase in the reading effectiveness score of the subjects. His methods align similarly to the example from the book written by Steven Frank, but differ in that Cole focuses more on the words themselves than the columns they fall into. He constructs only two columns of words in his book, and the first set involves only pairs of words. A brief excerpt about Basic Astronomy primes the brain of the reader for what follows shortly after it. The three word eye-hop details explorations of Ernest Shackleton and other famous explorers to the South Pole. The four word eye-hop tells the story of The Optimist and further challenges the brain to group words together. At this point, Cole predicts that most of his readers will experience 'the breakthrough', without pronunciation, grasping the full meaning of the phrase. If it does not happen at the four word level, Cole guarantees it will at the five word eye-hop, given the logistical challenge of pronouncing each of the five words in half a second. Therein lies the goal of the Ron Cole eye-hop. On top of ensuring the processing of five words at a time, Cole forecasts a 75 percent recollection of the content in a general, gist-of-it way, not necessarily word for word. He encourages reading as quickly as possible while maintaining at least that level of comprehension.

Follow the Text with a Guide

If this lengthy digression and topic does not work for you, I have good news, there is another useful method. Meta-guiding has been around for some time and can help you accomplish this goal of reading five or more words at a time. It sets the pace for your eye by guiding it to certain words using a pen, pencil, or your finger. By tracking your eye and standardizing the amount of time you spend on each word, you can keep your eye moving along the page. There is a reason that children use the technique when they learn how to read. It helps to move from one word to the next while boosting reading speed and retention. Albeit for different purposes, adults can benefit from it too. The difference is that adults use it much faster, and that is where the trick lies. Working your way up, the faster you can move your finger across the page and follow it with your eyes, the quicker you can read. Acting as a tracker for your eyes, it sets the pace for your eyes and helps you focus from word to word.

Jordan Harry, notable entrepreneur of StudyFast, talks about this exact issue and how, if you fixate too often on each line, you will not only slow down your reading, but tire your eyes as well. Familiarity mitigates this phenomenon, he says, increasing the efficiency of your eye movements and allowing for an increase in reading speed. Part of that increase in efficiency depends on your ability to co-opt your peripheral vision for reading purposes. Doing so, according to Harry, will reduce the number of fixations required per line to about three. By processing more information at one time, it should enhance the quality of the bigger picture of the information without sacrificing understanding. Regular work and addressing of these points should enable you to read quicker. Harry may just be the poster-child for speed reading since he is just 20 years old and has expanded Study Fast to 15,000 people in 147 countries. Overcoming a speech impediment, he now boasts a reading speed of 1,500 words per minute, the same speed this book promises. He offers everything from Online Courses to workshops to events and speaking engagements. Truly impressive, considering his age and childhood condition.

Jim Kwik espouses meta-guiding as well for biological and developmental reasons. He cites that children do it on their own until they are taught to not rely on it. You do it subconsciously when you count things or need extra focus on what you read. From an evolutionary standpoint, your eyes are pretuned to pick up on motion, essential for hunting and survival skills developed by our ancestors. Visual pacing improves focus by pulling our attention through the information rather than segmenting it. He also notes the inherent connection between sight and touch, similar to that of smell and taste. Smell is a large portion of taste, for evidence just eat anything when you have a cold. Your food simply does not taste as good. He quotes many people saying that they feel more tuned into their reading when they use a visual pacer. Perhaps the biggest point toward this connection, though, is the development of Braille, reading designed for those who are blind. Their sense of touch effectively becomes their sense of sight and the entire mechanism by which they read.

For those looking for a simple meta-guiding technique, stick with tracing each line with a pen, pencil, or your finger. If you, however, seek something more advanced than that, here is a preview of coming attractions. In Chapter ten: Learn Faster With Advanced Learning Techniques, you will find the complicated hand motions developed by

Evelyn Wood that released with her groundbreaking speed reading guide in 1959. Considered among the first documented speed reading specialists, she outlines several unique motions one can adopt to speed read, helping your eyes take in the words on the page faster. Stay tuned and read until the end for that, if for no reason other than curiosity.

Leverage Apps to Improve Your Reading

Rapid Serial Visual Presentation often gets used by apps that help with reading speed. By showing single words on the screen in front of you, this method removes the need for your eyes to move. This greatly decreases the time you need to process the information, much like the example MIT image processing experiment. As you get used to the system, the app will naturally increase the speed at which it shows you words, theoretically boosting your reading speed. The speed that words come up can surprise you, so much so that you do not realize that you understand them. However, the downside of this, given the sheer amount of words you see, your working memory gets overloaded. The words come faster than you can deal with them, and you skip some or simply do not process them.

If you decide that apps are the way to go, BookRiot has a list of apps that lend themselves to shrinking your TBR, or To Be Read. They are as follows; "Spreeder", "Reedy", "Read Me!", "Speed Reading", "Speed Reader", "Quick Reader", "Focus-Speed Reader", "Seven Speed Reading App", "Outread", and "Acereader iPad". Their compatible operating systems vary, some only on iOS, some only on Android, and a couple for desktop and browsers. Some are free, while others cost money in their respective app store. The range is far and wide, and I would be very willing to bet there is an app for your appetite, regardless of what your parameters are. If one works for you, download it and start using them to read! Keep in mind, new apps develop each day just as old apps leave the market, so some of these apps may be gone or replaced by the time you read this.

Another app that BookRiot does not mention but that a *MindTools* article does is "Spritz". Using similar RSVP, it released to much acclaim in 2014, even garnering an article in CNN Business that detailed the reactions people made to it, some awed, and some nauseated. Without beating a dead horse, the RSVP has skeptics, especially as one of many RSVP apps on the market, including at the time "Velocity". A minor difference, having one character in red as a focal point, leads to claims that "Spritz" more effectively capitalizes on RSVP while maintaining retention because the one-colored letter makes it easier to follow. The claim has some scientific backing, according to *Medical Daily*, as the brain takes 80 percent of its time locating the optimal recognition point for a given word and 20 percent actually reading it. That being said, speed reading expert Scott Young calls it improbable, considering that the brain can only grasp a 3-5 word "chunk" of information at once. He says our mental RAM just cannot sustain the levels of stimulation that "Spritz" utilizes. He also calls out "Spritz" for claiming research backs the application, but was unable to find any credible, independent, peer-reviewed research to support the claims. All of these apps share a commonality. You can supposedly read at 1,000 words per minute, but you risk comprehension loss and nauseation. The verdict: RSVP technology is not what it is cracked up to be.

A 2000 conference paper published by the University of Manchester in England concluded this very tradeoff. It admitted its value as a technique to facilitate information browsing and search but that it involves a drop off in comprehension. The human visual information processing system limits its use, and at the time, the paper added that much remains to be understood before wide and robust employment in practical applications.

Avoid Regression with Improved Focus

All of these practices, particularly the effective ones, assume that you don't pause or regress during your reading. Getting to the end of a page or halfway through an article and realizing that you have not taken in what you read usually forces you to go back and reread it. Similarly, coming across a word you cannot remember forces you to stop and regress to the technique you used as a child. Reread it for context and to try to understand what it means. With more difficult readings, this happens more frequently.

Jordan Harry, the aforementioned entrepreneur and champion of the effectiveness of speed reading, blames a lapse in concentration rather than a lack of understanding. Distractions cause this more than anything else, even when we think we have been diligently reading. Whether it is a comment by someone sitting in the same room, a text on your phone, or an errant thought, we often get distracted much easier and more frequently than we like to admit.

How do you change this? You can start by reigniting your interest in whatever you are reading. "When our brain wanders, it is because we have become passive. We need to be curious," says Harry. Get actively inquisitive — tap into your inner kid, the one who demands, "But what does that mean?" and "Who is that?" Other questions recommended by Harry are "What am I looking for?" and "What key words and figures do I need to find?" You might also check in every few minutes and simply ask yourself, "What have I learned so far?"

Don't Fixate

In addition to regression, the other bad habit to avoid is fixation. This happens when our eyes catch on a word or a phrase we read on a page. Often going hand in hand with regression, fixation causes us to linger on random spots, impeding our speed. Rather than going back and reading again, fixation freezes us as we think through what a word or phrase means. Harry refers anyone who will listen back to meta-guiding. A tool we use while we read, it helps maintain our reading speed, he says. Often we do not realize that we are reading too fast or slow until it is too late, and we have lost retention or speed. Harry also praises it for forcing our eyes to read faster.

Another bad habit to pay attention to when reading faster is reading out of control. What does that mean? Well, reading out of control entails not purposely reading at a certain speed. This can work both in the faster and slower direction. When you get swept up in a book and turn the pages faster and faster because you are enthralled in the text, that is reading out of control. When your reading grinds to a screeching halt and you labor through every sentence to try to keep everything straight, that is also reading out of control. Part of this is natural since some writing naturally reads faster or slower. The trick here is to try to moderate the reading speed, maintaining a balance between speed and moderation where the text calls for it. An article on the website *Develop Good Habits* debunks the misconception that speed is the emphasis of speed reading and encourages this focus on control. The speed aspect controls one part of how we read and is a supplemental ability, not the essence of speed reading.

Overlook Unimportant Words

That same article, "How to Read Faster: 9 Steps to Increase your Speed in 2020", offers much of the same advice we've seen: decreasing subvocalization, establishing a baseline, meta-guiding, minimizing eye movement, skimming and scanning, and a commitment to practicing and evaluating your speed. However, it offers an interesting and seemingly overlooked piece of advice. Skip small, unimportant words. Based on the premise that saving an extra thirty seconds per page equates to an entire hour and a half in the longer run, the article suggests overlooking small words such as articles and prepositions. You know, words that would benefit you much more in a game of Scrabble. The logic is that their contribution to the overall text is minimal at best. In rare cases when they are necessary, the context of the sentence generally fills in the blank for you. For instance, take that last sentence and remove the small words:

in, the, of, the, in, the, for. A decrease from 19 words to 12 does not seem very significant, but when every sentence is cut almost in half, it matters. You can get through each sentence about twice as fast and retain the essence of what it conveys.

If for some reason that train of thought does not work for you, flip it on its head. Rather than eliminating the less useful words, focus on finding the key words in a reading. Returning to basic grammar for a moment, find the subject and verb of the sentence. There is almost always more to a sentence than just those components unless taking, for example, the simple sentence about 'I ran', for instance. Identifying these parts, though, will give you important clues. Reading a sentence that begins 'the author demonstrated' will help your eyes look for the crucial third part of a sentence, the object. What is the author demonstrating? Recognizing the three building blocks of a sentence will help you process the sentence faster and allow you to focus on the substance of it. If you like, further grammatical analysis can help you decipher between dependent and independent clauses, allowing you to get to the point of a sentence quicker.

Even without any grammatical knowledge or assessment of a sentence, you can do as Abby Marks Beale does and just look at words that serve more than providing sentence structure. She gives a paragraph to her reader and tells them to read it as usual. Then she instructs them to just read the bolded words. Your eye will naturally focus on them, but not at the full expense of the other, less important words. You still see them, she says, but you do not read them, starting the process to expand your peripheral vision. Here is the paragraph I mentioned, for your benefit.

"The **best way** to **achieve** this is to **read key words** and/or **phrases. Key words** are the **bigger, more important words** in a **sentence, just like** the **headlines** of a **newspaper provide** the **essence** of the **content. Learning** to **stop** your **eyes** on the **words** that are **typically three**

letters in **length** or **longer** and **those which carry** the **most meaning** of a **sentence** are **keywords**."

Beale offers an alternative to this as well. Rather than picking out words, she suggests to pick out groups of them that form a thought. She provides another paragraph that contains two sentences with slash marks dividing thoughts. She urges her reader to go through the paragraph, ignoring the slashes the first time and using them the second. This method and the aforementioned constitute active reading methods that require focus on behalf of the reader to what they read and how their eyes move across a given page. Here is the second example, again for your benefit.

"Additionally, sentences contain groups of words/ that form a thought./ Looking for these thought groups/ encourages a wider visual swath/ while gaining higher understanding/ of the material."

As with anything, these techniques take time to learn. With proper dedication and practice, though, you can adopt them and use them for yourself quickly enough. It is a matter of conditioning your eyes and brain to act in certain ways and respond to certain stimuli.

Chapter Summary

- Before you start reading, set a goal and keep it in mind as you read. Doing so reminds you why you are reading and helps you look for words and phrases that will further your goal.
- Skimming aids this practice, as it can help you gloss over less important sections. It can also give you a preview of what you are reading.
- When skimming, subvocalization becomes an impediment to reading faster. But rather than focusing on stopping it, try to form a new habit to replace it.

- Read groups of words instead of individual ones. By taking in three, four, five, or however many words at a time, you can cut down on the amount of time you spend on each word.

- There are several tactics to help you develop this skill. Steven Frank sets up simplistic columns for you to train your eyes to follow only the middle column, while still being able to read the left and right ones.

- Ron Cole accomplished a similar goal with his trademarked eye-hop, progressing from the first word to the second, then the third, the fourth, and the fifth. He claims that his readers will experience a breakthrough at either the fourth or fifth eye-hop, since in the half a second your eye takes to jumps from the first to the last word, your brain simply cannot pronounce every word in between. Nonetheless, you still get the gist of the grouping of words.

- Meta-guiding tracks your eye movement across the page and moderates your reading by standardizing the pace. Use your finger, a pen, a pencil, or something else to lead your eye.

- Experts love this technique, particularly young phenom Jordan Harry, who by the age of 20 became an entrepreneur and developed StudyFast, a United Kingdom based company, of which he is the Chief Executive Officer. StudyFast takes the basic principles of speed reading and adapts them so that their nearly 15,000 customers in 147 countries can, well, study faster.

- Meta-guiding can consider Jim Kwik solidly in its corner as well, as he heralds the effectiveness because it is a natural thing we do. Children do it, you do it when you do not realize it, and it is a biological instinct to hyper focus on movement from our days as hunter and prey. He also notes the inherent connection between sight and touch, similar to taste and smell, and uses the Braille reading system as an example. Expanding your awareness of all that goes into reading, he also lists things that will help, beginning with checking your eyes and wearing any reading glasses you may have. Among the other recommendations, keep your surroundings cold to sharpen your focus, keep them positive with anchors to encourage your subconscious, read in natural light when possible, listen to music around the speed of a natural heartbeat of 60 beats per minute, practice good posture, with your body and the book, stay hydrated, and use your whole brain.

- Rapid Serial Visual Presentation (RSVP) usually comes with the latest speed reading software or app. By placing words one at a time in one location on the screen, it removes the need for your eyes to move across the page and can boost your reading speed. It can result in working memory overload, though, and inhibit retention.

- RSVP technology is one of those fad trends that took off at various points in the 2010s, and there are dozens of them out there, each a little different and claiming to be the silver bullet in speed reading. They are as follows: Spreeder, Reedy, Read Me!, Speed Reading, Speed Reader, Quick Reader, Focus-Speed Reader, Seven Speed Reading App, Outread, and Acereader iPad. They can help you get reading faster, but it is kind of cheating, since it is first and foremost not a practical text, and second, you only see one word at a time.

- Like every how-to guide, there are things to avoid as well. Regression is when you go back and reread what you just should have, seriously slowing down your reading. It comes from a lapse of concentration, according to Jordan Harry. His remedy? Renew your interest in what you are reading. Piquing your curiosity helps mitigate distractions and prevents passive reading.

- Fixation can also halt your reading, as your eye pauses on certain words or phrases. Harry recommends meta-guiding to keep your eyes moving.

- Focus on controlling your speed, not letting yourself go too fast or slow down too much. The average speed is essential to speed reading. It is no real use to read certain sections at 1,000 words per minute when the next one drops to 200 words per minute. That drops your average significantly to 600 words per minute, a fast reading speed but not the goal you may have set.

- Skip unimportant words to help you breeze through sentences. Some words are technically necessary but do not really contribute much to a sentence, especially when context more than suffices. Small words like if, is, so, the, to, and others only get in the way of your efforts to save time. It is a different skill and takes time to develop, but can assist you in your goal of reading faster.
- Conversely, focus on key words to facilitate your understanding. Often, it is easier to do something positive rather than eliminate something negative.
- Additionally, you can consolidate parts of sentences into thoughts to break the sentence into fewer parts that you need to understand, utilizing the capability of your eye to take in multiple words at once.
- If you just hate grammar, Abby Marks Beale has a method for picking up the important words on their own. Focus on reading words three letters or longer and move between them as quickly as you can. She also suggests grouping words into singular thoughts. These four, five, or however many word clusters can be processed as one and naturally go together, so she says they ease the ability to understand sentences in smaller parts.

These tips help improve the speed at which you read. The next chapter will give you complementary skills to better assist you in reading comprehension. Because what is the use of reading quickly if you do not understand it? Anyone can flip through pages quickly. A true master will almost completely comprehend what he or she reads on top of it.

CHAPTER SIX:

Reading Comprehension

Have you ever mindlessly flipped through the pages of a book that you really do not want to read? Maybe a textbook or assigned reading? Well, that is effectively what you do when you attempt to speed read without an accompanying focus on comprehension. There is a considerable difference between reading at high speeds mechanically for the sake of doing so and understanding what you read. Equally so, there is a difference between reading a text and comprehending it. When speed reading, your goal should not be to get through it as quickly as you can, particularly if you are learning a new skill. It is important that you understand the text you consume, particularly if you strive toward knowledge acquisition.

This may sound odd or counter-intuitive, but a tactic that helps with reading comprehension is to do more than just read the words on the page. Visualize what you read. There is such a thing as visualization and dynamic comprehension, meaning that as you read, you form visual pictures, instead of repeating the words within your mind, or 'listening' to yourself mentally. If you can manage to do this, it makes your reading more efficient. If you happen to be reading a story, you seem to be 'inside' the story. If you are absorbing facts, for instance about a new mechanical device, your reading will actually enable you to visualize just how that device works. Visualization forms the basis of the human condition. This makes sight a crucial function and tool for us to use to our advantage.

On the other hand, we learn to use language as a tool, making it somewhat unnatural to human development. It takes a conscious and deliberate effort to incorporate language into our quiver of skills as human beings. Different groups of people from different locations around the world developed language as a series of signs and symbols to communicate or record. These signs, symbols, and sounds have an arbitrary relationship with their meanings, which is why there are so many different languages. It's this arbitrary nature that makes languages difficult to learn, even if we have an innate capacity to learn them as an imperative to communicate. We are constantly translating to understand language.

In order to comprehend effectively while speed reading, you need to similarly 'translate' the language of words to the language of the mind, which is visualization. If you can adapt this somewhat abstract process to your reading practices, you will find that your reading comprehension can increase by a factor of 30% or more. So by bringing the mechanical aspect of reading 'up to speed' with that of the human mind, you can maximize both reading and comprehension. You will find your reading speed easily tripled and remember everything that you read effectively as well.

This seems like a particularly lofty goal. Can you really get to the point where you read upwards of 900 words per minute and still retain every last one? Do not let trying to retain everything phase you. If you are trying to memorize the entire book, you probably will not succeed. While some people take speed-reading to an extreme, there are others who TRY to take retention to an extreme. Unless you have an eidetic memory, also known as photographic memory, you will fail, even if by the slimmest of margins. More likely than not, you will get frustrated and contemplate giving up because you did not fully maximize your time and reading. Rather than shooting for a full and complete picture of what you read, when you read for knowledge acquisition you do so to form mental models in your mind. A mental model is essentially someone's world view of a certain concept, whether it works and aligns with physical reality or not. So when you read, you either develop an understanding for a new concept or you correct your understanding of an old concept, making your previous perspective more nuanced and complicated. As you get through more books, you will notice that authors are often redundant. In fact, several books will have the same overlapping information. Authors from the same category will often reference or quote each other. All this redundancy will drill the information into your head and automatically solve your retention issues. So simply focus on getting through more books and never stop.

Not knowing the meaning of a word can slow down your reading, making efforts to get through your reading quickly even more difficult. One of the secrets to overcoming this may seem obvious but takes a concerted effort to attain. Expanding your vocabulary will widen the range of words you can understand easily, but this takes the diligence to incorporate new words into daily use. The wider your vocabulary, the less you have to pause and look up the meanings of unknown words. Learn the meanings of new words when you have spare time. It will boost both your reading skills and your overall intelligence. In the same way you set a goal for your speed reading, you could set a goal to learn a certain amount of words per day or week. Before long, if you add three new words per day to your vocabulary, for instance, you will find your repertoire of words greatly expanded. There are plenty of excellent methods to learn a new word per day. I, for instance, use the Word Genius Word of the Day email blast. If you find two or three or however many more you like, use them to supplement each other and increase your vocabulary by the day. In conjunction with that, you will find fewer and fewer words you do not recognize in your reading, automatically increasing your reading speed.

A trick less for your overall reading speed and more for boosting retention when you read, play the "recall" game. At the end of each page in a book or the end of a few paragraphs in an article, pause and recall what you just read. Write a few key words in the margin to summarize what you just read. This will help for a couple of reasons.

First, you ingest the information on the page again. This mindful act of retention will increase your understanding almost automatically. Second, putting the information into your own words demonstrates an understanding of the information and represents some level of mastery of it. Each of these techniques constitutes an aspect of active reading. By doing things such as recalling, pausing, or taking notes rather than passively taking in information, you keep engaged with what you read.

Maybe the most important consideration and factor in reading comprehension is the environment you are trying to read in. Are you in a quiet place where you can focus? Or are you somewhere loud and noisy, with more distractions than you can deal with? There is a reason why libraries are so quiet and librarians enforce it so fiercely. It is just easier to stay focused and not get distracted when there is not much going on around you. One concession I will make, though, is that in a quiet environment, each sound and distraction gets amplified. A sneeze or bump against a bookcase, or whatever the source may be, can be heard by everyone and induces the stare of shame from anyone who can see you. Still, though, fewer distractions are easier to ignore. Compared to a coffee shop or your morning commute on the train or bus, a library is a sanctuary of silence. That is not to say it is impossible to focus when you find yourself in such an environment, but it is substantially harder. You require much more discipline and conditioning to keep from getting distracted. Be mindful of where you are and what kind of person you are when it comes time to focus. Find an environment that works best for you, and read there as much as you can.

Just as much as limiting the external distractions that you cannot necessarily control, eliminate those that you have full control over. Some people enjoy reading with some sort of background noise, like music or ambient noise. This can help, without a doubt, giving you something to intentionally block out, if that is how you choose to think about it. If this works for you, I encourage you to try it or adopt it. However, be mindful of the impact whatever device that plays this noise has on your productivity. Our devices, smartphones, tablets, computers, and so on and so forth, have so much functionality in this day and age. Odds are, whatever you use to play music or ambient noise will have some sort of notification buzzing or chiming to demand your attention. I do understand that sometimes you have to be connected in order to get important updates, but as much as you can, try to silence or ignore these pesky little interruptions. Dedicate time solely to reading and block out the noises of our digitally interconnected world for a time. Not only will it help you focus, it will provide some meditative time, as you quiet your brain from the constant stimulation. You may find yourself reading for that purpose just as much as the sake of reading. You will notice too that you can comprehend more when you make a concerted effort to focus on your reading.

More than anything, challenging your reading comprehension strengthens it just like any exercise designed to test and grow a certain muscle. This is true whether your concentration is speed or whether it is comprehension. You are more than allowed to read at reduced speeds if you want to tackle a difficult or new reading. In fact, I would encourage that from time to time. That way, when you go to speed read something similar or related, you can do so while sacrificing less retention. Challenging your reading comprehension will not directly help your speed reading, but it will help your overall reading and ability to recall information when you do apply speed reading techniques.

Chapter Summary

- There is a difference between reading quickly to speed through a text and reading quickly while also focusing on retention.
- Visualization can help with retention by constructing a broader perspective of the information and tuning into our visual nature.

- Do not try to retain everything. Even the best speed readers, or readers in general, cannot remember the entirety of what they read. Rather, they retain a percentage of it, between 60 and 85 percent for the most skilled speed readers. Instead, they form working mental models, which will enhance previous understandings or develop new ones.
- Expand your vocabulary to reduce the number of words you do not know when you read.
- Play the 'recall' game. Every so often within a text, pause and remember what you read. If you are so inclined, leave a note in the margin. Active reading in this way promotes a greater understanding of what you read as you process the information more times.
- Where you read matters tremendously. Think about yourself and your attention span. Try to read in an environment that suits your characteristics and matches your goals for reading.
- Challenge your reading comprehension when you can, at both high speeds and normal speeds. Reading with the intention of getting more out of it will help your speed reading, even though it will not necessarily increase your reading speed. Building your foundational reading comprehension makes retention when speed reading easier to accomplish.

This chapter should have helped you on your way to greater reading comprehension. In the following one, you will learn why you should use some of your free time to read, particularly if you find it laborious. After all, the more you read, the better you will get at it, particularly if you are reading actively and mindfully. Especially so if you are working on increasing your reading speed.

CHAPTER SEVEN:

Reading More in Your Free Time to Read Faster

Some people take to things much easier than others. Otherwise, we would all tryout for professional sports teams or symphony orchestras, or maybe write the next great novel. The reality, however, is that certain people are naturally better at some things than others, which is why you will never see me trying to guard Lebron James as he muscles his way toward the basket. It would take a tremendous amount of effort just to look even a little less helpless in that scenario, even if I wanted to do it. Similarly, if you find reading effortful, you would naturally want to do less of it. However, if you want to read more, you need to spend more time reading books which you like and find interesting. There is even more to it than that, though. Picking works that are easy to comprehend so prevents you from burning out quickly. This is, at least, where you should begin. Remember, challenging your own comprehension can improve your retention during speed reading. Nonetheless, there is a reason that people suggest reading books intended for children to help learn a new language. They read quickly, take little effort to follow, and contain words you probably already know, even if in another language. For those same reasons, minus the translation, you can start with quick reads like Harry Potter to boost your confidence and enjoyment in reading.

Stephen Krashen, highly relevant as a pioneer in second-language acquisition methods, conducted extensive research as a linguist about the various forms in which people learn new languages. He spearheaded a shift from previous rule-focused approaches to meaning-focused ones, particularly communicative language teaching, which is now the most widely accepted approach. In addition, he developed a controversial, but well-known, input hypothesis for language learning. This hypothesis argues that, when learning a new language, you need to accept high volumes of input at a comprehensible level. The application to regular reading, rather than with the goal of acquiring new language skills, lies in that if you understand less than 95% of the text, it will be too difficult to sustain your motivation to keep reading. When you think about it, this makes perfect sense. Struggling to understand something keeps you from enjoying reading it, and can frustrate or dissuade you from continuing. If you need a concrete example, recall a particularly convoluted book you may have read in English class and the themes, motifs, and character development your teacher smartly pointed out that you just plain missed. Or maybe you picked up an article from a high-brow publication and got lost in the nuance of some particular topic about which you know very little.

Again, this seems much easier said than done. Acknowledge that intention and action are two very different things, and one does not constitute the other. Sometimes intent does not turn into action. Sometimes it is because of lack of motivation, others because of lack of know-how. There is not much I can do about the former, but to help the latter, here are some suggestions for reading more:

Focus on building the habit. Reading is a skill — and skills take time to develop, they do not just appear overnight. When you just start out, you want to think about establishing the habit before anything else. Keep your expectations realistic, and keep yourself from getting too far ahead of yourself. Base your expectations on where you are, not necessarily where you hope to be, and set goals without making them unachievable. If you set unrealistic goals, you are going to crash and burn. If you fail to meet the goal, then you will feel discouraged and risk breaking the habit before you can really establish it. So focus on building the habit first. Tell yourself you are going to read for one hour a day no matter what. Or if that feels like it is too ambitious for you, start at fifteen minutes a day. Either way, work your way up to your target reading time. Meeting more little goals rather than fewer big ones may not give you as much momentary satisfaction, but will slowly but surely grow your confidence and abilities. Once you build some momentum, you will notice yourself get faster.

Reduce the barrier to entry. As human beings, we have mastered the art of procrastination, which may sound strange considering procrastination is doing nothing and putting off what you should be doing. We will come up with reason after reason to avoid doing something, even when we know better. To combat this, we need to eliminate resistance. One way to do this is to make "starting" the activity easier. Make reading so easy that it becomes almost unavoidable. Develop routines that lead you to read. You could read for however long when you get home at the end of the day since reading can relax your brain. Incentivize your reading somehow or another. Is there a particular activity you like to do or thing you like to have at a point in the day? Maybe you like to watch TV at night or eat dessert after dinner? Reading beforehand could give you an extra bit of satisfaction, tying them even closer to reading. Also, if you feel your TV watching gets in the way of your reading, doing so before would significantly reduce your guilt in watching TV rather than reading. If routines or incentivization do not work for you, you can keep a spare book or kindle in your bathroom or somewhere else that would turn idle time into potential reading time. This way, you can get at least 5–10 minutes of reading every morning. Another trick is to keep the book you want to read on the couch — opened to the current page you are on. You would have to actively choose not to read, picking up the book and moving it when all it would take to start reading would be to literally pick it up. If there is a smaller barrier to entry than that, I cannot think of it.

That is if the book you choose to pick up is one you're reading for pleasure. Have books that you genuinely want to read, which will encourage you to put in the time to read it. Think about what interests you most. Maybe there are certain individuals you admire or follow in the public realm. Picking up their autobiography, if they have one, could encourage you to read it. A book about their life could make you turn the pages as you learn more about their childhood, upbringing, education, and maybe a secret or two to their success. Are there certain things you have always wondered about but never really looked into? I guarantee you there is a book on it, if you look hard enough. Use your reading as a way to quench your curiosity, and make it a pleasurable thing to do.

If you find yourself in the middle of a book you do not like, switch books if you have to. Do not be afraid to leave a book unfinished and to switch books mid-reading. You do not have to commit to finishing every book you read. After all, life is too short to finish a bad book, and luckily you get to decide what constitutes a bad book. If you tend to get bored with one book or another, you can have around 3 to 5 books in your active pile of books you are currently reading. There is no universal rule that states that you have to read one book at a time, start to finish. You can have a book for any number of moods or mindsets you may be in. If you find yourself struggling to get through a certain hard book, switch to something you enjoy more, which may actually lead you to more important books down the line as you practice reading more.

Before you bite off more than you can chew with particularly difficult books, build up to harder books. If there is a really difficult book you want to read, start by reading more accessible commentaries, or related books that will make you familiar with the topic, ideas, and vocabulary. Research the book and the author to try to get a sense of the kind of language he or she uses when they write. This will give you some background knowledge which will make reading the harder book easier. Content knowledge is a big part of reading more fluently and efficiently, so if you struggle when you read a book, it might simply mean you need more background knowledge to process it properly. When you pick books that you want to read, the most important thing is that they are at the right level for you. It may have been considered cheating in school, but when you are reading for yourself there is absolutely nothing wrong with looking up Sparknotes, or any other summary or synopsis to help you keep track of what you are reading. This way you go into it with an idea and expectation of what you will read.

Build your foundation first. If you are having a particularly hard time with reading a book, spend the time to look up all the words you do not understand, search the concepts on Wikipedia or google around for the stories behind names and characters you do not recognize. This will initially take more time, but it will eventually help you read the rest of the book much faster.

Chapter Summary

- Reading comes more naturally to some people, but that does not mean that not everyone can do it. The more you do something the better you will get at it, and reading is the same way.
- Krashen's input hypothesis states that if you understand less than 95% of a given text, you will find it more difficult to keep reading it. Pick books or readings that are easy to understand.
- Start small and focus on building the habit before you make ambitious goals.
- Reduce the barrier to entry by making it easier to start reading. Place books in places you can not ignore them or read things that really pique your interest.
- Reading for pleasure will make reading seem like less like a choice and more like something you enjoy doing. Pick topics or authors you like. This is not a high school English class where you have to read a book assigned to you. You have the power of choice in the matter.

- You do not have to read every book cover to cover. You can switch between them, or stop reading them whenever you want.
- Start small and build big. You should not start with difficult books off the bat. Start with ones you know you can read at the speed and comprehension you want, then try ones that are a little harder, before you get to the hardest one you want to read.
- Build your foundation by doing a little research before you start reading. Whether it is major plot points or an overview of an article. A little bit of legwork before you begin will help you in the longer run.

Reading more will present one small detail, though. It will make keeping track of your reading hard since you have more to keep track of, naturally. The next chapter will give you some insight into how you can do this effectively. Providing multiple tactics and strategies to do so, you can choose which one best suits you. Adapting any of these will further your goal to read faster and ensure that you keep doing so actively.

CHAPTER EIGHT:

Tracking Your Reading Progress

Reading more will certainly boost your confidence. Like I said earlier, though, it will only have a limited effect on your reading speed if you're not actively tracking your progress and trying to improve. In order to truly increase your reading speed as I promised, you need to get serious and diligent about your speed reading practice. This involves setting goals and tracking your progress.

Try to consistently read sections of the same word-count and time your results. Calculate your reading speed using the calculation found in chapter four. Slowly push yourself to get faster. Start with a goal in mind for how many pages or words you want to read per-minute, and work until you reach that goal. Developing reading skills is the key to mental and professional growth. But remember not to empty the joy from learning. Success and growth should also be fun. Taking enjoyment out leads to resentment, but having fun helps you learn quicker. Studies consistently show that we learn more and progress faster when we enjoy what we are doing. As such, here are some ways to track your reading progress and keep engaged.

Goodreads

Take advantage of Goodreads Bookshelves. If you love reading and you do not have a Goodreads account, you need to change that. Now! Goodreads is basically social media for books. You can discover new books, track what you are reading, what you have already read, and you can interact with others through book reviews, comments, groups, and more. I spend much more time than I should on Goodreads, and it is my favorite way to keep track of everything I have read or want to read.

Goodreads tracks your reading for you each year. You can set a goal, and every time you mark a book as read in that year, Goodreads will update your progress, so you have a constant reminder of where you stand on your reading goal. Goodreads also publishes a reading report for you each year, so you can see a cool graphic about your reading journey.

Trello

Create a Trello Board dedicated to reading. Trello is a productivity tool that can be used for so many things, from school to work to life in general. It can be used to track travel plans, organize ideas, coordinate household to-do lists; and, of course, track your reading. If you are interested in trying Trello, the online tool is completely free and very versatile.

Pinterest

Use Pinterest for similar goals. Not quite the same functionality as Trello, Pinterest offers a similar objective to Goodreads, but in a format closer to Trello with a board of pictures, ideas, and thoughts. Incorporating the social media aspect, you can look at the boards that other people post for inspiration and log what you have read or what you hope to read using pictures. There are some interesting and famous people on Pinterest. Use their accounts or books for inspiration when you need some.

Spreadsheets

Create a custom spreadsheet to log your reading. Whether you choose to keep your spreadsheet online (using something like Google Sheets) or offline in Microsoft Excel, spreadsheets are a great way to keep track of reading goals and all of the books you have read. Using Google Sheets, you can also share with your family so everyone can track their reading in one place. Spreadsheets are a great way to actually visualize your reading goals. You can use a spreadsheet reading log to track what you read each year, what you purchase, and how you are doing for each challenge. It will boost your confidence in your reading as you see the list expand, particularly if using it as a friendly competition between friends or family. Not only that, it will help you figure out what books you like, what books you do not, how long it takes you to get through them, and if you are particularly adept at spreadsheets, create charts, graphs, and tables about your reading. Paper reading logs would be just as helpful, but not quite as informative.

Pen and Paper

If you've got an aversion to technology, all of this can be accomplished with a pen and paper, whether in a planner or loose leaf. Planners usually offer some extra pages in the back, as well as extra space on each calendar or diary page, meaning that there are plenty of options for how to track your reading.

Or, if you find yourself struggling with any of these, or need something more physical in your life, make your bedside table your reading list. Keep the five or so books, or however many, it does not matter, you are either currently reading or want to read next to you on your bedside table. It can be difficult to keep track of a reading list, especially if it is a mental list. Even physical lists on paper or a screen can be hard to track.

Of course, none of this matters much if you don't maintain sight of your goals. As you read, make sure you log your pace. Log how much progress you make toward your current WPM goal.

Chapter Summary

- There are many different ways to track your reading progress. It matters less which you choose than that you do it.
- Some people are just wicked smart and can keep track of their reading in their head. That is not realistic for everyone.
- Goodreads is an excellent way to keep track of your reading, as a social media platform dedicated to books and reading. It has all the benefits of a book club without the intermittent meetings, potentially annoying members, and having to read books chosen for you. It lets you document which books you read, rate them to show whether you liked them or not, and provides opportunities to interact with friends as well. It even gives recommendations.
- Trello can be a useful tool as well. This free and versatile application can be used for your reading as well as anything else needing organization in your life.
- Creating a spreadsheet to log your reading can enable friendly competition between those you share it with and help you visualize your overall reading better. Plus, if you are good, you can create actual visual representations of your reading in the form of charts, graphs, and tables.
- There is nothing wrong with good, old-fashioned paper. Get a planner or find space in your current one for reading logs or notes.
- If all else fails, use the pile of books you have somewhere as your reading list. It gives you a more tangible way to keep track of your progress. When it shrinks, you get encouraged, maybe to go out and get more books from the bookstore or your local library.

By this point in the book, you have been introduced to all the basics of speed reading. This will give you a solid start on your way to increasing your reading speed. Chapter nine dives deeper into the technique that most expert speed readers use. Skimming and scanning can be the two methods by which you can quickly and easily increase your reading speed the most.

CHAPTER NINE:

Skimming or Scanning

We've discussed skimming and scanning briefly, but it's such a useful tool that it deserves its own chapter. Unfortunately, skimming gets a bad reputation. Few people recognize it as a skill for reading and, rather, consider it quite the opposite of reading. Many consider skimming and scanning a tool to avoid reading, or simply a means of figuring out whether something is worth reading in full. This is just plain wrong. Skimming and scanning are not nearly that passive. In fact, as you will find in this chapter, both are difficult, intentional acts that require their own levels of mastery to do properly.

Skimming is a process of speed reading that involves visually searching the sentences of a page for clues to the main idea. It can mean reading the beginning and ending for summary information, then optionally the first sentence of each paragraph to quickly determine whether to seek still more detail, as determined by the questions or purpose of the reading. These sections are most important because they will tell you the most about what you read. The introduction gives you a preview of coming attractions for whatever the reading may be, giving you a chance to see what it is about and prepare you for what it is going to tell you. Similar to the introduction to the passage, the first sentence of a paragraph will generally tell you what the paragraph is about. It lays the foundation for the main points that follow or gives you an idea of what to expect. The conclusion will, assuming the author is good at doing so, wrap up the reading neatly as if in a bow. It should recap the main points in a succinct way. A well-written conclusion will tell you why you have spent your time well by reading everything that came before it. Lastly, it will leave you with something, hopeful resonant, that you have gained by reading.

Two techniques that involve looking only for the most relevant bits of information first will prime you for what is soon to come. Since you are already familiar with the main parts of the text, you will not be slowed down by confusing or surprising parts when you come to them in your reading. Keep in mind that, while skimming and scanning work best for non-fiction, it can be applied to fiction too. In a novel, skim the chapter for character development, key points of dialogue, and major plot points. Then read it at a faster pace than you normally would. Even though you are reading it twice, you are reading it faster, since you will have picked up the most important things on the first breeze through. Then, on the second read, you pick up more minute details that you missed on the initial skim. These two readings should be enough to parse any relevant information, but should you feel ambitious, a third go-around would be warranted, especially for more difficult books.

Okay, that sounds great! You say. But how do you do it? Here is a step by step process as to how to skim a text. Skimming — getting the essence from reading material without reading all the words — boils down to knowing what parts to read and what parts to pass by. Following are some tips and techniques for recognizing what is important to read in the act of skimming.

Know What You Want

Before you start skimming, ask yourself what you want to get from the text. Think of two or three terms that describe what you want to know, and, as you skim, keep an eye out for those two or three terms. Actively searching for them will help you find them easier than if you just passively read the text. Aimlessly skimming with no particular purpose is usually fruitless and boring. The lack of focus on an object leads to spacing out. I am sure you are familiar with this feeling. Skimming is not the same as passive reading, in fact, it is the opposite. Give your reading, and your skimming a purpose by looking out for keywords. Come into your reading armed with a couple of questions as well. Not only will they help you determine what you want to get out of the reading, if they go unanswered at the end, you have some fodder for more reading in the future.

Read Vertically

When skimming, you move your eyes vertically as much as you move your eyes horizontally. In other words, you move your eyes down the page as much as you move them from side to side. Skimming is a bit like running down stairs. Yes, you should take one step at a time, and running down stairs is reckless, but you also get there faster by running. And what happens when you walk only sideways down stairs? A whole lot of nothing. Nonetheless, this is still reading, not actually travelling down stairs. As such, to find what you're looking for, you've got to occasionally move your eyes left-to-right as well as up and down. This is both a caution against too much vertical reading and a reminder to move vertically as much as you can. Moving too quickly down the page will lessen the degree to which you understand each line. Not moving down fast enough will slow down your reading speed. It is a delicate balance.

Put Yourself in the Author's Shoes

Every article, book, and web page is written to make a point of some kind. Whether it is an academic article meant to present a certain hypothesis or a novel conveying a theme, everything has a point to it. Otherwise, it would not be worth the read. If you can detect the strategies that the author uses for making his or her point, you can separate the important from the unimportant material. Detecting the tendencies of the author requires you to put yourself in his or her place. Besides noticing the material on the page, notice how he or she presents the material. See whether you can recognize how the author places background material, secondary arguments, tangential information, and just plain frippery. Do the frills come before the point or the other way around? Does the author come right out and say it clearly or make you figure it out for yourself to some degree?

Another critical component of this is picking up on subtext that the author may have inserted, conveying ideas that are not explicitly stated. Some authors rely on their readers to make inferences and assumptions about the reading, particularly in literary or creative writing. This can often be just as important as the actual text. Many people think that a highly focused and sharp attention to detail can only pick up on subtext, but that is not true. Subtext can come in many forms from many techniques. The most important thing is paying attention to it and being able to interpret it the way the author wants you to. Additionally, interpreting the overall tone of the text, some believe, can get lost in reading too fast. Again, that is not true. Your brain still picks up punctuation at high speeds, and that is the key to unlocking the intonation that the author writes with. Lastly, be aware of the subject matter that the author writes about as much as possible and read with the big picture the author wants you to see in mind. This will improve reading comprehension dramatically. Determining the style of writing in this way can help you identify what's important.

Preread

If you are skimming for the purpose of knowledge acquisition, pre-read before you start skimming. For example, if reading an article, examine it before you read. By pre-reading an article before you skim, you can pinpoint the parts of the article that require your undivided attention and the parts that you can skip. It may seem counterintuitive since you then read it twice, but skipping the sections that do not pertain as much to your goal for reading cuts down pretty incredibly on time. *Speed Reading Lounge* offers four strategies to assist you in your skimming and scanning. Preview key sentences to pick up on one idea, perhaps the key idea, then practice honing in on the most interesting bits. Then scan names and numbers to get a narrative of the details about people, places and concepts. Identify trigger words to keep a lookout for important phrases and keywords. Use the pencil you may have for meta-guiding to jot them down. This will help ensure that you are getting what you want and need out of the reading. Lastly, read the title, including the headlines and subheadlines. In this world of search engine optimization, often the title will include key terms to look for throughout the reading, while subheadlines can give you an idea of the structure or anchor points in the text. Consider, for instance, this very book, Proven Speed Reading Techniques: Read More Than 300 pages in 60 minutes—A Guide for Beginners on How to Read Faster with Comprehension (Includes Advanced Learning Exercises). The title tells you what you will be reading and what you will get out of it, proven techniques for speed reading so you can read 300 pages in 60 minutes. The subheadline outlines the structure of the book, taking you from beginner status to reading faster while maintaining comprehension. Lastly, and more peripherally, it includes advanced learning exercises.

Pre-reading in this way will help you, as the article states, to differentiate which type of reading you will be doing, deciding whether to use speed reading or full comprehension modes. In a helpful analogy, author Mark Ways distinguishes between microwave and oven reading. Microwave readings refer to contents that include technical information, detailed explanations, guidelines or instructions. In this case, you care less about how it is written than the information included so that you can apply it in a real-world sense to your life. Oven reading compares closely to baking in this analogy and requires more time to heat and digest than microwave. Ways uses the example of biographies, success stories, or life experiences as things you would want to digest fully to better understand. Skimming and scanning will give you the main ideas but depth and diligence yield the most from this type of reading. Identifying which books you can skim and scan your way through will help you focus your reading and spend your time more wisely. Skimming or scanning a book that does not lend itself to those techniques will result in frustration more often than not, impeding your reading progress.

You may say, 'this seems a lot like just skimming to me, how is it different?' Well, pre-reading involves understanding the outline and construction of a text before you read it. For instance, you would glance over it without digging into the actual paragraphs. You would notice the chapter titles, subheadings, and then the chapter summary at the end. You would not engage this particular as a part of a pre-read. That's when the skimming comes into play. The different types of reading Mark Ways identified that are mentioned above can only be determined after a thorough pre-read. The purpose of it is to gain as much of an idea of the text before you skim it or scan it.

Read the First Sentence of Each Paragraph

The introductory sentence of each paragraph usually describes what follows in the paragraph. When you skim, read the first sentence in each paragraph and then decide whether the rest of the paragraph deserves a read. If it does not, move on. This works much better for non-fiction writing since fiction paragraphs do not follow the same constructs and can contain important plot or story enriching details in them. It would also be helpful to read the last sentence of the paragraph because it often succinctly summarizes the paragraph and segues into the next paragraph. The first and last sentences in a paragraph are often the most important ones. Sometimes you'll find it's completely unnecessary to read what's in between.

An article in the Journal of Experimental Psychology tested the effectiveness of skimming while reading. The authors conducted three experiments to determine this, using expository texts and only allowing for enough time for readers to get through half of each text. The first experiment found that skimming allows readers to obtain important ideas from each document at the expense of less important details. It also showed that they missed some inferences from the information included in the text. The second experiment determined that skimming and reading the first or second half of the paragraphs lead to the same amount of retention. This confirms what the paragraph above says, that skimming and reading the first sentence or so are both equally effective methods for speed reading. The study also found that due to the Website-like layout of the texts provided to the readers, skimming predicates on how pages link together, an indication of the ease of navigation through the document. Most interestingly, an analysis of reading times based on page and eye-tracking indicated that the text early on in the paragraphs, toward the beginning of a page, and at the front of the document received more attention from the readers. Again, this supports the assessment that skimming suffices when reading through a document under time pressure, according to the authors of the study.

Do not necessarily read complete sentences

The point of skimming is that you need not read every word on the page. If the start of a sentence holds no promise of the sentence giving you the information you want, skip to the next sentence. Read the start of sentences with an eye to whether they will yield useful information. For example, you do not need to read **this** entire sentence, or even the next few sentences, because it is just a pointless ramble about how if you had skipped the rest of it you would have saved yourself so much time and effort. It was not necessary at all, and when you take the sentence at its face value in the first few words, you do not get frustrated, especially when the sentences get long and convoluted and you start to question their grammatical correctness; and then they start to throw things in, like semicolons, which you have to harken back to English class to figure out if they are used right or not—that before you know it makes the sentence not worth your time.

As a case in point, "For example, you do not need to read this entire sentence" took me less than a second to read. It took me about 11 to read the rest of it. In this case, the sentence literally told you that you do not have to keep reading, but there will not be many of them that do in your general reading. A better example may be: "The Stone Age was defined by an innovation in tools, as early humans began to incorporate things from the world around them to develop new ways to complete their tasks." The first part of the sentence, the independent clause, tells you the point of the sentence. The second part only serves to provide more information in the form of an example. Reading the first part but not the second gets you about as far as reading both.

Skip examples

There are some things you just don't have to read, much like the one I just provided. Authors often present examples to prove a point, but if you believe the point does not need proving, you can skip them. I could put an example here, but after that lengthy one, you would probably skip it anyway.

When skimming, do not be afraid to take a few more seconds and re-skim what you just read to ensure comprehension. You are already saving time by skimming rather than reading in-depth, so you would just save a little less by going backward for a short bit. You could also pre-skim, so you know a little of what to expect in what follows.

Chapter Summary

- Contrary to popular belief, skimming and scanning are active skills that do not rely on obtaining information through osmosis. That is to say, it is an active process that does not just happen on its own.

- Skimming prioritizes certain information at the expense of others. Scanning a text before you read it will help you identify which information will help you and which will not.

- Unproductive though it may seem, reading something twice in this manner, glancing over it then reading the parts you thought interesting quickly, will reduce your reading time because details don't bog you down.

- It works for both fiction and non-fiction writing. You have to identify different things in your first pass by, though. Whereas non-fiction is based on points helpful to the argument, fiction consists of plot points, dialogue, themes, or character development. You could skip things like descriptions, particularly wordy ones, for instance.

- Know what you want to read beforehand, going off of a title, headline, or something related that you have already read. It can be helpful to think of terms you want to learn or concepts you want to grasp better. Knowing what you're looking for always helps to find it.

- Read vertically. That is, do not move your eye so much side to side. Reading words in clusters will help with this. Careful not to move too far or fast vertically because you may miss information you want to read, which hopefully you have already identified.

- Think like the author. Much easier in non-fiction writing when there is a thesis you can identify but also practical in fiction, figure out what the point the author wants to prove. There is always at least one. More than that, try to figure out how they present it. Where is the evidence relative to the point?

- Preread. Evaluate the text. Big paragraphs or little ones? Are the sentences long or are they really short? Identify what you think will be the keywords and phrases. Come up with goals or questions you hope to fulfill by the end of the reading.

- Read the first sentence in each paragraph. Particularly in academic or scholarly texts, it may tell you all you need to know about the point the author makes in the paragraph. Read the last sentence too, it will often tell you what the paragraph said and lead you into the next one.

- Only read full sentences when the information serves you. When the information in the beginning piques your curiosity and makes you want to read more, do so. But do not keep reading sentences that do not give you much information, they only serve to bog you down and keep you from moving on to ones that actually fulfill the purpose you set for reading them.

- Skip examples. Particularly when they use phrases like, for example, for instance, as evidence, to demonstrate this, or anything else that can signify information that only supports the point. They can be harder to identify than that sometimes. You may just have to use your gut or intuition and skip the rest of the paragraphs at the risk of missing something important. Chances are, though, you will not miss too much. For instance, if you had only read 'skip examples', you probably would have gotten just as much out of this bullet point without reading my intentional rambling. It should show you what a sneaky, hiding example looks like, though. I hope you enjoyed this small, exemplary aside. You're welcome.

Congratulations! You have come to the end of basic speed reading. You can now go out into the world an intermediate speed reader and try these tips and tricks for yourself if you like. What was that? You want to know what the rest of the pages in this book are for? Since you asked, these are only for the daring. Chapter ten has more secret, advanced techniques that will help your speed reading even more. Okay, they are not so secret, but they are advanced. Read on to find out what they are. You are closer than you have ever been to becoming a master!

CHAPTER TEN:

Learn Faster with Advanced Techniques

Thank you for reading this far. In doing so you have demonstrated a desire to get the very most of this book. Some people see a chapter title like "Learn Faster with Advanced Techniques" and quit because they question whether or not it will be worth their time, or maybe they do not think they will be up to it. Or maybe they already got what they wanted out of the book, which is fine.

Here is your chance to get ahead of the pack. Gaining more knowledge has always been important for success. But the pace of modern life has become so quick that by the time you learn new facts they are already becoming outdated. So, we have to learn faster. And the most effective way to do that is to improve your reading speed and comprehension.

Metacognition

These advanced techniques require a careful look at your reading tendencies, analyzing them as much as possible to improve them. Metacognition is the first step to this end, as inaccessible as it may seem. In reality, simply thinking about how you think will help you understand what topics you do not understand. This awareness of your shortcomings allows you to take a step back and look for ways to improve them. Improving your language skills will also lend itself to improving your reading. After all, the better you can apply language yourself, the better you will be at reading and identifying the other applications that people use for the same purpose. For instance, understanding a semi-colon and how to use it requires knowledge of what constitutes an independent clause. Improving your grammar in this way boosts your reading comprehension and keeps you from being confused when authors throw weird grammatical structures at you. It will also boost your self-confidence, making you a better writer, conversationalist, or public speaker. Your first impressions will be stronger with greater language skills as well.

Here are 6 exercises to improve your reading speed and comprehension in other ways. Some of these are a review of earlier techniques, others are new.

Size-up the Task

Assess the work you are about to do. Skim the text first and look for important points. Catch the headings and subheadings; read the first and the last paragraphs of several chapters; get accustomed to the writing style unique to each author. Grasp the forest before focusing on the trees. Not only will you keep an eye on the big picture, but you should be able to identify the main ideas after a quick skim.

Ask Questions

As you read through the text, create questions you are wanting to find answers to. Then anticipate finding the answers to your questions. Focus on your interests and what you want to take away from the reading. Skip the irrelevant information. It is impossible to remember everything you read, so learn to pull out what is relevant to your needs. You know exactly what you need to take away from the reading. Then, at the end of the reading, you will have either answered questions, and gained something from it, or you will have more questions, thus, more reading.

Decrease Subvocalization

As discussed earlier in the book, while subvocalization can help with comprehension, it greatly slows your reading speed. When children first learn to read, they whisper the words or say them softly. At the next level, they read silently but still move their lips as if saying each word. As adults, we say the words in our minds—it is called "subvocalization." However, subvocalization does not allow us to read faster because we can only go as fast as we speak. The average speaking rate is about 150 words per minute, while the average reading speed is about 200-300 words per minute. So, to read faster, we need to silence that voice inside. How? Listening to music while reading helps. At first, it will affect your comprehension. But soon you will notice your concentration increases. Paradoxically, the music that distracted you earlier will help you to focus and learn faster. Think about when you put music on as background noise, for when you are doing chores, or at a party, or anywhere else for that matter. Generally, you notice it at first, but then it fades away into the scenery. You only notice it once in a while. The same will happen when you read with music playing.

Read Groups of Words

I mentioned earlier that you should read phrases not words. Here is how you can actually put that into practice. Children learn to read starting with joining syllables. Later, they join words to understand sentences. We often stop there. But, there is another level—absorbing groups of words at once. Remember the columns from chapter five? Grab a pencil and divide the page into 3 columns, so each of them has 2 to 4 words in a row. Try to read them together jumping from one column to another. It is easier than you think. Once you get the hang of it, you will not need the columns. We are just applying the same rule from comprehending words. We do not read every letter but we recognize the whole word. Now, instead of reading separate words, you are reading groups at once.

Quiz Yourself

Ask yourself, "What is the author trying to say? How is this different than other things I have read? How does this relate to other material I know?" When you are making sense of something, you start learning it. Employ this method when you stop in the middle of reading, rather than rereading a section. Summarize what you just read as if you had been stopped by a teacher in class and been given a pop quiz. If it feels right, keep reading.

Do Not Just Consume, Create

Knowledge is not just something you absorb, but rather something that you create as a learner. You develop new meanings, new neural network connections, and new patterns of electro/chemical interactions within you. Learning happens when you integrate your new knowledge, then apply it in some way to enforce a new work process or create something new. Practical application of your newfound knowledge is a great way to practice a new skill.

Take notes and write. Do not type on a computer. While typing your notes into the computer is great for posterity, writing by hand stimulates ideas more effectively. The simple act of holding and using a pen or pencil may seem old-fashioned in this day and age, but just think of all the visionaries it has worked for throughout the years. Not only that, despite the fact that typing is faster than handwriting notes, the multi-functionality of a laptop lends itself to distractions way more than handwriting. Even though it makes taking notes on large amounts of information easier, all it takes is one notification, or one sound, or one errant thought, and a couple clicks later you go down the rabbit hole of distraction. An article from National Public Radio (NPR) cites a study that Psychological Science published, determining that longhand notes forced note-takers to select the things they write down more carefully. So while it is possible that laptop users take down more notes, odds are handwriters take better notes because they identified the most important information while ignoring the less important points. The study tested this by showing TED talks to students about various topics before asking questions about facts, which both groups accomplished equally well. Concept-based questions, however, significantly favored the handwritten notes. The temptation to write things verbatim, that is word by word, was simply too much to overcome when using a laptop.

This was just one hypothesis tested to determine whether the act of taking notes by hand or by typing affected memory and retention. The second allowed students the chance to review the notes they had taken between the lecture and the test. Handwritten notes still yielded stronger results. The conclusion was that taking notes by hand requires 'mental lifting' on the part of the brain, fostering comprehension and retention. Typing notes induces a more mindless, get-everything-down-while-I-can approach. This study removed the variable of distraction, disconnecting the Internet on each laptop. Even the most diligent students can get distracted, and most waste 40 percent of class time on things unrelated to the lecture or their coursework. One study of law school students showed nearly 90% of those with laptops used them for at least five minutes to do activities with no relation to the coursework. Maybe even more shocking, 60% spend half the class distracted. Long story short, the overwhelming evidence suggests that old-fashioned pen and paper benefits your retention.

Skimming Motions Recommended by Evelyn Wood

Beyond that, other experts offer strategies and techniques that lead to greater reading speed and do not sacrifice retention. Many consider

235

Evelyn Wood as the pioneer who popularized speed reading with her *Seven Day Speed Reading and Learning Program*. Similar to this book, she promises things like doubling current speeds of reading, improving reading comprehension and recall, sharpening concentration, and notably, since she gears her book toward students, adhering to deadlines. She asks readers to use a series of unorthodox hand motions to keeps their eyes engaged and moving as they peruse the information on the page.

Motion 1: Altered Metaguiding

Palm on the page, fingers together but relaxed, all flat, you move your hand along the page much as you would with regular meta-guiding. Use your hand to pace your eyes. The major between her advice and the meta-guiding we've discussed in prior chapters lies in how you transition between lines. Wood encourages lifting your fingers above the page ¼ to ½ an inch, no more or less, and diagonally bringing your hand to the place where the next line starts, repeating this motion all the way down the page.

Motion 2: S-shape

The second motion she describes is an S-like motion down the page, fluidly moving between the sides of the page without jumpiness and skipping a line or two in the process. The motions she describes seem to increase in difficulty.

Motion 3: ?-Shape

The third motion involves a similar motion as the first, but instead of tracing lines, you trace the lines down the page in question mark shape.

Motion 4: X-Shape

As the fourth motion, Woods suggests using an X-shape, starting at the top left part of the page and moving diagonally about five lines down to the right margin. Once you reach the right margin, move your finger up two lines of text and repeat the first motion in the opposite direction (to the left margin of the page). Again, you'll move up two to three lines, and move down diagonally five lines. Effectively, you'll repeat these zig-zag, "X" motions until you reach the bottom of the page.

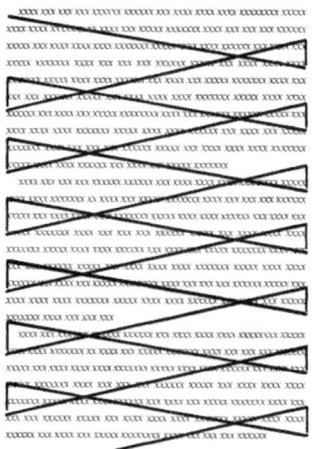

Motion 5: The Loop

The fifth motion makes a loop and follows a similar path to the X, only the motions are smoother, more fluid. Imagine making a figure 8. Create these loops, moving down the page five lines and circling back up a couple (from left to right then right to left) until you reach the bottom of the page.

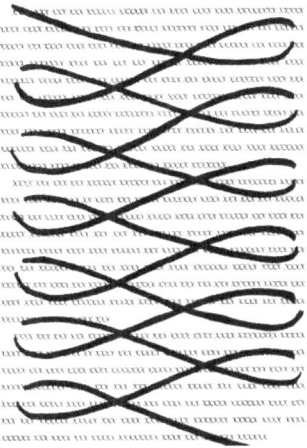

Motion 6: L-Shape

The last she motion she suggests is the L-motion, which would confuse anyone who does not know how to write in cursive. Similar to the loop motion, you move down the page with loops. However, rather than moving to the right margin diagonally down the page, you read straight across a line before looping up and moving down five lines diagonally on the backstroke (to the left margin). For those interested, she provides four more, the horseshoe, U, brush, and half-moon. For risk of losing you further in this digression. I will provide the diagrams and move along.

Another similar meta-guiding technique, much more simplistic than the elaborate hand motions Evelyn Wood uses, involves using a blank white index card. It makes sense. The index card helps to focus your eyes as they track words along the page. This improved focus is coupled with an increase in retention. However, you must be careful doing this not to inadvertently regress. To do as much, you can follow the advice of the article from *Fast Company*. Place the index card above the line you want to read. This not only prevents your eyes from returning up the page, it encourages and even forces them to continue moving down. This adds a barrier to regression, as you must conscientiously remove the index card from preceding text to look over any information you already passed. There is a small catch, however. This above-the-line index card technique does not work too well for reading on a computer since you have to hold your arm out for long periods of time. Even though the index card weighs next to nothing, your arm will get tired before long and keep you from using the technique. Better to not do it at all and save yourself the frustration. Plus, it looks a little ridiculous. In any case, if you are reading for speed, you are much better off reading from a paper source anyway, since on-screen text slows your reading by about 25%.

Other Meta-Guiding Techniques

Sticking with the theme of using a meta-guiding visual pacer, Kwik offers nine more tricks to reading faster and mastering information overload in an article for *Alive.com* in 2017.

First, he suggests visiting an optometrist to get your eyes checked, if you've not done so recently. If not, he says, ensure that your eyesight is at its full potential. Use your prescription glasses or reading glasses.

Next, he emphasizes the importance of finding an appropriate reading place. This often means striking a balance between sleep-inducing comfort and distracting levels of alertness. You could opt to recline with blankets and pillows, but you'd likely fall asleep before you get far. On the other hand, you could blast the A/C, but too much cold would be distracting. Instead, you want to be comfortable, but alert. Keep the room cold, which supports alertness, but not so cold it's distracting. Use a pillow if you need, but don't recline or lay down, as too much relaxation leads to drowsiness.

Another point Kwik makes is that you should find positive anchors that can influence your reading since they can reinforce good self-images about yourself as a reader and discredit bad ones you may have developed along the way. Positivity calms your nerves and relaxes you, essential components to taking in information. Many of these positive anchors involve relaxation and comfort, but they likewise help maintain attentiveness. Try using natural light, for example. You strain your eyes when you read in dim or fluorescent light. Kill the lamps and overhead lights, pop down beside a window, open the curtains, and let the sunlight settle on the pages. In absence of that, some lightbulbs can mimic natural light. Playing music close to a regular heartbeat, about 60 beats per minute, can similarly relax your body and induce a heightened state of learning. The best relaxation method, perhaps, is sitting up straight with good posture to avoid strain on muscles and draw long, deep breaths. Try using a 3-2-4 breathing technique, inhaling through your nose for three seconds, holding for two seconds, and exhaling for four seconds. This keeps your brain well-fueled and running at peak capacity. Related, keeping your book upright will discourage hunching over and promote a direct facing of the page. Staying hydrated will help your brain too, as it functions less effectively when dehydrated. Not only that, your stomach will try to trick you into eating, when in reality, you are just thirsty. Keeping water near you will lessen your trips to the kitchen to snack and keep you focused on the task at hand.

Right Brain and Left Brain Distinctions

Kwik's last point, as it pertains to visual pacing: Use your whole brain. Meta-guide your reading with your left hand to engage your right brain, balancing out your neural function and enriching your reading experience. Any person familiar with left brain versus right brain science will tell you that this makes sense. Children, particularly those who have been diagnosed with dyslexia, struggle when learning how to read because elementary teaching methods cater more to left brain processes. Rather than learning to read the word by addressing each part and arriving at the whole, right-brained students do the opposite. They learn by seeing the whole word and then dissecting it into its component parts. This means that they learn the word based on how it looks, "sight word" approach, rather than how it sounds. Phonics help these children very little since the process involves identifying parts of words that are or sound the same or different. On a big-picture scale, right brain processes lean on context rather than sequence. Left brain students generally read each word in a systematic and orderly fashion, gradually developing an understanding of the passage as they put together words to construct meaning based on each word as a part of the whole. Right-brained children, however, will take multiple words and sentences before processing them as a whole, then search for context clues and develop a mental image of what each word and sentence means. On a practical rather than pedagogical level, this means incremental exercises like phonics bore right-brained children since there are no smaller units to divide them into. They would prefer to learn through real, meaningful books. To borrow an analogy, left brain students may be more likely to want to learn the exact movements and techniques involved in swimming before even getting themselves wet. Right-brained children, however, would be more inclined to dive right into the pool and figure out the finer details later.

Engaging your right brain just as much as, if not more than, your left will take advantage of the tendency to read from an overview perspective, looking at the global picture of what you read to ascertain the overall context. Like a right-brained child, this will include missing details, skipping words, skimming quickly, and not wanting to stop and sound out words. After gaining enough information from the reading to establish an overall picture of the messages, themes, and points conveyed, the right-brained child moves on, leaving the nonessential details behind and not wasting time to focus on them. Right brain processes involve the formation of visual clues, and tend to adhere to silent reading, though occasionally they will read aloud to themselves, making Kwik's point about the reading environment that much more important. So good news, right-brained people, your neural tendencies may be a critical factor in your ability to speed read. Left-brained people, fear not. Although we tend to categorize people as left or right-brained, everyone has the capacity to use both sides of the brain. Just because you favor the side that does not naturally do all of these things does not mean that you are incapable of doing them. It may take some more practice and hard work, but you too can master speed reading effectiveness, for which side of the brain you lean toward does not determine the limit of your abilities.

How do you unlock the capabilities of this magical right brain, you ask? The right side of the brain awaits the arrival of textual information via the corpus callosum, says David Butler in his book *Speed Reading with the Right Brain*. Even though most writing about brain function in general address the left brain, the right controls effective comprehension. To get a sense of what exactly that means, concepts and visual images form as a result of right-brain activity. Overall, as evidenced by the explanation before about how different children learn, the right brain looks at entire images or ideas together and deciphers the patterns and connections within the information. Comprising higher order cognitive processing, the right side interprets information at greater speeds and with more holistic attention to the big picture. This explains the reason behind the monopoly of the right brain over imagination, intuition, facial recognition, and artistry. The right brain simply processes data faster and at a higher volume than the left, meaning reading with the left brain is about as useful, as Butler notes, as squeezing information through a straw.

There is more to it than just that. After processing occurs in both and between the right and left side of the brain, the prefrontal cortex takes over. Consciousness resides here, regulating information, modulating impulses, and coordinating data from the other parts of the brain. In this central location, plans get formulated, decisions made, errors spotted, and habits broken. Most importantly for the exercise of reading, working memory operates in the prefrontal cortex. This is not a perfect system since emotions can affect this area of the brain. That does not have to be a bad thing though, since dopamine, the neurotransmitter that conveys joy and pleasure in the brain, serves as a primer for action and actually strengthens its informational signals, something Butler intentionally points out in the book. Repeated, rhythmic, structured, and easily visualized information aid the prefrontal cortex in remembering information easier.

So, to engage your right brain, Martha Beck offers some exercises to wake that portion of your brain that gets somewhat overlooked in our hyper-rational world. First, she recommends signing your name in every way you can think of. Right to left, upside down, backward and upside down, every direction should be explored to the best of your ability. Second, have a bilateral conversation by writing a question with your right hand and then answering it with your left hand and whatever pops into your mind, regardless of which hand is dominant. Your non-dominant hand will almost certainly write shakily, but do not worry, that is not the point. What is important, though is noticing that your left hand has its own personality. It may sound strange, and it kind of is, but what may be stranger is that your right brain knows things you do not know that you know. It assesses your physical and mental feelings, often offering solutions.

Learning new moves will help your right brain activate since the motions will be unfamiliar to it. Having a hard time thinking of something? Beck uses the example of walking, but instead of swinging your arms opposite your legs, swing them on the same side. Try it in different variations, backward, closing your eyes, any that you can think of that is hard but attainable. Then, throw the kitchen sink at it. In this case, once you activate your right brain, start reading at a blistering pace, faster than you thought you could before. In other applications, you can try to tackle a problem that has been irking you. Instead of stewing over that problem, with your right brain activated, read a few different things, relax, do chores, or anything other than mull over the problem. Do, though, engage it intermittently before dropping it and continuing to do anything else. According to Beck, this provokes epiphanies, similar to eureka moments on television. By engaging more ideas through activities, your brain comes up with the first few potential solutions that may not be any good. Encouraging the brain to churn out solutions yields more and more of them, particularly when the right brain takes over. Rather than being the end goal, activating the right brain for speed reading allows you to deposit more information in that part of your brain. When you activate it again to solve a problem, the information you obtain speed reading with the right side of your brain should be there and become an important factor in increasing your speed reading effectiveness.

Triage-based Reading

Abby Marks Beale believes that choosing the text and picking your battles may be the most important factor in your speed reading effectiveness. Given your limited time, regardless of your speed reading prowess, you need to make choices about what you have time to read and what you do not. Similar to an emergency room, some things, like a heart attack, get precedence over others, such as indigestion, to keep with the example she uses. In other words, you need to perform triage on your reading list. In your large pile of books and articles to be read, you have some heart attacks and some indigestion cases. Identifying the heart attacks advances you further in your reading than the indigestion cases do. That is not to say you should not read books that are not important. Indigestion cases need to be resolved as well. They just have lower priority.

Purpose Setting

Not only should you have a firm idea of what reading is more important, Beale also recommends you know exactly what you want to get out of the reading by having questions readily available that will comprise your purpose in reading. These questions guide your reading and actively engage you with it by seeking out the answers. She calls this "Purpose-Setting" and writes 8-10 questions down on whatever index card or notebook she has available before opening the book. She takes it one step even further, saying that reading alone does not suffice. According to Beale, you need to apply what you read in order to best retain it. My high school English teacher would give us a word of the day before every class. Without fail, every day she said we need to use it three times before we own the word and can use it for ourselves. Similarly, knowledge without application does not get you far. To take full advantage of your reading you need to manifest it into the real-world in some way. Beale offers a litmus of being able to add three tasks to your to-do or projects list that reflect what you have gained from the reading. Reviewing the list to reflect on how well you adapted the reading to your life should relate back to your purpose-setting step and demonstrate a new skill or piece of knowledge.

Assessing your progress, be it in a sort of abstract way that Beale does, or in a more tangible process like the PX Project, a single three-hour-long cognitive experiment, is necessary to your overall experience. Without figuring out where you end up, you do not truly understand your improvements, which could be a reading speed increase of up to 386 percent as in the case of Tim Ferriss. The results of the PX Project are astounding, almost too good to be true. To showcase the efficacy of the project, it comprised speakers of five different languages and incorporated dyslexics. Each of them underwent conditioning that produced reading speeds of highly technical material at a rate of 3,000 words per minute, or 10 pages every minute, 1 page every six seconds. The PX Project bases its methods on a basic understanding of the human visual system, eliminating inefficiencies while increasing speed, without the cost of retention. Ferriss outlines the mechanism of the project in a series of exercises in an article for the Huffington Post. The target areas, minimizing fixations, eliminating regression and back-skipping, and using conditioning drills to maximize horizontal peripheral vision span and the words you register in each fixation, will be familiar to you from the previous pages in this book.

The first technique entails reading two lines in one second with the assistance of a tracker or a pacer, regardless of comprehension, throughout the page. The second expands your perception by beginning one word in from the first word of each line and ending one word from the last, again disregarding comprehension. Ferriss prompts the reader to repeat this task twice more, once using the second word in from the beginning and end of each line, and the other using the third word in on each end, once more ignoring comprehension. He then asks the reader to calculate their new words per minute reading speed. He qualifies this by saying that even though you can read at rates up to triple your previous, you should not use this ability to read three things. Instead, read the same thing three times, and bolster your comprehension.

Wade Cutler promises to *Triple Your Reading Speed* in his so-named book, spending the first thirty or so pages on your current reading skills and the blocks to achieving higher reading speeds. He identifies many of the same things that this book has: failing to preview whatever material in front of you, wasteful eye movements and regressions, poor vision span, vocalization, and subvocalization. General vocalization is not one we talked about much, but includes lipping, tongue warbling, jawing, adam's appling, and diaphragming, various manifestations of reading along inaudibly. He adds more miscellaneous weaknesses, such as pointing/marking, hand-scanning, and slow page turning. While Cutler spends a lot of time on the impediments to speed reading, he has just as many drills to increase your reading speed. From following the middle of three columns of letters while reading from left to right, to progressively more complicated variations, he follows similar eye span increasing theories as Cole and Frank. He expands the range of the letters and jumbles them up into groups of three and four. The columns increase to as many as seven, while the innermost columns get more and more complicated. He then gives the reader drills in the same model to learn pacing and block reading. Shifting to a thin, newspaper-style column, Cutler provides a more practical application of skills. The goal here is one fixation per line. He then ups the difficulty to one fixation per two lines.

Cutler introduces in the next part of the book something he calls the Two Stop Method, resembling something like an S or a Z. Repeating the trend of widening the columns, he first makes your eyes bounce back and forth between two wide ones. They slowly come together as the columns widen. Modulating there after, this is designed to exercise your eyes and help them track consistently between columns. It closely resembles the Eye-Hop method that Ron Cole developed. As a test, Cutler provides excerpts from readings to illustrate his point so that you can apply your newfound skills instantly and test them to see how well you picked them up. He adds a poem from Edgar Allan Poe, the well-known *The Cask Amontillado*, *A Short History of the Civil War*, a chapter from *Treasure Island*, another from *The Time Machine*, *Dr. Jekyll and Mr. Hyde*, and *Money Signs*. Each progresses in length and difficulty, and the tests mimic reading comprehension quizzes from a high school class. He assigns book-length features to give the reader a list to follow and more tests to determine their reading ability.

Chapter Summary

- To keep up with the accelerated creation of information, reading can be your weapon in the arms race of knowledge, and reading this far has gotten you one step closer. Here are six more tips to further advance your speed reading.

- Measure your task before you tackle it. Do not go into it blind. Take a good look at the text you are about to read and make mental notes about what you can expect.

- Ask questions while you read. Odds are the author intentionally made you curious so that he or she can satisfy that curiosity later in the text. Not only that, it will help you keep track of the big ideas and perhaps leave you with questions that will lead you to more reading down the line.

- Decrease subvocalization. Your reading speed is much faster than your speaking speed. When you speak the words, even cognitively, you limit your potential. Silencing that voice can boost your rate of reading. Do not worry about comprehension because at this point you are employing other tactics to compensate for any you lose.

- Read groups of words. Divide each page into three or four columns with a pencil and practice jumping through them in sequential order, line by line. Just do not use this on a book you can not mark up.

- Quiz yourself as you go to keep your memory fresh. Bounce around with your questions and make connections to as many points in the reading as you can.

- On that theme, create as you go. Reference related reading and develop new associations that your brain can follow. Knowledge is not just absorbed, it is created. Active reading facilitates this.

- Take notes by hand. Studies show this helps memory retention much more than typing at a keyboard. If you are still skeptical, think of the countless people who hand wrote things before the invention of the computer or typewriter. You will find some pretty smart people.

- In her book How to Fly with Your Hands, Evelyn Wood issued one of the first speed reading guides in 1959 with some interesting hand motions. She designed them to move your eye and track it across the page in different manners. This sets the same goal as meta-guiding, to pace your eyes across the page and standardize your reading speed.

- Try placing an index card on the page as a meta-guide. Below the line you are currently reading is an acceptable method, but be careful not to regress to any of the information you just read above it. A more effective tactic would be to place the index card on the line above the one you are trying to read, so that your regressions will be greatly reduced, if not eliminated. Also, this will force your eyes to keep moving forward and down the page, increasing your progress compared to the alternate placement. The only catch, the index card does not work well with a computer screen, since you have to hold the index card out with your arm stretched. It can tire you out quickly, but that is okay because reading on paper rather than a screen keeps you from losing 25% of your speed anyway.

- Jim Kwik, who I mentioned earlier in chapter five, has some interesting tidbits that deal with more than the act of reading. The environment in which you read affects your reading about as much as anything. So too does your posture, and something as basic as how you hold the book. Staying hydrated will have an effect too. His most insightful point may be the way he suggests to use your brain, that is, to fully engage it. Reading is often associated with the left brain because of the logic that it relies on. However, in analyzing how right-brained children learn, and specifically learn to read, the very things you look to do in speed reading appear. Focusing on the conceptual big picture, missing minor details, skipping words, and most of all, moving on with inessential details behind, all sound like speed reading best practices.

- Engage your right brain when you read. Kwik suggests you use your left hand to meta-guide, potentially an effective method to awaken that side of your brain. However, a more substantial effort to activate your left brain, by signing your name every way you can, having bilateral conversations, learning new moves, then throwing the kitchen sink at it, as Martha Beck advises, will fully activate it. Right brain activation will not necessarily speed up your reading. That is a more conscious choice you make. The byproduct, however, will reveal itself in a higher comprehension of what you speed read since speed reading activities align with right brain ones, as mentioned before.

- Abby Marks Beale encourages you to choose your battles and prioritize the most important reading you want to get done, similar to how an emergency room treats the most important cases first. She recommends you have 8-10 questions before you read to set your purpose and guide you toward your goal for reading whatever it is you have in front of you. Then, actually use what you obtained from the reading because application boosts retention significantly. Like my English teacher used to say, use it three times, and you own it. She referred to the words of the day, but the premise remains the same. Beale adds three tasks to her to-do or project list that reflect her reading. Reviewing the list makes you reflect on what you have added to your life by reading that text.

- Tim Ferriss proclaims the benefits of the PX Project, boasting a 386 percent increase in his reading speed after the 3-hour lesson. Incorporating meta-guiding, visual perception expansion, and grouping of words, he offers techniques that, when repeated enough, result in astounding increases in reading speed. Through a thorough understanding of the human visual system, the PX Project eliminates inefficiencies to increase speed and maintain retention.

- Wade Cutler claims he can triple your reading speed too through a series of techniques that resemble the columns that Steven Frank provides in his book. Cutler, however, varies them by width, number of letters, and difficulty, working your way up from three columns of single letters to passages from novels. Spending a lot of time focusing on how to remove blocks to speed reading, one area Cutler addresses that none of the other experts do is vocalizing. Similar in principle to subvocalizing, it involves ticks or habits readers have that mimic speech. He identifies movements of the lips, tongue, jaw, adam's apple, and even as far down as your diaphragm. These have the same effect as subvocalization, slowing down your reading in some circumstances

CONCLUSION

Pause a moment. Think back to your mindset as you opened this book. You have come quite a long way. You quite possibly began this journey to speed reading prowess with a vague idea of what speed reading entailed. After reading, you learned about some of the benefits speed reading can bring you. The range is far and wide, from simply being able to take in more information to boosting your confidence, advancing your career, or improving your meditation practices, whether you know it or not. I gave you a preliminary look at what you can expect from this book, and what gains you may be able to make by this point here, the end. Only you know the truth of this. I hope that you remained engaged, applied the techniques, and tracked your progress. At the start, you may have held onto some myths about speed reading, which we debunked right away in chapter two. Namely, they were that you can read 10,000 words per minute, subvocalization inhibits you in your quest to read faster (it does, but not you need not worry about eliminating it until you're at an advanced learning stage), and that you automatically practice reading faster when you read normally.

I encouraged you to embrace whatever reading ability you had coming into this book. An understanding and evaluation of yourself allows you to analyze how you can improve most, and the areas that need more focus. Being honest with yourself can be challenging, and so can reading, particularly since it is not a factory default setting to the human condition. With this as an abstract baseline, chapter four gave you a more concrete one by calculating your reading speed. It also gave you a benchmark by providing speeds for a variety of different reading levels.

Chapter five started the transformative process of turning you into a speed reader. It gave you all sorts of techniques to try when you practice your speed reading, from first and foremost setting a goal, to skimming, cutting down on subvocalization, reading phrases, meta-guiding, rapid serial visualization, avoiding regression and limiting fixations. These may have originally boosted your reading speed significantly, but you may have noticed a drop in comprehension.

Chapter six remedied that by giving you counters to a drop in retention. These included visualization, allowing some words and phrases to go because they were too complicated, expanding your vocabulary, and playing the recall game.

These tips and tricks alone are not enough, though, as chapter seven lays out. One of the best ways to get better at reading is to do more of it. The one caveat is that you have to read mindfully. A good place to start is books that are easy to read, as the input hypothesis developed by Stephen Krashen suggests that texts with words that fall under a threshold of 95 percent knowledge make a commitment to continue reading even more difficult. This chapter gave some helpful ways to build a routine for reading, like focusing on the building blocks of the habit, making it easier for you to start, reading books because you enjoy them, keeping your options open by switching books and building up to harder books by expanding your foundation first through research.

Keeping track of your reading may be most important, especially if you need the positive reinforcement to keep up your habit. There are so many ways, first and foremost timing your reading regularly to keep checkpoints of where you are. A good old-fashioned reading log in a planner or notebook will never fail to keep you on track, as long as you keep up with it. In the digital age, more and more productivity and functionality can shift to the online forum, where Goodreads, Spreadsheets, Trello, and Pinterest boards can document your reading and engage you with other readers or more content. When in doubt, to either supplement or replace any of these, a tried and true pile of books can make an adequate reading log, especially if you like to juggle multiple books and keep one or two to look forward to handy.

The best way to get through them, and a tactic that many people probably already utilize, skim and scan your reading while retaining the important information. It is important to discredit the misconceptions. Skimming and scanning are not quickly glancing over pages and turning them, expecting information to flow easily and effortlessly. There is an inherent trade-off between speed and retention, but skimming and scanning account for this. It is not a temporary fix, nor does it undermine the author's tone and disrespect their careful word choice. On the contrary, they require a dedicated and mindful approach to any reading. They start with something simple, knowing what you want to get out of it, through pre-reading or your own assessment. Then you read vertically as much, if not more than, horizontally, while putting yourself in the place of the author to figure out the strategies and reasons behind the text. Be selective about what you choose to read, for instance, read the first sentence in a paragraph, but not necessarily every complete sentence or examples.

Lastly, chapter ten should have left you with more advanced methods for speed reading. Staying ahead of the pack in a competitive digital world involves sizing up your tasks, asking questions, decreasing subvocalization, reading groups of words, quizzing yourself, applying your reading by creating knowledge after you read, and taking notes with your hand and not with a computer. A chief strategy among the ones listed in this chapter, and not mentioned in chapter five, is making use of your right brain, which can potentially improve your comprehension several fold. Doing so will allow the information to process through both sides of your brain. The left contributes to logical functions and facilitates your efforts to deposit knowledge into long-term memory banks. The right side of the brain processes information at a substantially faster rate, making it wise and effective to hand over as much information to it, especially as you read for speed. Expert testimonies bolster this chapter and introduce you to unique and constructive methods, building off of some of the ones earlier in the chapter or that resurface from chapter five.

As you may have noticed, these tips build on each other in just that way. Some simple techniques introduced in the exposition of the book come back later in different and more complicated ways. Do not confuse them for the same thing, for instance, meta-guiding with your pen is different from doing so with an index card which is different from using your left hand, or using some seemingly ridiculous hand motions as Evelyn Wood suggests. If you employ these tips in conjunction, you will find yourself reading faster and retaining more without actively trying to do so (although that's beside the point, you should most definitely be actively trying to improve your reading pace). I cannot guarantee that you can now magically be able to read anything you pick up at a rate of 1,500 words per minute. It is not a snap of the fingers that time leaps you into the next morning where you'll roll out of bed, pick up a book, and read it as a superhero would. We've already dispelled such fantastical notions. You yourself need to take charge of your own reading and incorporate the methods, techniques, tips, and tricks I have provided in a way that works best for you. Consider these solutions to your problem, an instruction manual for your project, if you will. But this is a do-it-yourself type of project, and I cannot do it for you. Develop your own routines, rituals, habits, or tendencies. Whatever you do, take note of each of these tips and tricks and work your way up to 1,500 words per minute reading. You have the tools and instructions. Now build your way up to that goal. I have every faith in you.

RESOURCES

Beck, M. (n.d.). Creativity Boost: How to Tap into Right-Brain Thinking. Retrieved December 23, 2019, from https://www.oprah.com/spirit/how-to-tap-into-the-right-side-of-your-brain-martha-beck-advice/all

Booth, A. (2014, February 4). 10 Reasons Why You Should Learn Speed Reading. Retrieved December 22, 2019, from https://www.lifehack.org/articles/lifestyle/10-reasons-why-you-should-learn-speed-reading.html

Burke, S. (2014, March 13). The Spritz app lets you read at 1,000 wpm -- but at what cost? Retrieved December 22, 2019, from https://money.cnn.com/2014/03/13/technology/innovation/spritz/

Butler, D. (2017). *Speed Reading with the Right Brain: Learn to Read Ideas Instead of Just Words*. ? CreateSpace Independent Publishing Platform.

Capuano, R. (2019, April 23). Right-Brained Reading. Retrieved December 23, 2019, from https://www.thehomeschoolmom.com/right-brained-reading/

Cole, R. (2012). *SuperReading for Success: The Groundbreaking, Brain-Based Program to Improve Your Speed, Enhance Your Memo ry, and Increase Your Success*. New York: Penguin Publishing Group.

Cutler, W. E. (1993). *Triple Your Reading Speed*. New York: Prentice Hall.

de Bruijn, O., & Spence, R. (2000). Rapid Serial Visual Presentation: A space-time trade-off in information presentation. Retrieved from https://www.researchgate.net/profile/Oscar_Bruijn2/publication/220944929_Rapid_Serial_Visual_Presentation_A_space-timed_trade-off_in_information_presentation/links/09e415112db90c75ed000000.pdf

DeRusha, B. (2019, August 23). 10 Speed Reading Apps to Help You Tackle Your TBR. Retrieved December 22, 2019, from https://bookriot.com/2018/10/19/best-speed-reading-apps/

Doubek, J. (2016, April 17). Attention, Students: Put Your Laptops Away. Retrieved December 23, 2019, from https://choice.npr.org/index.html?origin=https://www.npr.org/2016/04/17/474525392/attention-students-put-your-laptops-away

Duggan, G., & Payne, S. (2009). Text skimming: The process and effectiveness of foraging through text under time pressure. *Journal of Experimental Psychology: Applied*, *15*(3), 228–242. https://doi.org/10.1037/a0016995

Ferriss, T. (2014, July 13). How I Learned to Read 300 Percent Faster in 20 Minutes. Retrieved December 23, 2019, from https://www.huffpost.com/entry/speed-reading_b_5317784

Frank, S. (1998). *Backpack Series-Speed Reading Secrets (The Backpack Study Series)*. Holbrook, Massachusetts: Adams Media.

Frank, S. D. (1994). *The Evelyn Wood Seven-Day Speed Reading and Learning Program*. Fall River, MA: Fall River Press.

Grothaus, M. (2018, May 24). How to train yourself to become a speed reader. Retrieved December 22, 2019, from https://www.fastcompany.com/40574769/how-to-train-yourself-to-become-a-speed-reader

Halton, M. (2019, April 1). A speed reader shares 3 tricks to help anyone read faster. Retrieved December 22, 2019, from https://ideas.ted.com/a-speed-reader-shares-3-tricks-to-help-anyone-read-faster/

Hammond, B. (2018, March 22). What is the Strengths Perspective? :: Speed Reading Study Explained Better Than Ever. Retrieved January 1, 2020, from https://www.isogostrong.com/strengthsfinder-speed-reading/

Harari, Y. N. (2015). *Sapiens: A Brief History of Humankind*. New York: Harper.

Harry, J. (2018, December 28). 5 Things Holding Your Reading Speed Back. Retrieved December 22, 2019, from https://medium.com/@studyfast/5-things-holding-your-reading-speed-back-aac6405fc5c0

Kaufman, J. (n.d.). 10 Days to Faster Reading - Abby Marks-Beale. Retrieved December 22, 2019, from https://joshkaufman.net/10-days-to-faster-reading/

Kraushaar, J., & Novak, D. (2010). Examining the Affects of Student Multitasking with Laptops during the Lecture. *Journal of Information Systems Education*, *21*(2), 241–251. Retrieved from https://eric.ed.gov/?id=EJ893903

Kump, P. (1998). *Breakthrough Rapid Reading* (Revised ed.). New York: Prentice Hall Press.

Kwik, J. (n.d.). Kwik Brain 007: How to Read Faster. Retrieved December 22, 2019, from https://jimkwik.com/kwik-brain-007/

Kwik, J. (2017, January 21). 10 Tricks for Speed-Reading (That Will Save You So Much Time). Retrieved December 22, 2019, from https://www.alive.com/lifestyle/speed-read-like-a-boss/

Larsen, L. (n.d.). *Does Speed Reading Improve College Student's Retention Level and Comprehension?* Retrieved from http://leannlarsen.com/Portfolio/Speed%20Reading%20Research.pdf

Macalister, J. (2010). Speed reading courses and their effect on reading authentic texts: A preliminary investigation. *Reading in a Foreign Language*, *22*(1), 104–116. Retrieved from http://nflrc.lll.hawaii.edu/rfl/April2010/articles/macalister.pdf

May, C. (2014, June 3). A Learning Secret: Don't Take Notes with a Laptop. Retrieved December 23, 2019, from https://www.scientificamerican.com/article/a-learning-secret-don-t-take-notes-with-a-laptop/

Montgomery, C. (2018, November 4). How to Improve Reading Comprehension: 8 Expert Tips. Retrieved December 22, 2019, from https://blog.prepscholar.com/how-to-improve-reading-comprehension

Nation, P. (2005). Reading Faster. *PASAA*, *36*, 21–37.

National Research Council. (2012). *Improving Adult Literacy Instruction: Developing Reading and Writing*. https://doi.org/10.17226/13468

Nelson, B. (2012, July 30). Do You Read Fast Enough To Be Successful? Retrieved January 1, 2020, from https://www.forbes.com/sites/brettnelson/2012/06/04/do-you-read-fast-enough-to-be-successful/#2db68dab462e

Olson, S. (2015, January 7). The Science of Speed Reading; Benefits And Consequences Of Reading 1,000 Pages In 10 Hours. Retrieved December 22, 2019, from https://www.medicaldaily.com/science-speed-reading-benefits-and-consequences-reading-1000-pages-10-hours-316828

Peterson, D. (2019, July 3). How to Read Faster and Have More Study Time. Retrieved December 23, 2019, from https://www.thoughtco.com/how-to-read-faster-31624

Rayner, K., Schotter, E. R., Masson, M. E. J., Potter, M. C., & Treiman, R. (2016). So Much to Read, So Little Time. *Psychological Science in the Public Interest*, *17*(1), 4–34. https://doi.org/10.1177/1529100615623267

Rodrigues, J. (2019, September 6). 5 Reasons Why Speed Reading Is Good For Your Brain. Retrieved December 23, 2019, from https://www.irisreading.com/5-reasons-why-speed-reading-is-good-for-your-brain/

Scott, S. J. (2019, December 17). How to Read Faster: 9 Steps to Increase Your Speed in 2020. Retrieved December 22, 2019, from https://www.developgoodhabits.com/how-to-read-faster/

Super-Speed Reading. (n.d.). Retrieved December 10, 2019, from https://tvtropes.org/pmwiki/pmwiki.php/Main/SuperSpeedReading

The Mind Tools Content Team. (n.d.). Speed Reading: – How to Absorb Information Quickly and Effectively. Retrieved December 22, 2019, from https://www.mindtools.com/speedrd.html

Thielen, J., Grochowski, P., Perpich, D., & Samuel, S. (2016). *Speed Reading and Reading Retention Workshop - Poster and Active Learning Exercises*. Ann Arbor, MI: University of Michigan Library.

Trafton, A. (2014, January 16). In the blink of an eye. *MIT News*. Retrieved from http://news.mit.edu/2014/in-the-blink-of-an-eye-0116

Ways, M. (2019a, April 2). Reading Comprehension Strategies. Retrieved December 22, 2019, from https://www.speedreadinglounge.com/reading-comprehension-strategies

Ways, M. (2019b, November 6). Skimming and Scanning – 4 Strategies. Retrieved December 22, 2019, from https://www.speedreadinglounge.com/skimming-and-scanning

Young, S. (2019, August 18). I Was Wrong About Speed Reading: Here are the Facts. Retrieved December 22, 2019, from https://www.scottyoung.com/blog/2015/01/19/speed-reading-redo/

Accelerated Learning Unlocked

40+ Expert Techniques for Rapid Skill Acquisition and Memory Improvement.

The Step-by-Step Guide for Beginners to Quickly Cut Your Study Time for Anything New in Half.

John R. Torrance, Productivity Coach

TABLE OF CONTENTS

INTRODUCTION

If you've ever found yourself in a quagmire as you attempt to learn something new, you've come to the right book. Learning something new can seem like a daunting task, especially given the range of sources that exist on the topic. With the wealth of information available today, you have more opportunities than ever to discover nearly anything. You can jump on your computer or pick up a book and learn whatever you want. The human mind has that kind of unlimited potential. There's a catch, however: knowing the right techniques that will help you access those parts of your brain that best work for you rather than against you.

The purpose of this book is to get to the very core of accelerated learning and improved memory basics. This guide will prepare you for a new learning adventure. Each chapter is based on proven principles that will help you learn as quickly and as effectively as you can. It will provide a solid foundation for you as you embark on your learning journey, allowing you to understand the "why" behind the theory so you can achieve greater success. It is a roadmap for practical and immediate action so that you can see real results. Ultimately, this text is a balance. It aims to be a combination of both theory and practice in a way that will ultimately give you the understanding required to achieve the outcomes you're looking for.

These words will help stimulate your thoughts, inspire discussion, and lead you towards positive action. Like with many topics, this book covers core principles, so if you want to go more in depth on any one chapter, know that there is plenty out there that will go into greater depth. This book is intended to go in-depth only in ways that are immediately practical to you as a learner. It is liberating, however, to know that none of us (and certainly no one book) will ever be able to explain or instruct the full potential of learning that we as human beings hold. There are so many creative possibilities for learning and for life; the key is it all starts with that critical first step! The longer you wait to take this first step, the longer it will take you to finally achieve what you've only dreamed of accomplishing.

I hope you commit to reading, and make this commitment to yourself: take it one chapter at a time. Doing so will enable you to get where you've always meant to, but never thought you could. I guarantee you have it in you. With the proper tools, focus, and work ethic, you will get there, and I will show you how. I hope this book gets you started, not only on learning a specific new skill, but also on a fascinating, limitless journey that comes from being a life-long learner.

CHAPTER ONE:

Debunking Five Popular Myths On Learning

You've made it this far, in life and in your career. In some ways, you may think you know enough. Maybe you think you already know what will work for you when it comes to learning new skills and retaining information. This is, at least in part, true. You do have methods that work and that have brought you to where you are in life. You have a baseline of learning that has served you well. However, chances are you are here because there is more to know, to learn, and you are interested in finding an even better way of doing it.

Regardless of what you know - or what you think you know - there are also certain falsehoods about teaching and learning that most of us have been exposed to and that we, in some ways, carry with us throughout our lives. In this sense, what you have built over time as your understanding of how you learn may be completely wrong - or at the very least, incomplete.

Research on learning and memory in the recent past has demonstrated how our beliefs and intuitions about how we learn are more often than not absolutely incorrect. Trial and error is apparently less scientifically helpful for more complex forms of learning, however helpful it may have once been for our early ancestors' survival techniques. As human beings, we are notoriously bad at rating (or predicting) our own performance. We tend to think we know more than we actually do! Actual comprehension or understanding, the cornerstones of real learning, are more often replaced by our impression of knowing something based on a feeling of familiarity or ease in how the information is presented to us.

Human beings are born with an amazing capacity to learn, and more often than not we barely tap into our full potential. We have an incredible ability to learn a variety of different topics and to go in great depth in specific domains.

In this first chapter, I will overview five of the most popular myths about learning that threaten to mislead you as you set out on your new learning venture. By better understanding these myths, you will be able to analyze where you may have been misguided in the past, and ways you can correct yourself along your learning path. I'll follow up on each myth with new and improved methods of learning you can replace them with that will actually work.

Myth #1: Learning Styles Are Essential To Learning

You may have heard about learning styles as a method for teaching and learning new things. Many people, educators included, believe that learning styles are set for each learner and can be used as a tool for a person's academic and professional career.

The concept of learning styles has come to encompass a large body of commercial materials and educational resources, in theory as a means of primarily helping teachers in the classroom. There are slight variations to models and schemes, and over seventy of them exist in total. Each one in some way classifies learners into a category and provides teachers with tools to assess students and tailor lessons to feed into each of the designated styles. The influence of this view is far-reaching within the educational field, from kindergarten to graduate school, and there is an industry that thrives on providing tests and workbooks for schools and professional development organizations.

A recent study indicates that more than ninety percent of the broader public believes they would learn better if they were taught in one of the designated learning styles. This is, however, based more on what has been referred to as "essentialist" and an automatic way of thinking versus evidence that it actually produces those desired outcomes. Advocates in favor of it claim learning will be less effective (or even ineffective) if learners do not receive instruction that takes into account their learning style. In some way, they believe learning styles will promote better learning outcomes. In the past several years researchers have seriously questioned the extent to which the learning styles method has practical implications in educational contexts. Overwhelmingly, studies suggest that there is very little validity to applications of learning styles as well as too little empirical evidence of its benefits.

On a basic level, there is no adequate evidence from current research that can justify learning styles as the best way to teach and take in new information. Studies that do have an appropriate methodology for testing it (which is a rarity) have even found using this technique can have negative outcomes. Learning styles, in short, are widely believed in and yet unfortunately not supported by scientific study because they don't yield the results they promise; the learning styles model can actually undermine education and learning new skills.

Think about it this way: if you spend time and money tailoring your learning to one particular method, you are neglecting the other methods of learning that would enrich your knowledge base more holistically. You aren't just a visual learner and nothing more. As with many things, this may be a default you are drawn to in certain scenarios or contexts, but it would be limiting for you and your ability to learn new topics if you were to classify yourself as only a visual learner.

What To Do Instead

Researchers have pointed to more action-based learning strategies that involve a customized approach for tackling new skills and topics. When learning something new, it is best if you identify the optimal approach for each kind of subject matter that is based on that particular subject. For instance, if you're an English teacher who has to make a writing course curriculum, you will want to include a heavy verbal emphasis, whereas the most efficient and effective method of teaching geometry will require materials that relate to visual and spatial techniques for learning. Different people will always learn in different ways; that is perhaps the primary lesson we can learn from the learning styles model. What will be more helpful for you moving forward in your learning is how you apply different learning methods to the different skills you want to learn. If you're learning music, you want to engage your auditory learning style. If you want to learn painting, you'll want to choose your visual learning style tool, and so on. The more dextrous you are as a learner, the more likely you will be to find success.

Think of learning as having a toolbox. You want to have as many tools (learning styles) in your toolbox as possible so you can choose the most appropriate one for the situation at hand. To continue with the example above, it would be a much better practice for you to accept that you are primarily drawn to visual learning, and then bolster your capacity for auditory and kinesthetic learning (and so on), so you can better position yourself for learning based on content and context versus a habitual preference. This will, in turn, build your neural elasticity and allow you to more easily adapt to learning new things. Just remember: the content is the key to learning.

My suggestion for learning new skills is to work backward. Start by matching your learning strategy to the content you're studying instead of basing it on style. If you are trying to improve your reading skills, step one is simply to read more - and read correctly. Take your time to really understand the words you are reading, the syntax, the sentence structure, everything. This may appear tedious, but real learning is based on the content that you are studying, not an unsupported standard practice. You are pursuing an outcome, which means you want to start first with where you want to go, and then begin inching towards it incrementally.

Studies have also indicated that using your prior knowledge will help you learn new things. What you already know will have a strong effect on how well you can retain new information. When we connect new and old information, part of the brain associated with learning is activated. The implications of this are that learners can build stepping stones from what they know to what they don't yet, and that will improve and quicken their ability to take in new information. If you want to get better at reading, choose a subject you know fairly well or have some interest in. Did you play a sport in school? Do you like learning about different geographies? Choose a book you know will be "easier" for you to read so you can motivate yourself to stay the course with your learning.

Staying motivated will help keep you focused and committed to new learning. Learning based on what you are interested in is useful because it builds on what you want to do. It's a way of tricking yourself into really liking what you're learning. As with anything, the more fun we have doing it, the more likely we are to continue to do it.

Myth #2: Re-reading & Highlighting Will Help You Learn

Let's say you have an important meeting coming up. Is the first thing you do to refresh your memory on your talking points or re-read your materials? Do you have bullet points? Or maybe you memorize lines to share with the group. Whatever your approach is, you may be surprised to hear the statistics on what does and doesn't work.

Highlighting and underlining, in particular, have been found to be fairly ineffective learning strategies. Research indicates this approach is, in fact, a passive way of learning, and will likely not provide desired results. Passively reading the same text over and over again won't do anything for your comprehension or recall unless it's spaced out over time. While these practices are common, they offer very little benefit beyond what reading the text does. You must be actively engaged with the material.

Some research has even suggested that highlighting can interfere with learning because it distracts from the reader synthesizing connections and gaining a big-picture understanding by instead drawing attention to individual facts. Highlighting or underlining can also be detrimental if the wrong information is selected. Re-reading was also found to be ineffective at best, distracting and time-consuming at worst. Summarizing or writing down your ideas as you read was found to be more helpful than highlighting or underlining, depending on your relative skill level at doing so. Overall, all of these were deemed less useful exercises for learning by the scientific community.

Despite this, in a study conducted by Ulrich Boser, author of *Learn Better: Mastering the Skills for Success in Life, Business, and School, or How to Become an Expert In Just About Anything*, more than 80% of respondents believed that rereading is a highly effective approach to learning. Similar to broad beliefs on learning styles, public opinions on re-reading, highlighting, and underlining as a means of learning is more rooted in standard practice than it is in empirical evidence.

It's easy for us to assume we operate similar to computers because our brains serve as a kind of hard drive for our mental functioning. However, we are more than a database that collects various data points that flow past us. As humans, that's not how our learning works. Boser found instead that learning is often a "form of mental doing" and supported more active, engaged methods of learning. We need to make sense of the content we seek to learn, so it can integrate within our mental systems as a wider understanding.

What To Do Instead

In contrast to more familiar practices like highlighting and re-reading, active learning strategies carry the most relevance and support, even if they aren't as well known. For instance, distributed study practice is a tactic that involves spreading out study sessions rather than engaging in one marathon, commonly referred to as 'cramming.' This may help you get through a meeting or test, but it will not stay with you as lasting learning. It is more effective to spread your learning out at intervals where you allow yourself to digest the material. Longer intervals mean longer-lasting learning.

In the shorter term, instead of re-reading, highlighting, or underlining important information, you can turn the information into a short quiz. This more active strategy will allow you to both process and integrate what you're learning. You can do this by asking yourself what the author is telling you at the end of every paragraph, in your own words. Summarize in the moment, and then compare it to what you already know. How is it similar to what you've read before? How is it different? How does it relate to other materials you've encountered on this subject? As you begin to make sense of what you're reading, you will deepen your learning potential.

Myth #3: Focus On One Subject At A Time

Historically speaking, we've been told it's good to practice one skill at a time. For instance, if you are a beginner pianist you may be told to rehearse scales before chords and to get one down before attempting to learn the other. If you're practicing a new sport, you may be told to break down learning based on one move at a time. In research terms, this is called blocking and is seen as common sense and easy to follow. It's also the dominant teaching practice in schools, professional training programs, and the likes.

Especially when it comes to learning a difficult subject, people widely believe you should practice one thing at a time. If you're learning to use a new suite of software, these people will suggest you practice one program one day and another the next, that way you can focus on fully understanding each one before moving on to something new. However, research shows you're more likely to confuse similar information if you study a lot of the same subject in one day like this. Blocking as a learning technique keeps you from distinguishing between two similar concepts.

Think about it. When you encounter a set of concepts (or terms or principles) that are similar in some way, you have a higher likelihood of confusing them with one another. You may mistake one word for another word with a similar spelling, or choose the wrong strategy for a math problem because they use a similar equation. You will make more errors more frequently when you expose yourself to only one main concept at a time.

What To Do Instead

An alternative approach is to expose yourself to different concepts by interleaving (or mixing) them together, so that one concept is followed by a different one. Learning related skills or concepts in parallel like this has been found to be a surprisingly effective way to train your brain. It's more effective to study multiple subjects each day than it is to do one deep-dive into a subject or two (especially if you're "cramming"). By mixing subjects, you are allowing your brain to have more time to consolidate new learning. Commonly called the "interleaving effect," this gives you a chance to see the core idea or big picture because, as you shift concepts, you gain a better sense of what each one means.

So, instead of a beginner pianist practicing only scales and then chords and then arpeggios (as with blocking), interleaving would involve alternating between practicing all of the above on a given day. Studies have shown this mixed method of learning tends to outperform blocking in a variety of subjects, from sports to categorical learning (such as math). Most recently, one study even found interleaving benefits critical thinking skills, as students who were trained with the technique were found to make more accurate assessments than those who used blocking techniques in complex learning scenarios.

The interleaving effect has also been found to have long-lasting effects on learning because it reinforces neural connections between different tasks and correct responses, which enhances your learning over time. This can often feel slow and difficult at the beginning, but what this means is it can generate better long-term results. You have less likelihood of forgetting what you learn because it improves the brain's ability to discriminate between concepts through a series of practice attempts that are different from the last. In this way, automatic responses aren't applicable, as with blocking, where once you know what solution fits, or which move works, the learning is over and your brain disengages. Interleaving makes your brain consciously focus on finding the correct solution based on the context of the problem. This process can help you improve your ability to learn critical features of new skills and concepts, so that you can select and implement more appropriate responses.

Myth #4: The 10,000 Hour Rule

Journalist and author, Malcolm Gladwell, popularized the idea of the "10,000 hour rule," which states you need 10,000 hours of deliberate practice in order to become world-class in your chosen field. Recent research offers a counterpoint to this trend, however, suggesting that the amount of practice accumulated like this over time does not seem to play a major role in explaining individual differences in performance across all learning domains, including music, sports, and professional (or adult) education. Although practice is certainly essential when you're learning a new skill or studying a new topic, there's no magic number of hours that will turn you into an expert or bring you to the proficiency level of a professional athlete or musician.

In reality, practice alone doesn't make it perfect. What has been coined "deliberate practice" has been found to have less influence in building expertise than previously thought. Researchers have studied deliberate practice as a means of understanding whether or not experts are "born" or "made" - or maybe a bit of both.

Overall, studies have found that deliberate practice is important, but not as important as advocates have claimed it is. There is a positive relationship between practice and performance, meaning the more people practiced, the higher their level of performance in a given domain. The difference is, the domain in question makes a difference in how well it effective it is. Deliberate practice is highly effective for games like Scrabble or chess, but less effective for sports, psychology, and related subjects.

What To Do Instead

The important question to consider moving forward is what else matters besides practice? Researchers at Princeton University point to the age a person begins an activity, along with individual variances in ability and commitment to learning as explanations for differences in human performance.

While researchers focus on determining why deliberate practice is not the answer, you can focus your attention on not convincing yourself there is a magic number to your success. Don't beat yourself up trying to meet an arbitrary number that may or may not actually help you reach your goal - and most likely will not. You won't become an expert this way, and you'll exhaust yourself in the process.

What works instead isn't just about time either; it's about seeking outside advice and input. Having this kind of feedback will be critical to your learning and will help keep you accountable. This is why hiring coaches or tutors can be so beneficial for your success.

Myth #5 You Are Either Right Or Left Brain Dominant

The idea that some people are right-brained while others are left-brained has been around for some time now. According to the theory, left-brained people are more logical, analytical, and methodical, while right-brained people are more creative and artistic. It is the basis for a myriad of personality tests, self-motivation books, and pseudo-psychology quizzes, and yet again this is not supported by any actual science. In reality, there are connections between all brain regions that enable humans to engage in both creative and analytical thinking; these things are not confined to only one side or another.

A recent study at the University of Utah has effectively debunked the myth through an analysis of more than one thousand brains. The study suggested that people do not typically prefer to use either their right or left side of the brain. Instead, they use their entire brain equally throughout the course of the entire experiment. We do prefer one side or the other - again, based on context. Scientists call this phenomenon "lateralization," or when we use one brain region more than others depending on the specific function required. For instance, speech comes from the left side of the brain for most right-handed people, but this doesn't imply that great writers or speakers use the left side of the brain more than the right, or that one side is bigger or richer in neural activity.

What To Do Instead

Don't divide yourself into one of these misleading categories. Understand that we all use our entire brain equally, and the fact that our brain is connected is what allows us to think both creatively and analytically, depending on what we are learning. Focus on how you can pursue the skills or expertise you've been meaning to conquer. Even if you tend to be more analytical than creative, or vice versa, this is not because you are relying too much (or too little) on a specific region of your brain. You aren't helping yourself by trying to fit into an existing (and incorrect) category of learner or thinker. What you want to do is enhance your learning in ways that will strengthen your ability to be flexible and to take in new information in longer-lasting ways.

Chapter Summary

Learning myths are extremely harmful in the way in which they have infiltrated into majority practice. The substance behind these beliefs is lacking and misleading for us as we approach learning new skills and subjects. Regardless of what you're trying to learn, you will need to come up with a strategy that works for you. You are regulating yourself, which means you have to set your own study rules. You are in charge of your own learning, so you will have to monitor your cognition, motivation, behavior, and learning environment in order to stay organized and focused. This process begins by knowing what not to do, which I have just covered. In the next chapter, you will learn key principles to prioritize that will accelerate your learning.

CHAPTER TWO

Seven Key Principles That Optimize The Learning Process

Learning something new may at first seem pretty difficult - and it can be. The good news is you can do something about it. You can improve your ability to learn by developing a good strategy that will work for you, and by following some basic guidelines that will help you accelerate your learning process.

Accelerated learning is not a new concept, and has been used by educators for decades now as a means of achieving a faster learning rate in students. To achieve desired learning outcomes in a shorter time frame (compared to conventional teaching practices), we have to first understand it is a holistic approach to learning. It integrates a mixture of teaching pedagogies and psychological theories to enhance and expedite learning. Perhaps most importantly is how it uses a learner's emotional and intellectual state as a basis for learning. It relies on intrinsic motivation to propel learning forward by focusing on learner needs, goals, life conditions, and so on, so that it truly offers a human-centric, practical approach to learning.

A leading expert in this methodology is Dave Meier, who wrote *The Accelerated Learning Handbook: A Creative Guide to Designing and Delivering Faster, More Effective Training Programs*. Meier describes accelerated learning as the use of music, color, emotion, play, and creativity in a way that involves the whole person in their learning to enliven the entire experience. The principles overviewed in this chapter come directly from his comprehensive guide on learning new things more quickly.

I will focus on the seven leading principles that overview the highlights of Meier's handbook, so you will have a window into how your mind can acquire the knowledge you want. Each principle is derived from detailed studies on the human mind and leading methodologies of learning. You can use these principles to develop more substantial learning practices that will engage your whole brain and optimize your learning process. Once you understand these basic principles of accelerated learning, you will be able to properly implement them into your learning techniques.

Engage The Whole Mind & Body

Learning is not just in your mind; it is a combination of your body and your mind, and the connection between the two. This means you must use your whole self for learning: your mind, body, emotions, and all your senses. Science has shown us how using our entire brain is critical in order to make our learning faster, more interesting, and longer-lasting. The brain and body are inseparably connected. Moving your body, for example, can significantly improve your brain functioning, and certain brain states can have a profound effect on your body.

Your thinking, learning, and memory are not just all in your head, but are rather distributed throughout your body. In her book, *The Molecules of Emotion*, Candice Pert writes how much of our thinking, learning, and decision-making actually takes place on a cellular and molecular level. It is troubling, then, how we are almost always taught to separate our body from our mind. Traditional learning focuses on more conscious or rational, left-brained processes, or are strictly verbal. It tends to ignore the other senses by creating learning environments that do not engage the body, which would include our feelings and senses. In a learning context, moving our body helps stimulate chemicals essential for engaging our brain's neural network. This form of learning is referred to as "somatic learning" and denotes tactile, kinesthetic, or hands-on learning.

Somatic learners tend to be at a disadvantage in Western culture because our educational traditions tend to disregard the body as central to learning. We historically have told children to sit still and be attentive listeners in class instead of encouraging exploration, movement, and activity-based learning. There are many ways you can physically get your body involved in your learning; your learning doesn't have to be only, or even primarily, physical. It is, however, important to integrate some kind of body movement into your learning in a way where you alternate from physically active to physically passive learning.

Don't Just Consume - Create

Meier writes how knowledge isn't just something you absorb, but rather what you, as a learner, create. Learning happens when you fully integrate new knowledge by applying it in some way that makes it especially meaningful to you. You can make basic content more meaningful by creating a new significance for it that makes it relevant to you. This happens when you form new neural network connections and new patterns of interactions on a molecular level within yourself as you connect different concepts together. In turn, this will help you enforce a new work process or create a more practical application of newfound knowledge.

As you prepare yourself for learning, something you should do is take care to embrace a natural, more childlike state of wonder so that your innate ability to learn is engaged. This state is characterized by openness, freedom, fearlessness, joy, and curiosity. When you arouse your sense of curiosity, you open yourself up to new possibilities and connections; in essence, you make yourself fully ready to absorb and process new information. Learning, much like life itself, will stagnate if there is nothing left to be curious about or to engage with. Spark your curiosity by asking questions about the content you want to learn and you will find yourself learning and growing in ways you never imagined. If you approach your learning like a problem or a puzzle, you will engage your curiosity and find more motivation to learn.

You can also access and develop your sense of curiosity by using play as a means of engaging with learning content. When we have a sense of play, we release positive endorphins that bring us good feelings and help our bodies and minds engage in whatever it is we are trying to do. In terms of learning, this means we develop a creative intelligence that drives our ability to learn and grow.

Collaborate With Others

Traditional learning has created a tendency towards competition and individualistic learning that is steeped in isolation. Teaching pedagogies and universities have historically embraced individualism and the struggle to win, advance, versus a more tribal-based, collaborative approach to learning and interacting with others. Education has tended to emphasize individual achievement through individual grading that is strictly based on how students perform as everyone competes for the best grades. In theory, this was to create self-reliant individuals who work independently and in competition with one another as a motivating factor that educators hoped would lead to greater individual achievement. This over-emphasis on individualism in education, however, prevents the collective whole from being utilized to its fullest potential, which also means individual learners suffer. Isolation often creates an environment of stress and tends to reduce the speed and quality of learning. The competitive approach creates silos between learners instead of bridges from which information, intelligent, and real feedback is more readily possible.

Collaboration among learners enhances learning. Working with others engages us in a process of interaction that creates a social base and a network of support. This social base aids learning because, as humans, we are social learners. Collaboration between learners, such as learning through a learning community, creates space for individuals to really interact with each other and the content in a way that isn't distracted by hierarchy. Competition indicates there is a winner and a loser, whereas with collaboration there is a nurturing, understanding environment where learning can take place safely and openly. There is no longer a sense of competition between slower learners and faster learners, which inevitably creates avenues of cooperation that help speed up skill acquisition. It will help learners awaken their social intelligence when they collaborate, which researchers have found improves learning significantly.

Finding a genuine and collaborative learning community, where everyone can share their own particular experience or unique knowledge acquired, can work better as a learning tool rather than learning in isolation. If you have tried learning in isolation and felt drained, tired, or like you have mixed results, try collaborating with others who are also interested in your area of study and see what happens.

Learning Occurs On Many Levels, Simultaneously

Accelerated learning attempts to address the linearity of learning that comes from traditional teaching methods and the foundation of psychology. Behaviorism as a science seeks to explain human behavior in a systematic way, and yet it also has introduced a worldview of learning that is more mechanistic and disassociated rather than inclusive and interconnected. Modern formal education is based on learners as separate and disconnected which creates fragmentation to the learning process. Learning is divided into separate subjects, individuals are separate learners, and we as students are taught to learn one thing at a time.

Researchers have shown us, however, that learning isn't linear; rather, it involves absorbing many things at once. Effective learning engages you on many levels simultaneously: consciously, mentally, and physically. People take in knowledge with all of their senses and with their whole selves. We learn on many levels simultaneously. We have such a greater capacity for learning than has yet to be fully recognized on a wider scale by our methods of formal education. The rational consciousness of our minds is only part of our mental capacity; we utilize other cognitive functions such as verbal processing, creative imagining, and visual stimulation to aid our learning as well. The brain doesn't work in sequence; it processes information in a parallel way and thrives when it is challenged to do multiple things at once.

When you use multiple ways to learn something, you'll end up using more regions of your brain to store information about that subject. This makes information more interconnected and embedded in your brain, meaning it basically creates a redundancy of knowledge within your mind which helps you truly learn the information rather than only memorizing it.

Remember learning styles from Chapter One? Try mixing up different types of learning styles in order to absorb information in numerous ways. You can do this by using various kinds of media to stimulate different parts of the brain. For example, you can read notes, read a textbook, watch a video, and listen to a podcast (or audio file) on a given topic. The more resources (and variety) you use, the faster you'll learn.

Do The Work (With Feedback)

We know, unequivocally, that people learn best when content is rooted in real-world contexts. Contextual learning is non-linear, experiential, multi-layered, and uses the entire brain. Our brains are wired to digest entire contexts, not one isolated thing at a time. Noncontextual learning is piece-by-piece, fragmented and reminiscent of mechanistic thinking of the past. It would train us to have robotic responses in a narrow framework of learning, but would more often than not leave us feeling unfulfilled and lacking in abilities to think critically.

Lasting learning comes from doing the work itself, with feedback. Information that can be applied is far better than hypothetical constructs or abstract concepts. Facts or skills that are learned in isolation are harder to absorb and more quickly evaporate from memory. Doing the work itself provides the richest avenues for learning in a continual process of immersion, feedback, reflection, evaluation, and re-immersion. We will learn to sing by singing, how to swim by swimming, and so on. As learners, we need to immerse ourselves fully in a subject and to make it activity-based. Try and make it as authentic and based in real-world context as possible, because experience is the best feedback. It will enable you to learn on many levels, involve your whole brain (and body), and include the senses in your learning.

Think of ways you can create meaningful content relative to the subject matter you want to learn, and then deal with new learning material in a way that allows you to integrate it into your existing knowledge, skill-set, and sense of meaning. If you have the time and capabilities, you want to apply what you've learned. Find ways of getting quality feedback from trusted individuals, reflect on that feedback, and re-immerse yourself in your learning.

A quick word of warning against too much computer-use: computers tend to be isolating - albeit in some capacity helpful - learning machines. They are, overall, socially isolating devices that keep us separated from others and disengage us from collaborative learning. And again, as social creatures, people learn best not in isolation, but rather by interacting with others in a real-world context.

Be Positive

Studies have shown the effects of positivity, music, and involving play as a means to help people learn significantly faster and more effectively. The power of positive suggestion and supportive environments, in particular, cannot be understated. Our emotions, as verified through extensive research, have a profound effect on the quality of what and how we learn. Think back to some of your previous learning experiences, and you will probably be able to find examples of how this is true for you. Positive feelings are a catalyst for learning; feeling joyful as you learn new content will accelerate your learning. In contrast, negative feelings delay or even cease learning altogether. When feelings are positive and you are in a relaxed, open state, you will be able to access the higher levels of your brain. When your feelings are negative and you are stressed, you will tend towards using the shallower, more reptilian parts of your brain which are more dedicated to survival than complex cognitive processing. It is very difficult to learn in this state of mind.

Unfortunately, many people have negative feelings about learning. Perhaps they associate learning with memories involving previous pain, stress, humiliation, or other negative experiences. However, these negative suggestions (or assumptions) will have to be challenged with positive ones, or else learning will be stifled. Assumptions, in general, tend to color (or even create) our experience. Generally speaking, negative assumptions lead to negative experiences and vice versa.

As you approach learning new skills or subjects, it is then extremely important you focus on feeling positive. This doesn't mean an easy, superficial, or frivolous self-assurance. Real positive talk is essential and rooted in an honest, matter-of-fact attitude. Tell yourself what is good about what you're doing and why. What is valuable about what you are trying to learn? What will you be able to achieve after you have learned it? Be open and honest about your strengths and how they will help you accomplish your learning goals. As Meier puts it, "a positive feeling toward the learning experience is the necessary first step in learning." If you're feeling frustrated, stressed, uninterested, or bored, it's better for your learning if you take a break and return when you feel more motivated and positive.

It is also important to consider the environment in which you are learning. Much like your mental environment (or attitude) and your social environment (or collaborative learning scenario), your physical learning environment plays a role in how well you learn, and each of these factors feeds into one another. Think back to the various classrooms you've been exposed to. Did they inspire you to be there? Did they stimulate you to learn and grow? Traditional classrooms have historically been underwhelming at best. If your physical learning environment inspires negative feelings it can have an impact on your attitude, which will then affect how well you are able to integrate new information. Try - if you can - to create a space for your learning that you will want to occupy. This space should evoke feelings of curiosity, inspiration, and excitement. Doing so will help both relax and energize you for your learning.

Brains Love Visual Content

What Meier calls "the image brain" refers to the way in which our brains prefer visual stimulation because they absorb visual information instantly and automatically. Images are instantly memorable to us. Visual stimulation is easier for us to retain because it is concrete, whereas auditory and verbal stimulation tends to be more abstract. Think about it. You can probably recall, through imagery, thousands of your favorite (and least favorite) experiences. You can remember these so well not because you were concerned with memorizing them as they were happening; your image brain was doing it for you, in the moment, automatically and on many levels at the same time.

Studies have shown how courses that integrate imagery into classroom learning tend to produce students that have higher recall and long-term retention than courses that do not. Recall and retention rates were even higher in classrooms that used collaborative learning in addition to imagery to teach scientific content. This imagery can take a variety of forms, from graphics and other illustrations, to mnemonic devices or stories. In addition to these, you can always come up with your own creative method that works best for you.

Incorporating images into your learning is a natural way to teach yourself something faster and with higher quality. If you can translate verbal or auditory abstractions into concrete images of some kind, you will be more likely to retain that information and it will be easier for you to recall later. Words are important to us and integral to teaching; however, if you can associate words with images it will have a much more positive effect on your learning.

Chapter Summary

Remember: learning happens when you fully integrate new knowledge by applying it in some way that makes it especially meaningful to you. As learners, we need to fully exercise parts of our brains that emotionally connect us to new material for optimal performance. This means you must think critically as you navigate new information, decide how you want to approach your learning, and use your imagination to engage yourself in building these new skills. Therefore you want to: engage your entire body and mind; create rather than consume; collaborate with others; understand learning happens on several levels; do the work and seek feedback; have a positive outlook; and prioritize visual learning content. Doing this will ultimately help you to create more value out of the entire learning experience. Now that you have the principles you will need to consider your learning journey, the next chapter will focus on how you can structure your learning practice to more quickly acquire the skills you desire.

CHAPTER THREE

Rapidly (& Painlessly) Acquiring New Skills

As you learn a new skill it may seem like the path to mastering it is long with many twists and turns. You may feel powerless at times, like it's useless for you to carry on trying. The good news is this is only as true as you allow it to be. There is a way you can learn a new skill quickly and effectively. Your brain tends to want you to master new things as quickly as possible, which can lead to frustration as you may want to skip the necessary steps to actually mastering it.

How fast you can develop a new skill depends first and foremost on your understanding of the stages of skill acquisition. If you understand the three learning stages of skill acquisition, you will be able to push yourself forward faster because you will be able to see where you are on your learning journey. As you progress, you will be able to map how you are doing more accurately. Everyone passes through these stages, so knowing which stage you are currently in will, in the end, actually help speed your learning along. It will save you lots of energy, frustration, and feelings of hopelessness. The three stages of skill acquisition sit on a continuum of skill learning, and move you from novice to expert. There is first the cognitive stage, then the associative stage, and finally, the autonomous stage.

The Cognitive Stage

The cognitive stage is usually characterized by frequent errors because it is a time when you as a learner have to think about the skill and how to execute it. As a learner, you are absorbed in mental processes associated with how you will gain this new skill. If you are an athlete, you will be thinking about your body position, which muscles to engage, and what each step of the skilled movement should look like. At each step, the learner will be fully focused on execution, which typically results in choppy movements that are incomplete. Imagine a child trying to learn a new motor movement. This is similar to adult learners attempting to improve a new motor skill: there is a lot of observation, attempts at mimicry, and likely frustration at their errors as they make mistakes. As such, this is a critical stage where the learner will benefit from frequent feedback. An instructor or coach will need to provide that feedback as well as demonstrations during the cognitive stage of skill acquisition. If you are teaching yourself, you will want to look for videos or other visualizations that will help show you what the skill looks like when it's well done. Break it down into various skill sections that you can gradually put together as you progress through your learning.

The Associative Stage

The associative stage of skill acquisition is the time when you as a learner have progressed from thinking about what you are doing to thinking about how you are doing it. This means you are no longer thinking about your body position and muscles, but rather where you are directing your movement. Where are you passing the ball? What's the end goal of your movement? You transition the focus from whether you can manage to do the movement you want to instead focus on what you want to achieve by doing so. During this stage, the movement becomes more fluid and smooth as the learner provides their own feedback instead of relying only on outside help. Most learners will still have errors as they continue along the skill acquisition continuum; however, these will not be as large or as frequent as during the cognitive stage of skill acquisition. As you progress through this stage, you will still benefit from immediate feedback on your performance and technique through a knowledgeable source. This will help you make critical adjustments and begin to increase the complexity of the context in which the skill is executed. For example, instead of hitting a tennis ball from a stable stand, you may have a partner hitting moving targets at you to return. From there, you will need a lot of frequent and large chunks of practice to move on to the autonomous stage.

The Autonomous Stage

The final stage, the autonomous stage of skill acquisition, is when you as the learner no longer think at all about the skill. In this stage, the movement comes naturally and is fluid and intuitive. You can now focus on other aspects of the skill movement, such as who to pass the ball to, where to move after the play, or think a few steps ahead of the current skilled motion. An autonomous athlete knows what the movement feels like and can consistently provide their own feedback. As with the previous stage, external feedback on skill execution will still be beneficial. Coaching an autonomous learner usually focuses on the execution of the skill under pressure and with various cognitive processes being completed simultaneously. This stage of skill acquisition is the mastery stage, and learners have characteristics such as kinaesthetic sense, good anticipation, consistency of performance, and sound technique. You will be able to correct your own movements, even midway through moving, as you adjust to oppositional movements or certain environmental interferences. You will be able to consistently perform the skill well with errors occurring very infrequently.

Now that you know a bit more about the three stages of skill acquisition, think back to something you've been meaning to learn -

some new skill or talent. Maybe there are objects scattered about your house, anything from a textbook or that guitar you've been meaning to learn how to play. They may remind you of an abandoned potential project you were once so enthusiastic about that now you feel actual pain remembering how you gave up attempting to acquire it. Perhaps you've even tried again, only to fail yet again.

When you consider the stages of skill acquisition above, you have to understand you have never moved through the most painful ones: the cognitive and the associative stages. You're still a newbie so you've gotten stuck in committing errors and as a result, you have given up. Your brain is actually designed to protect you from pain during the first two stages. It wants to just skip ahead to the autonomous stage right away where you've already mastered the skill, or at least where your skills have plateaued. Keep in mind, this is all about leaving your comfort zone. You're stretching yourself beyond what you're used to, so hang in there. You're still in these earlier stages of learning, and you can avoid some of the growing pains.

Time is such a valuable resource for all of us, so I've included some of the leading research on rapid skill acquisition. Josh Kaufman has outlined key principles on how to do this in his book *The First 20 Hours* (we'll return to this concept in the next chapter). The following six recommendations will help you learn the basics of anything in less time. Here's how you get there.

Choose a Passion Project

Think about what you are most passionate about. What gives you a sense of meaning? Is it designing for accessibility? Becoming a great leader? Where do you find pleasure? Is it giving customers a great experience? Providing excellent products? Acquiring skills rapidly is all about finding and developing new strengths by leaving your comfort zone, so if you are trying to learn a new skill, you must leave your comfort zone. This means you leave your old strengths behind as you focus on growing new ones. As you choose a project you are passionate about, ask yourself where you find meaning in your life and what activities give you pleasure. Build out a visual that will help you pinpoint these necessary ingredients. You can even map out where your current strengths are so you have an accurate picture of what you would like to further develop.

When we pick something we're interested in, we'll have the discipline to push through the cognitive and associative stages of skill acquisition, to put forth the necessary time and effort to acquire the skill, and to reach the finish line. Once you know why you're passionate about this project that you love, you can plan around it. Set goals for your success. Research and acquire the proper equipment and resources you will need for your learning journey. Then, plan your schedule around this chosen path. Get organized and pumped for the path ahead.

Focus Your Efforts on One Skill at a Time

You only have so many hours in a day, and learning a new skill can be difficult. If you try to divide your limited time and cognitive resources across learning a variety of skills, you will likely burn out; unfortunately, burnouts do not learn very quickly. When the world moved at a slower pace, multitasking was a valuable skill to claim. Nowadays, however, it has been proven to make you a less effective individual and a less efficient learner. If you try to do two or more tasks at once, it will actually decrease your productivity by forty percent. Remember, just as you should avoid multitasking at work, you should absolutely avoid it as you dedicate yourself to learning a new skill. You need to immerse yourself in your skill acquisition process so you can reach your skill potential.

There are likely many different skills you'd like to acquire, but an important first step of rapid skill acquisition is for you to choose one to focus on first. Start by making a list of all the skills you're interested in, and then pick the one that is most exciting to you right now. This excitement will help you stay motivated through your practice.

Though it may be tempting to try and dive into several skills at once, you should focus all of your energy on learning a single skill at a time. For instance, you may have been tempted to combine learning Python coding with learning Spanish, search engine marketing, and video editing. Studies have shown this is not how you will gain a new skill the fastest. You must use your time wisely when trying to learn something new since you may only have about an hour each day to dedicate to it. Try not to try to learn multiple new things at once, because you'll progress much more slowly, which will in turn not help motivate you to continue.

Decide Your Target Performance Level

How skilled at this do you truly want to be? Once you've decided you are obsessed with learning this new skill, you will now have to decide just how much being great at it matters to you - and how great you want to be. Do you want to be an upper echelon master, or do you want to just be pretty good? For intense competitors, the answer will always be "I want to be the best," but it's completely alright to know the basics and stick in the middle if it's just a hobby to you. If you want to take up soccer mostly to socialize and know you can hold your own on the field, then great. This principle is completely up to your preference and where you want to be.

Break Your Skill into Sub-skills

Begin with setting and mastering sub-skills that you can build upon. This will help you begin to visualize your learning success. Planning is critical as you do this because if you have no path or vision for what your success looks like, you will be stuck in the preliminary principles wondering when you'll figure it out. A new skill is rarely one thing to achieve. There are tactics you can use to break it down, deconstruct the skill you're trying to learn into separate parts. You can then order those parts in a way that will allow you to accomplish your target performance as quickly as possible.

Provide Proper Tools to Optimize Your Skill

Sometimes when we're learning something new, we throw ourselves into the ring without doing the proper research. If you want to learn a new language, chances are you won't find the best resources that will help you do so for free. If you really want to learn how to play the guitar, you're definitely going to need a guitar and, most likely, guitar lessons. This means you should be sure you budget your process just as you would with any other important life decision. You want to make sure you have the right tools with you for your success. What will you need at each step to get there? Alternatively, what will get in your way, or serve as a barrier to your learning? Identify the necessary resources and potential obstacles you may encounter.

Quantity over quality

In my opinion, this is the most important principle for learning new skills as quickly as possible. We've been told time and time again to focus on "quality over quantity," and that may be true in some circumstances, like when it comes to having friends or buying fewer items. With rapid skill acquisition though, it's the exact opposite. Before you enter every learning session you have to understand that you are not an expert, and won't be for a little while. You will have to work on being less critical about your performance from session to session. You have to realize that you are slowly progressing. Practice as much as you can with consistent feedback. Keep yourself motivated and engaged. Plan your practice schedule out so that you have dedicated time for what you need to do. This will force you to put in the hours necessary to achieve your target performance goals. Try also practicing at the same time for consistency, as this will help you actually keep with it.

Chapter Summary

Now you know the three stages of skill acquisition (cognitive, associative, and autonomous) and my key recommendations on how to learn the basics of anything new in less time. These are: choosing a passion project to give you greater discipline and motivation; focusing your efforts on one skill at a time to reach your full learning potential; deciding your target performance so you have realistic learning expectations; breaking your skill down into sub-skills so it's more attainable; identifying proper tools for your success, and obstacles to it; and lastly, practicing as much as you can with consistent feedback. If you prioritize learning a new skill using these points as a guide, you will be on your way to success. In the next chapter, you will learn how best to approach your first - and most important - twenty hours of your learning.

CHAPTER FOUR

The First Twenty Hours

As previously mentioned, Josh Kaufman is a noted rapid learning expert who has suggested twenty hours as a magic number for learning a new skill. The six principles I just overviewed are critical for a new learner to consider throughout this twenty-hour learning journey. According to Kaufman, everyone will hit a wall early on in the rapid learning stage, so by pre-committing to twenty hours new learners will have a sure-fire way to push through that wall to acquire a new skill. This won't necessarily mean you become an instant master at a new skill, but rather that you will reach a higher competency level more quickly and more surely.

The first few hours of learning something new are always the hardest, and this is where the majority of people give up. It's essential, however, to continue to push through the first twenty hours of practice, regardless of whatever bumps in the road you may run into. Once you get through the first twenty hours, you'll have a significant amount of practice under your belt, so subsequent practice will not be as difficult. Here are my recommendations for how to approach your first twenty hours of practicing a new skill.

Start by Setting Your Goal

First, decide what skill level you want to achieve. I briefly talked about setting your target performance level in the last chapter. Now really consider where you want to be and how you want to get there. One key idea of *The First 20 Hours* is to begin by deciding how good you want to become at a skill. Once you have an idea of the skill level you are eyeing to achieve, then you will break it down into smaller steps to reach it.

For example, say you want to become good at marketing copywriting because you need to write an email to land a deal with a high-ticket potential client. You don't need to extensively study copywriting in its entirety. You can look at the best practices for writing sales emails, instead. You can figure out the steps and bite-sized pieces that you will need to write that perfect email for your use in this scenario. Make a plan. Begin by first studying how to write subject lines, then how to properly personalize your emails, and finally the proper tone and voice, maybe even suggestions on how to avoid landing in the spam folder, and perhaps some principles of influence to ensure that your email converts. You can also research different templates that you can then tailor to your use, and so on.

Keep in mind, with the right goal set you're more likely to succeed in acquiring the skill you've set your sights on. It may help with your accountability if you share your goal with a friend. Having a social implication for your learning will help keep you motivated along the path to achieving your goal. There are also huge benefits to learning in a group. Remember collaborative learning? When you learn in a group, not only are you able to learn from others, but you'll also be encouraged to make progress together. Whether it is a chess club, a mastermind group, or an online meet-up group, try to connect with other like-minded individuals, if nothing else for feedback and support.

Decide What Resources You Need

Since we're talking about learning a new skill within twenty hours, it's important to decide what you will need to get you started.

How can you stay focused? You will have to work to limit distractions and make sure that you have the tools you need to learn and succeed at your desired skill. While it may seem like a simple step, it is of utmost importance for you to do carefully and correctly. Begin by figuring out what types of materials and environments - even tools or apps - will be able to support you in your success in learning this new skill. Perhaps you simply need a pen, paper, and highlighter for marking passages in textbooks. Or maybe you'd rather automate your learning sessions by gathering online references and reading them on your mobile tablet. Alternatively, maybe you prefer learning in wide open spaces, such as outdoors or in a park, or maybe you prefer learning in the comforts of your own home, listening to music or next to your favorite window.

As you make sure the environment you are in is perfect for your rapid-learning progress, you have to take care to ditch any social media or related distractions, including the temptation to check messages or emails. As the saying goes, "out of sight, out of mind." Before you sit down to practice or study, make sure all potential distractions are far from sight. You can plan ahead by setting a specific place for learning that doesn't have a TV, talkative friends, or other temptations. Taking control of your environment like this also doesn't necessarily mean you always need to do it alone. Sometimes working with friends in study groups can be a useful way to influence your environment.

Once you have your ideal environment down, you can move on to identifying potential barriers or roadblocks that may interfere with your learning process and work to eliminate them. You want to create a distraction-free environment so you can focus on your learning. Remember how your brain will look for shortcuts, and any excuse to not practice. It will try to turn back at any barrier because you are in the early stages of learning, which can be painful. You have to work to remove these barriers. If you're learning how to play the guitar, leave it in the middle of your room so you constantly see it and are reminded of your commitment to practice. You want it to be as obtrusive a reminder as possible so you can't avoid it.

You should also try to anticipate emotional roadblocks as well. For instance, maybe you are beginning to feel overwhelmed or anxious. Remember how having a positive attitude aids your learning process? Take a break if you find yourself struggling to feel optimistic and relaxed, and then return to your process when you have a renewed sense of motivation to learn. This is not the same as commitment. You have to make yourself power through the first twenty hours, according to this theory, so you have a higher likelihood of acquiring your new skill. Sometimes that means committing to even the smallest amount of work even when your motivation is lacking.

Practice, Practice, Practice

When planning your skill acquisition process, you have to make sure to allot time for practice. In order to become an expert, there is no substitute for this. It takes dedication, discipline, and focus, as well as a sincere, genuine desire to do the work. If you aren't passionate about something, you won't become an expert at it. You must stay consistent, or you'll backtrack. Ideally, you will practice or study at the same time every day. If you're struggling on how to make time for this, start by cutting out any other activities that aren't directly necessary to learning this new skill. Fill that time with practicing.

Obviously, you can't completely clear your schedule like this; there are adult responsibilities you have to do and emergencies that arise day-to-day and week-to-week. However, if you're serious about learning a new skill, cut out most of the fluff in your schedule and re-dedicate it to this. Your goal is to free up sixty to ninety minutes a day to dedicate to practicing. Don't forget to receive feedback on your progress so you can find out whether you've gone wrong anywhere, or if you should be approaching your learning in a different way. Feedback is critical in the early stages of skill acquisition. You may even want to hire a coach to help you with this. Coaches can guide you and give you feedback throughout the process in ways that may be difficult for you to do yourself. In some instances, you can monitor your own learning. For example, if you're learning a new language, you could try using a voice recorder to listen to yourself speaking. This will make it easier for you to hear mistakes in your pronunciation or grammar.

It can be easy to get caught up in reading and gathering information on how to do something and never actually get around to doing it. Just remember: the best way to learn how to do something is to actually do it. Regardless of how unprepared you may feel, make sure you are continually physically or actively engaged. Keep yourself alternating between research and practice, with lots of practice in between research stints.

Practice in Short Bursts

If you're like me, you dread the end of the weekend. The workweek looms ahead on Sunday night, promising to bring endless new tasks to complete. If you're learning a new task, this can be even more daunting. The good news is there's a better way for us to approach these long periods of work without feeling overwhelmed. Learning something new that is difficult, or even working on activities for long periods of time, is draining and often inefficient. Research has found that it's actually better to work in short bursts with frequent planned breaks. This is commonly referred to as the Pomodoro Technique.

The Pomodoro Technique calls for us to take a five-minute break after every twenty-five minutes of work. Set session goals so you accomplish three to five of these work sessions throughout your day. Once you do this, you'll be amazed at how quickly you progress. By prioritizing quantity and speed, you're much less likely to get frustrated - and as a result, demotivated - during your initial stages of practice. When you first start to learn something new, the hours of practice it takes to really start making progress can feel like an eternity. You may even think you've spent more time working on something at the beginning of learning a new skill, just by how hard the learning task itself is. Using the Pomodoro Technique will help you avoid frustrations as you begin your learning process. It will help keep you focused and motivated, as you'll be able to track your time working.

When you work on a task without a break, you're more likely to lose focus and as a result, get sidetracked from doing real work. When you take a break, however, you force yourself to have a few seconds to re-evaluate or reflect on your work. You give yourself the necessary space so your attention can rest before returning to your task. You may find that you need to adjust what you're working on, or make some necessary change. It will increase the quality of your work as well as the speed at which you're able to do it. When it's time for your break, it's important for you to take it seriously and really move to a new activity. You can treat them as a reward for your hard work where you walk a bit, do some stretches, grab a cup of coffee, or do something that relaxes you (like meditation). You can experiment with how long you prefer to work before you take a break, although research tends to suggest that somewhere between twenty-five and thirty-five minutes is the sweetest spot. Keep in mind that longer work periods can lead to burnout, which is especially harmful for your motivation if you're trying to learn a new skill.

Kaufman also suggests that you practice your new skill within four hours of going to sleep. According to him, practice done within this timeframe causes your brain to integrate the learning more rapidly into your brain's neural pathways because your memory and the motor-mechanics needed are ingrained at a quicker level. You can also help your brain by celebrating the little wins along the way. This will result in more endorphins and serotonin released which will, in turn, encourage you to continue. Have a piece of chocolate or watch one of your favorite music videos as a treat so you keep having fun. Learning a new skill should be exciting and something you cannot wait to practice every day. Keep your good attitude and motivation strong!

Chapter Summary

Inspired by learning expert, Josh Kaufman, this chapter covered how you can structure your first twenty hours of learning a new skill. Remember that by pre-committing to twenty hours, you will have a way to push through the learning wall everyone experiences and achieve your learning goals. My four key recommendations for how you can approach the first twenty hours of your learning are to: start by setting your goal; decide what resources you need to succeed; consistently practice and seek feedback early on; and finally, break your practice periods down into digestible intervals so you don't lose your motivation. All of these work together in a way that will increase the quality and efficiency of your learning. In the next chapter, you will learn about my all-time favorite learning principle and how it can serve you on your learning journey.

CHAPTER FIVE:

The Life-Changing Pareto Principle

You may have never heard of the Pareto Principle, but you have most likely heard of the eighty-twenty rule or the law of the vital few. The Pareto Principle suggests that, for most things, approximately eighty percent of the effects come from twenty percent of the causes. This has been applied to everything from land ownership, to taxation, to mathematics. This rule is based on a power law distribution and has been proven true in business, in relationships, and most importantly, in how we learn. In terms of learning, it means that you want to identify the twenty percent of work (or causes) that will give you the eighty percent of results you want (the effects). The main concept lies in identifying the few most effective strategies and materials that will allow you to quickly become adequate in the chosen subject.

For example, if you're learning a language, it does not take long to realize there are a few key words that tend to pop up over and over again. You can do a quick search for "most commonly used French words" or "typical French phrases" to begin to learn how to speak French before going into the more technical or grammatical details. When applied to athletic training, you can use the Pareto Principle by practicing around twenty percent of the key exercises and habits for a particular skill in order to have eighty percent of the impact. The learner should not focus so much on a varied training or learning very technical aspects of a skill. It's basically telling you what to start with first - not that the other eighty percent doesn't matter. For instance, having a healthy diet and going to the gym regularly are still important for athletic training, but they are not as significant as the key (or twenty percent) activities.

The Pareto Principle will change the way you learn. Depending on your chosen skill, the amount of study material can be immense. You will need a strategy to choose the most effective material that will help you achieve your goal, as well as put it in the right sequence. Applying this principle to your learning can be done in various ways. You can use it to choose the most effective approach for studying that is available to you. Beyond studying methods, the eighty-twenty rule can be extremely useful in choosing the right material. I've compiled some helpful tips for you to consider as you use this approach to rapidly acquire a new skill.

To begin with, identify the skill that you are currently trying to learn. It doesn't matter if it's a sport, a language, a motor skill (like playing the guitar or another kind of instrument), or learning a new game (such as chess). No matter which field, skill, or expertise, just choose something you are trying to improve in. It could even be a new task that's been recently assigned to you by your boss or a teacher. It could be a new specialization or hobby. Identify the learning subjects in your life and be open to discovering more than one simultaneously. Compiling this list will help you organize yourself in your learning process.

Now make a list of the five to ten resources you use in your learning process. For each of the topics or skills you've thought of, now you want to consider five or more things you are currently doing in your learning with each one, or that you are actively working on improving. For instance, if one of the skills you are trying to learn is how to play guitar, list out five or more actions you are taking to help your learning. These can also be resources you are using that are helping you improve.

Once you've done this, you can choose the one or two items that provide you with the best results. Choose carefully and as unbiasedly as possible. Even if it's something that you find difficult or to be somewhat of a struggle, if it's helping your learning, it goes on the list. Remember that the goal at this point is not to get to mastery, but rather getting to your eighty percent as quickly as possible. Excitement and motivation will help you go on from there. In addition, you will now be more familiar with the subject and will be able to make more educated decisions from here on out. After you choose the two items that will provide you with a quicker fluency, you will be in a much better position to incrementally learn more and learn faster. If nothing on your list fits this description, head back to the beginning of your resource list and add some new ones. It may take some trial and error at first, but don't worry! Reach out for feedback from a trusted friend or mentor or do a quick Google search if you need to. We live in an era of information. Everything you need is at your fingertips.

The final step in applying the Pareto Principle is to practice the two items you've chosen to be the most effective and efficient in providing you with your results for the next two weeks. You've done your process of elimination, now it's time to practice. You will see, over the course of this practice session, how much further along you come than you may have initially expected. You can also apply the Pomodoro Technique and keep in mind the stages of skills acquisition as you do this phase as well. All of these principles play together in a way that will both deepen and quicken your learning.

Beyond learning, you can use the Pareto Principle in any area of your life where you feel there may be an imbalance of effects. It may not be applicable to all areas, but many situations you may find are out of balance (for instance, financial, health, marital, social, or professional). You can think of the top ten to twenty percent of inputs you put into your life on the whole to get eighty percent of what you want out of life. Maybe you'll discover you value relationships more than you thought; maybe it will improve an aspect of your professional life.

You can then find ways to emphasize the key percentage that brings you that eighty percent of joy or satisfaction. Decide to spend more time in those activities and place them first in your schedule. Maybe you meet with more of your key friends or reinstate date night into your relationship. Or maybe it's investing more of your money in the experiences you want to have. You will also want to find ways to downplay or eliminate the rest of the activities that don't give you the same payoffs. This may mean you cut some toxic people out of your life, or redirect your money to smarter or better investments that have better results and give you an overall higher quality of life. Whatever the case, the eighty-twenty rule can be a guiding light for you in overall creating more balance for your day-to-day.

Chapter Summary

The Pareto Principle is my favorite learning principle. It serves you by helping you identify the twenty percent of work that will give you eighty percent of the results you want. Learning this is truly life-changing. It will help you prioritize the most effective learning strategies and materials that will guide you towards your learning outcomes. You can use this amazing tool in other areas of your life as well to find more overall balance. In the next chapter, I'll give you an overview of key points to consider in the art of effective note-taking.

CHAPTER SIX:

The Art of Effective Note Taking

Research on memory has indicated that we easily remember ideas or information that we turn our attention to often, and conversely how we can quickly forget the ideas or information that we mentally touch only once or twice. This is intentional and developed as humans evolved. It's a natural forgetfulness of information because our brains are filtering out the data we're telling it isn't important. It's simple: the less we expose ourselves to something, the less we will retain it in our minds. We tell our minds what's important to keep by introducing it and reintroducing it into our days through practice and study. The more we practice, the more permanently information is stored in our minds.

When we try to learn something new, our recall is strongest right off the bat. Imagine you're studying vocabulary in class, and you're introduced to twenty new terms. If you were tested immediately, you would likely have a recall of near one hundred percent. One day later, your recall would be down by forty percent. As learners, if we don't return our attention to new material, within the first twenty-four hours we will have lost forty percent of that information. Even one day later, and we lose another twenty percent of recall ability. So in two days, we will have forgotten sixty percent of our new learning. This effect is called the "forgetting curve" and was developed by Herman Ebbinghaus in 1895 as he conducted early research on memory and forgetfulness.

In short, our temporary memory can be deceiving. We hear something and we think because we can immediately think about and repeat it that we will remember it later as well. Think of it like this. Our brains have attached a drop of glue to a thought (as temporary memory). Gradually the glue loses its adhesive quality, and because it was only a drop, the bond disperses and we no longer remember the thought. However, if we constantly return to that one thought, and apply additional drops of glue to the original drop, the adhesive is strengthened over time. Eventually, the information will become part of more permanent memory.

Because information is lost quickly over time, learners need to develop an effective strategy to retain new information. Note-taking is a good tool to help with this; however, just plain taking notes will not be enough to do the trick. Effective note-taking is designed to help you recall what you have learned and to retain that information well over time. If we take notes effectively we can retain and retrieve almost 100% of what we learn.

How To Take Notes

One easy place to start is to always write your notes by hand. Although it might seem like typing your notes on a laptop during a conference or lecture would be more thorough (and maybe even help you learn faster) the opposite is in fact true. It is better for your learning if you take notes with a pen and a piece of paper. Doing so will both speed up your learning as well as help you to retain it. Research has shown that learners who type their lecture notes process and retain the information at a lower level. Those who take notes by hand in contrast actually end up learning more.

While taking notes by hand is slower and more cumbersome than typing, the act of writing the information fosters higher levels of comprehension and retention. Reframing the information in your own words helps you retain the information longer, meaning you'll have better recall and will perform better on tests. This happens because we have different types of cognitive processing associated with taking notes by hand versus typing. When typing, learners can easily produce a written record of the lecture without necessarily processing its meaning. Faster typing speeds allow students to transcribe a lecture word for word without putting much thought into the content or deeper meaning behind what was said. Because learners can't write down everything they hear by hand, they have to make choices on what to prioritize and focus on. You will have to instead listen, digest, and summarize what you're hearing so that you can succinctly capture the essence of the information. Taking notes the old-fashioned way forces the brain to engage in heavier mental lifting than if you were typing, and these efforts then lead to higher rates of longer-lasting learning.

Studies on taking notes have found note-taking is more effective when they are organized and transformed in some way, or when a teacher gives examples of how to take good notes on the given material. Either way, it requires effort, and half the battle is understanding the reasons for needing to take and interact with notes. The most effective note-taking skills involve active as opposed to passive learning, which means the responsibility for learning is placed on the learner. Research has shown how actively involving and engaging students in the process of learning is critical for lasting learning. Despite these findings, traditional classrooms tend to mostly encompass listening to formal presentations versus reading, writing, discussing, solving problems, or otherwise engaging with the learning material. What's important to note about this form of learning is that it involves higher-order thinking tasks such as analysis, synthesis, and evaluation.

These learning strategies promote active learning because they involve the learner in learning things and then actively thinking about what they are doing as they are doing it. This is commonly referred to as thinking about thinking, or metacognition. While learners are engaging with their content, they should also be considering how they are learning it, what works, what causes confusion, and how the thinking changes as the topic of learning changes. This will help you as a learner discover what is working well for you, and what adjustments you should make next time. It will help you learn from your mistakes faster and more effectively. Metacognitive practices will also increase your overall ability to transfer and adapt your learning to new contexts and tasks.

In regards to note-taking, these concepts have several implications. It's an interactive process and involves using the original notes many times over in order to build a memory of the content, as opposed to just assuming taking notes is a one-time copying activity. One leading strategy for note-taking is called the Cornell Method, which provides a guide for taking notes that will help you organize your notes into more easily digestible summaries. This method outlines four stages of good note-taking.

#1 Note Taking

To begin with, you will want to prepare a page to take notes and do so the same way each time. Write an essential question at the top of the page that is relevant to the topic of study to focus on a key learning objective that you should be able to discuss after your study session. You can then divide the page into columns. One will take up around a third of the page and will be left blank for questions and related notes that can be added later when the notes are revisited. The other side is for notes captured during a conference, lecture, or learning session (this can include notes from a textbook, video, podcast, or related source as well).

Throughout the learning session, you want to listen and take notes in your own words rather than writing down verbatim what you hear or see. Paraphrase what you're hearing so it makes sense to you. You can leave spaces in your notebook between main ideas so you can return to it later and add information. As you listen, make sure to write in phrases rather than complete sentences (using bullet points and lists where possible), and develop your own consistent style of abbreviations or symbols to save you time. As you engage with the learning content, you will get better at how you can listen for important information versus trivial information. It will help you to take cues from the instructor or source. If it says this is critical or a key theme, that's a sign for you to pay extra attention to what follows. Finally, you can use highlighters or colored pens or pencils as you take notes to indicate key changes in ideas, concepts, or any links between information. Getting creative like this will also keep you better focused and on task because you will be finding ways to stay interested and engaged in the content.

#2 Note Making

Now revisit your notes and revise the content. Review what you've written and see if there's anything you need to edit or adjust for accuracy or clarity. Write questions in the column you left blank from before that correspond with the answer (your original notes) on the other side. Use highlighters or symbols to connect key chunks of information or material together in a cohesive way. This is also a good time for you to seek feedback. You can exchange ideas and collaborate with other learners, or even better, an instructor or coach, so you can check your understanding and test the comprehensiveness and correctness of your notes.

#3 Note Interacting

Once you have reshaped your notes, now you want to link all your learning together by writing a summary that addresses the essential question, and that answers the questions you wrote in the column during your note-making. Remember that a summary is a general overview of the content you are learning, which is different than a reflection that instead focuses on your response to the learning task or content. You can learn from your notes by building in regular times for revising your notes for each topic of study you have. When you return to study them later, you can use the questions and answers to quiz yourself.

#4 Note Reflecting

The final stage of note-taking incorporates reflection on the content you have written down. You should seek out written feedback from a peer, tutor, or instructor to check for your comprehension and accuracy as it is still the initial learning phase. You should then should address the feedback by focusing on one area of challenge you are experiencing in their learning that is related to this content, and any questions that arise from it. This will help you deepen your overall understanding of the content in the long run. As a learning tool, reflection is helpful to do periodically throughout the entire learning process, especially leading up to major exams, presentations, or other performance measures.

Additional Study Tips

As with many things, note-taking is only the first step in your study process, so I want to close this chapter with a few additional helpful tips that you can use once you have your notes at the ready. In general, keep in mind the more times you touch new information, the less you will forget it.

1. **Study in a Question/Answer Format.** Whether you are reading a textbook chapter or going over your lecture notes, try to always be looking for an answer to a salient question you have created to focus your attention on deepening your understanding of the content. Oftentimes the format of a test is in question/answer, so you're also priming yourself for important benchmarks on your performance. You will be learning the information in the way a test will likely ask it.

2. **Use Flashcards When Applicable.** Use your notes as a guide, and then put any information you can on flashcards: a term, a question, etc, on the front of the card, and the definition or answer on the back. Remember, only one idea, term, or question per card. This is another way for you to use the question/answer format.

Flashcards are also very portable. You can take them with you everywhere and use any spare five to ten minutes here and there each day to quiz yourself.

3. **Study in Small Chunks.** The best way to learn something well is to introduce it gradually into your mind in brief intervals over a period of time. This is the opposite of cramming, when you try to absorb large amounts of information in one or two long sessions. Cramming is the least effective study method for long-term retention; however, as I'll discuss later, there is a place for it in rapid skill acquisition. In general, you will retain information better if you break your study session down into four or five ten-minute study periods. If you do this every day learning up to a performance review, you will do very well.

4. **Make a Schedule.** It will help to have a study plan and for you to study according to your priorities. You want to decide how you want to divide your study sessions and organize your time. It may be worthwhile to keep a calendar of tests and assignments (either that you're assigned or that you make for yourself). Study and schedule your learning periods for when you are most alert. If your life allows you, give yourself breaks between learning new content and going to work or moving on to another activity. These breaks will allow you to review what you've just learned and even potentially preview what you're going to do or learn next (if applicable).

5. **Distribute and Modify Your Practice.** Research has found that it's better to use short study sessions to learn a topic over a period of time. This will encourage meaningful learning that is longer lasting. The more you space out your practice sessions the more effective they will be over time. It will help you retain the information and stay motivated to keep learning. Additionally, making slight changes during these repeated practice sessions will help you master a skill faster than if you did it the same way each

time. This only works if the modifications you make are small. Big changes in practicing a new skill won't help in the same way.

Chapter Summary

When taking notes, prioritizing a few simple things will go a long way. Take notes by hand because the act of writing out the information fosters higher levels of comprehension and retention. Reframing information in your own words will also help you retain the information longer, meaning you'll have better recall and will perform better on tests. Note-taking is also an interactive process, and involves using original notes many times over utilizing a process called the Cornell Method (note-taking, note-making, note-interacting, and note-reflecting). Besides the Cornell Method, I also gave you a few additional study tips to consider as you structure your learning sessions, such as: studying in a question and answer format; using flashcards; studying in small chunks; making a schedule; and distributing and modifying your practice. In the next chapter, you will learn how to take your learning one step further and accelerate your expertise.

CHAPTER SEVEN:

How To Accelerate Your Expertise

When you're new to learning something, it can be tricky as you work to upgrade from moderately skilled into the level of expert. You've started from a basic level, and depending on how steep the learning curve is for your given topic, it may take a little while for you to get where you want to be. For starters, you'll want to get in the right mental shape. Prepare yourself mentally and have a good attitude. It will be challenging, but with the right help, you can get there quickly and surely.

With the incredible rise in technology these days, rapid learning is more of a reality than we realize. This generation of learners lives in the age of knowledge and information. Just think: through the internet, we are able to access all kinds of knowledge so we can answer almost any conceivable question we may have. What's more, is the notion of people being natural-born geniuses or savants is constantly being questioned and replaced by research that suggests we are much more naturally programmed to learn. All we need is the right guidance so you can figure out your own unique code for learning. The following recommendations will help you discover this, as well as stay on the right track in quickly becoming an expert in your chosen field.

Find a Mentor

Remember: success leaves clues. The best shortcut to becoming an expert is to find an expert who already does what you want to achieve, and then form a relationship with them so you can learn from their story. This is as much about the failures as it is about the successes. You want to try and not make the same mistakes that your mentor has made on their road to success. Finding out what not to do from the expert will fast-track your learning of a new skill. It will be a huge win to have this person more personally walk you through what needs to be done.

Many people misunderstand how to approach finding a mentor. You may want one but not quite understand what it even means. You'll want to really do your research and select a couple of candidates you'd like to have as a mentor. Take a minute to consider a few things before reaching out to them. Chances are this person is a leader whom you admire, and the way in which you approach them could be the make or break in whether or not they accept your invitation. The last thing you want to do is to put someone in an awkward position where they may feel bad for saying no or obligated to say yes.

Remember first and foremost that mentoring is not all about you. The person you want as your mentor will likely also not be looking for you, so you have to assume an active attitude to your approach. Really consider what you want from this person. They should be someone you want to be like, not just someone who has a job that you want. This person should have a similar set of strengths and skills that you want to adopt and learn from. Having several candidates isn't a bad idea before you decide to commit to one (or two, depending on your availability). Once you've selected who you'd like to have as a mentor, get to know them. Read articles they've written, follow their blog, and so on. The more you know about this person and their public persona, the more realistically you'll be able to set your expectations.

Now that you've done your research, you're ready to make the ask. Try not to mention the word 'mentor' right off the bat. It's a little bit of a tall order for a first meeting. Instead, ask for an initial meeting, and personalize your message with something that drew you to them in the first place. Don't go for flattery, just be honest and insightful. Maybe you read an article or a quote from them, or you are a fan of the organization they work for. Then choose a place that's informal, like a coffee shop, and keep the first meeting to under an hour. Prepare some questions or conversation points you want to cover and that you think would make the meeting more enjoyable for them. The key is to let the conversation flow relationally. Be sure to thank them for their time; they're a busy professional, like you aspire to be.

In his book, *How to Win Friends and Influence People,* Dale Carnegie talks about how you can get influential people to meet with you. You have to disregard your insecurity and at the same time proceed with humility. He writes how you should show genuine interest in the person, remember their name, really listen to them, be sincere, and smile. In other words, you should approach the meeting as though you're trying to make a friend. That's something really anyone can do.

After meeting, you can decide whether or not you want to take it another step. Did the person reciprocate your relational demeanor? Did they offer too much unsolicited advice or talk down to you? Did they ask you questions and seem sincere? Did you leave the meeting feeling inspired, interested, and engaged? In other words, did you feel like a real connection was made? If not, let it go as an attempt and nothing more. Then redirect your efforts to someone else. You don't want to waste your time forcing something that won't be good for either one of you in the long-run. If the meeting went well, however, then you'll want to immediately put together a follow-up plan.

Unlike with dating, it's okay to appear ambitious with a prospective mentor. You want this person to know A) very clearly what you're looking for and B) that you're serious and wouldn't be wasting their time if they take you on as a mentee. As such, it's appropriate to follow up immediately, and to thank your prospective mentor for their time. You can do this via email or text - or a phone call if that's the communication method they prefer. At the end of the call or message, mention that you'd like to meet again, and if they agree, offer to get something on the calendar. Be prepared to suggest a couple of days and times (usually three or four is standard). Remember, you're both still vetting each other at this point, so you want it to feel relaxed and not contrived.

Now is perhaps the hardest step. You have to let the relationship evolve organically, like with any other friendship. You don't want to place too high of expectations on your mentor, or even on yourself. You may be tempted to jump right into calling it a mentorship, to give it a sense of status and importance, but in reality, it's a relationship like any other. It needs to evolve at a healthy pace for both of you and will need to be based on mutual respect and trust. Just give it time for it to grow as it will. It may get challenging at times, which is just as well. This is when your mentor likely feels comfortable enough to really begin to sculpt something about your habits or ways that will give you lasting results. You may be tempted to push back, which is a normal reflex. Remember, what you do in response to this is crucial to your growth; this is what you signed up for. Rise to the challenge and develop some resiliency. This is where the good stuff happens. Also note this is not a matter of right or wrong. You and your mentor can have differing opinions; it's how you communicate about them that matters.

It's important to take initiative in different ways to help guide the relationship. For instance, you can set a regular schedule, adapt to your mentor's preferred meeting times or places, and come to every meeting with talking points and questions you'd like to cover. This will make sure you're making the best use of your time. It will also be good for you to learn how to anticipate problems and to offer solutions (when appropriate) for your mentor as you would for anyone else you're close to. You want to understand their professional and personal priorities much the same way you'd like them to do with you. You can ask more from your mentor without demanding it; this won't bother them, quite the opposite. It will make them feel honored and appreciated for their expertise. Finding ways to solidify the bond you've created will only strengthen the relationship.

Be sure to periodically ask your mentor for feedback. This can be a difficult pill to swallow at times, but it's also good for you. This will be the number one way you grow over time and will be a highlight for both of you. Asking for feedback may initially feel weird, but eventually, it should become almost second-nature, and you'll find yourself thirsting for words you used to fear. A good mentor will also treat these times with great care and sensitivity. Keep in mind that this entire process will take your continued commitment to it. It's not like a summer internship; mentoring takes more time and energy. Only when you dedicate yourself to the process will you be able to understand what it means to be a student on the path to expertise.

Know the A-Listers in Your Niche

Similar to the research phase in finding a mentor, you want to, more broadly, understand who in your field is making waves. If you want to get spotted on the radar and learn the things that you should definitely know, then your best bet will be to learn from the professionals who are in that niche. It will be fairly easy to spot them because they're basically the most referenced or active people on the scene. If they're not, then you can easily Google keywords for your niche and look at the top-ranking blogs, articles, or book authors. Finding these professionals is just the beginning. Following and being recognized by them is the next step, and much more difficult.

You need to follow these people, first of all, because they matter (at least in your niche). Sure, you can ramble that you have ideas worth hearing all you want on various spaces throughout the internet, but if no one knows you, no one cares, and so it's all fairly pointless. Instead, you can follow these people and learn from their ways. How they do the things they do is the standard for your field. If you want to rise, you have to either meet their quality or surpass their skills. Of course, getting recognized by them is a bit tricky, because why do they need to recognize you? What do you offer them? Try and build something worthy as you create your own network. Decide where your value is and show it.

Their opinion matters, and so does their social circle. Simply lingering around their blogs won't be enough. You want to always remember to leave a mark. Comment, join anything that's happening online (such as a webinar or comment on videos or something similar), and better yet, correspond with notable authors or bloggers. Most likely they'll be too busy to answer, but at the very least you're trying by reaching out and creating an avenue of connection. You can help your case by making sensible, response-worthy messages to help get your replies. While more difficult than meeting in person, you can approach this in much the same relationship-building way as you would with a mentor. If your niche is one that has in-person events you'll also want to attend as many as possible. Meet-ups, conferences, happy hour groups, or any other kind of social networking events; make it a point to attend as many as you can. You can bet these are the places where the experts and A-Listers will be, which means you definitely want to be there as well.

This also means you should rigorously follow trends in your niche. Every field undergoes change, some more rapidly than others. Experts are those people who always stay at the forefront of what's happening. They explore new trends to understand where their industry is headed. This provides you with foresight as well as insight. While others are unaware of the shifting waves of progress, experts can more easily and quickly connect the dots so they can take advantage of the change that's coming. You can stay abreast of trends by setting up specific Google Alerts for trends you are following, or subscribe to blogs and websites like TrendHunter. Another big thing you can do is to commit to reading more. Look for and read industry analyst reports, as they try to predict industry trends over the next ten years. It doesn't hurt to ping your network if you see a new trend, to see what they think.

Define (& Re-Define) Your Network

Networking is an important part of enriching your personal and professional life. It could be the key to you landing your dream job. However, even the most extroverted people struggle with how to network in an effective way. The idea of making connections with strangers can be intimidating, and knowing where to start can be tough. Despite these challenges, sculpting a network that really does work for you will be invaluable as you dedicate yourself to learning something new and becoming a valued expert in the field.

Let's start by defining what it is. Your professional network is a group of people that have connected over a common theme that is relevant to your work. You are all coming together for business or career reasons, searching for avenues of professional connection. This could be a way for you to find out about job leads, but in reality, if done right, it is so much more than that. Besides being a place where you can solve work-related problems, find recommendations for vendors or suppliers, and be exposed to information about prospective employers, employees, and clients, your network is where you go to learn. Members of your network are who you go to with questions and concerns, and more broadly who you learn from. It's your learning community for you to bounce ideas off of and integrate within as you discover new information and deepen your existing knowledge about your field.

So who should be in your network? This unique group can be made up of almost anyone you've ever met, as long as they check a few boxes. You want these people to have a good character and to somehow bolster your goals. Start by looking in the obvious places: your previous and current workplaces. Current and former coworkers are people with whom you already have some point of connection, so it's an easy way to begin. Chances are they can introduce you to someone else who has similar interests or who may be a helpful contact as you grow in your field.

Additionally, you'll want to research and attend professional conferences and events where you can be exposed to and connect with like-minded people with similar career goals. See what kinds of professional associations exist in your area that will introduce you to attendees of interest. Many conferences have a list of organizations or employers who are attending their upcoming conference, so, with some diligence, you can see who you may want to connect with beforehand. Before attending a conference, make sure you have updated business cards with your non-work contact information and bring them with you. If you especially enjoy the conference, and if it's an option, you may opt to become an active member of the association or organization that held it. You could serve on a committee or volunteer for the next conference. This will give your colleagues a chance to see you in action.

In addition to events and conferences, you can use your LinkedIn page and/or Facebook to make connections with others, although studies show in-person meeting is typically best for longer term connections. As a starting point, though, these can be helpful in getting your foot in the door with someone. Keep your LinkedIn page maintained, much the same way as you would your resume. Post about your accomplishments, newsworthy developments in your field, and make connections with others from your field, your school, or your favorite companies.

Keep in mind your friends and family are also valuable parts of your network. Talk to these people about your career goals and aspirations. Chances are they know someone through their own network that has some helpful information for you. You never know who will be able to give you guidance and support, so speak up! Doing so can also build bridges in your personal life as well, as it will help you get to know your extended or in-law family. In a similar vein, remember your former professors or instructors from college, graduate school, or even high school. If you were close with a teacher, or a memorable student in some way, keep in touch. These people can either connect you to other contacts or be mentors to you in some way. Former classmates can do the same. If your university has meet-ups or reunions, try to attend as many as possible, and to connect with other students who were in the same classes or graduated with a similar degree. As you get older, these contacts will continue to get more and more valuable. If you were a member of a fraternity or sorority, you can look here as well.

Volunteering for charity is another way you can network to meet people who are engaged in the community while also working towards social betterment. It's a great way to casually get to know others from a non-professional vantage point that may feel a bit more natural to some. You may even discover something you didn't know about yourself, or find a new skill or field you want to grow in. Plus, when you volunteer, you not only gain experience and exposure to other like-minded people, you make a difference for a group of people. Besides looking great on your resume or LinkedIn, you can feel good about the good you are doing.

It will be important as you define and redefine your network that you keep it alive and healthy. Don't treat it like a dusty old book on a shelf that you only access every year or so to reference one or two things. Think of it as an organism. It is a living, breathing thing that must be tended to or it will fade. The last thing you want is to reach out to someone who doesn't remember you or to miss out on a great opportunity because you have a contact who knows about it but doesn't think of you. You'll want to make plans to stay connected with people in your network. If you have people who aren't local to you, then make sure they know they have a standing invitation to meet up if they're ever in your city. Send a few key emails or notes to your core network every year so they know what you're up to. The holidays are an ideal time to do this, as are times when you're making a change such as starting a new job or moving to a new city.

As you continue to sculpt your network, keep in mind who you know is more important than how many people you know. This is where "quality over quantity" rings true! Jim Rohn, personal development guru, says that we're the average of the five people we spend the most time with. That can be a scary thought for some of us. Think about who those five people are for you. If you want to up your professional game, you will need to surround yourself with people who elevate and inspire you. The people around you have a huge impact on your life, so it is important for you to surround yourself with the right people. It is critical for you to find people who inspire you, who share a similar mindset with you, or who can act as mentors. You need people in your life who will push you rather than pull you in harmful directions that can hold you back.

Take a minute to consider who you spend the majority of your time with. Who are your closest five friends? How do you support them? How do they support you? Do they inspire you and challenge you to be better? How do you feel around them? Do they build you up? Do they in some way hold you back? The values that people you spend time with have will seep into your life and your values system, for better and for worse. That is why it is so important for you to be in alignment with people you are around. Otherwise, you will be dissatisfied or lose sight of your own goals and values. If you spend time with people who are motivated, hard-working, happy, successful, and healthy, then you will begin to experience some of those positive side effects yourself. You will feel inspired to grow and develop to match those traits so you better emulate them yourself. The more you emulate them, the more you attract them back into your life. It becomes a positive feedback of giving and receiving goodness and inspiration.

As you grow and prune your network, just remember to be genuine and keep an open mind. You never know who you could meet.

Be bold and respectful. If you're attending an event with hiring managers, ask one for an informational interview. Reach out to professionals in your network and beyond. Most importantly, don't let your shyness stop you. Those who struggle with shyness are in danger of missing out on the benefits of professional networking. Keep in mind, everyone struggles with this; it is not easy to reach out to others. Start with resources like LinkedIn and Facebook, and gradually work towards reaching out for in-person meetups. You can also begin by looking for situations in which you feel the most comfortable and to then use those opportunities to form relationships. For example, when you participate in an activity you enjoy you will meet other people who also enjoy it. Likewise, doing volunteer work will give you the opportunity to meet people with whom you have something in common. Start small and build from there.

Never Stop Learning

This one is huge. You would think at some point experts would have learned everything they could learn to be where they are as experts. That's just not true; experts never stop learning. Ever! As a matter of fact, most people, once they become an expert, will actually commit to learning more. The reason for this is simple. Once you are an expert and begin to enjoy the benefits of being an expert, you will want to stay an expert. Beyond being proud of this accomplishment, experts have the drive to stay knowledgeable and to be informed. Typically, experts read more, continue to educate themselves through courses and workshops, regularly gather knowledge from other experts, and are constantly looking for new ways to learn and grow.

Experts tend to want to digest new information on different topics as often as they can. They never want to stop learning. As you commit yourself to develop into an expert, you will want to visit new blogs every now and again, and to try something new. Doing so will help you think beyond the box. If you are still interested in learning, why not go beyond your niche and invest time in understanding another, related niche? Try designing, or internet marketing, or coding. The options are endless! I've grown so much from trying new things. You have no idea how powerful it is to integrate SEO, blogging, and internet marketing together until you try it and see the results. Learning new things like this can (literally and figuratively) open yourself up to a lot of opportunities. There's nothing better that can improve your existing skillset, and overall make you more competitive, than combining several multi-disciplines into one mind. The results are incredible. It will be such a breakthrough for you, both personally and professionally. It is the key to your success.

The more you learn, the more people will want to listen to what you have to say. You may even find yourself becoming a thought leader in your field. Experts are never content with what is, or the status quo. As a rule, they're always looking for the next step or evolution of their profession. They are constantly trying new techniques, improving on existing concepts, exploring new ideas, and adding value wherever and however they can. They strive to push the boundaries and expand the limits of their field. Experts devote themselves to leading the way for the future of their profession with true vision. To get to this point, you'll have to start small with a big vision. Perhaps you can begin a blog or do very specific updates on your social media channels around your area of expertise. Or you could consider writing a simple ebook, submit a white paper to a professional organization, or write articles for online publications. Keep in mind that becoming a thought leader is not a sprint; it's a marathon. You get there by doing lots of little things well.

As you grow in your learning, you also want to be sure to share your knowledge with others. Experts become more valuable by sharing their skills and knowledge with people around them who could benefit from it. They always want to be of service to their professional community. If you want to be seen as an expert, put your expertise out there for all to benefit from, and do not be afraid of being judged. Try to let go of your fears, and put your thoughts and ideas (based on your expertise) out there. One way you can share your knowledge is to train others, say by speaking at a small event or industry conference in your local city. Remember as you seek these opportunities out that it's not about you. Consider your audience and the ways in which getting your message out there will improve the field. You have to be seen as someone who confidently shares information and expects nothing (within reason) in return. Sharing your knowledge also helps you absorb the information better to help you further your study.

Chapter Summary

To move from a basic level into expertise, you will have to prioritize a few key actions - and stick with them! These are: finding a mentor in your field with whom you can form a quality relationship and who challenges you in productive ways; knowing the A-listers in your field who are at the forefront of what's happening and understand where your industry is headed; sculpting a network that really works for you and your pursuit to becoming a valued expert in the field; and digesting plenty of new information on different topics as often as you can - so you never stop learning. In the next chapter, you'll learn actions you can take to improve your memory that will help you along your learning path.

CHAPTER EIGHT:

Improving Your Memory

In many ways, memories shape who we are because they make up our internal realities. They are stories of ourselves, and they are the stories of what we are capable of learning through our ability to recall necessary information at relevant times. There are several factors that have been tied to reasons for improved (or easily degraded) memory - anything from genes to nutrition to meditation practices. In general, reducing your sugar intake, avoiding high caloric foods, and getting plenty of exercise is highly recommended in order to have better memory function.

Living both a physically and mentally active life will be important overall in your ability to retain your brain function longer because, just as the rest of your muscles grow stronger with use, so too do mental exercises help maintain mental skills and memory. Exercise is tied to stress reduction and improved positivity, which are both crucial to prioritize as you commit to learning something new. Some sources even call for an increase in caffeine to help boost memory (and performance) even if only in short-term contexts (such as during a study session, or for a test or a big presentation). Beyond that, the core practices below will help you improve your memory as you learn a new skill.

Sleep More (& Better)

Many people find themselves cutting back on sleep the busier they get, even though they recognize how important sleep is for their overall health. It can be tempting to convince yourself that sleeping isn't productive and that sacrificing a good night's sleep before an important presentation, exam, or workday will yield positive results. We tend to think of sleep as a luxury versus a necessity; however, when it comes to learning and memory, sleeping is actually one of the most important things you can do.

Research has found that people who suffer from sleep disorders often have impaired memory functions. Cognitive scientists at Washington University have found evidence that people who sleep after processing and storing a memory carry out their intentions much better than people who try to execute their plan before getting some sleep. This gives new meaning to the phrase 'sleep on it!' Researchers have shown that sleep enhances our ability to remember to do something in the future, something referred to as prospective memory. Our ability to carry out the future actions we intend is not so much based on how those intentions are embedded in our memories, but rather a trigger we encounter later on by some particular context that sparks our recall of those intentions. Prospective memory, or things we intend to do, include such things as remembering to take a pill, remembering to buy our friend a gift, or bringing home the right groceries from the store. We use this form of memory every single day. Researchers believe the prospective memory process occurs during something called slow wave sleep, an early pattern in the sleep cycle that is very conducive to memory strengthening. These findings convey the importance of making sure you get to sleep after making plans or to-do lists before you execute the plan itself. In short, sleep helps us strengthen our associations between the task that we intend to do and the context that triggers the memory of this task.

Sleep also helps with memory consolidation and improves our ability to remember what we learned during the day. Deep sleep, or non-REM sleep, can strengthen memories if the sleep occurs within twelve hours of the initial learning. This has important implications for how you time your study and sleep schedule. If your current schedule doesn't allow you to get the recommended seven to eight hours of sleep every night, then you can prioritize sleep on the weekends. Research has found sleep deprivation to be detrimental to attention span, alertness, and reaction times, which are clearly things that you need in order to have a productive workday. What's good is that getting just one full night of sleep will restore your cognitive functioning back to normal. These recovery periods are not the ideal replacement for getting good sleep consistently throughout the weeks, but they do work as long as they are fairly regular - for example, every weekend for at least nine or ten hours.

Studies have also shown how memories that are associated with a reward are also reinforced by sleep. Sleep helps strengthen memories, and it also helps you choose and retain the memories that have a rewarding value because rewards act as a mental tag that works to seal information into your mind as you learn it. During periods of sleep, the information is solidified, which means taking a short nap as you learn can help you cement new facts and skills in your memory. In other words, taking a nap after a period of learning is beneficial for your long-term retention.

Try Mnemonic Devices

Memory can be broken down into sensory memory, short-term memory, and long-term memory. Sensory memory is when our senses help us to receive and record and recall information. Short-term memory is when we remember what we have recently seen or heard. For instance, you may recall a phone number you just looked up or the name of a person you just met. Long-term memory, in contrast, is when you transfer short-term memories into your deeper, more lasting memory that has no capacity on the amount of storage. Information gets into long-term memory through repetition or visualizing information so you can recall the information later, much like a filing cabinet. We often need cues to help trigger us to recall information from our long-term memories. That is where mnemonics come into play.

Mnemonics are techniques we can use to help us improve our ability to remember something. They are memory devices that help your brain better absorb and recall important information. Mnemonics are simple shortcuts that allow us to associate the information we want to remember with an image, a sentence, or a word. Think of mnemonics as ways to give your brain a boost with tasks it can do anyway. Often, the information you want is in your brain somewhere, and all you need is a tool to help you reach it more quickly when it counts. As we age we'll experience a decrease in memory function. This results in slower thinking, decreased concentration, slower memory processing, and a higher need for more memory cues. In these instances, mnemonics can also be used to help keep memory sharp. In any case, these memory techniques make it easier for us to remember facts and can be applied to nearly any subject.

Mnemonics will help you simplify, summarize, and compress information to make it easier to learn. It can be especially handy for students in medical school or law school, or people studying a foreign language. Basically, if you need to memorize and store large amounts of new information, you can try a mnemonic and you'll find that you remember the information long after you pass your test. The following is a list of the most popular mnemonic devices you can use.

The Method of Loci

Loci is the plural of 'locus,' which also means location, and in Ancient Greece, they used this mnemonic device for easy memorization. The method of loci involves the mental strategy of imagining yourself in a room you are familiar with, and then taking note of items around the room, such as the couch, lamp, piano bench, photo album, and so on. You then pair the items that you mentally place in the room with the pieces of information that you are trying to learn, such as a list of things that you need to remember in a certain order. You can visualize yourself walking back through that room and then picking up or passing by each item that you placed there, thus triggering your recall for that information. The method of loci has been proven to be a very effective method for learning. Research has demonstrated how it leads to a significant improvement in the ability to recall information in multiple cases, from college students to adult learners. Some research has also suggested that using mnemonic techniques such as the method of loci is effective in improving the ability to learn and remember information for people with mild forms of cognitive impairment. This is likely because the method of loci uses elaborative rehearsal, which involves manipulating information by adding meaning to it and using it, rather than only studying a list and repeating it.

Acronyms & Acrostics

Acronyms are typically the most familiar type of mnemonic strategies, ones you're most likely fairly familiar with. They use a simple formula of a letter to represent each word or phrase that needs to be remembered. Think of the NBA, which stands for the National Basketball Association. While an acronym is a word formed from the first letters or groups of letters in a name or phrase, an acrostic is a series of lines from which certain letters (such as the first letters of all lines) form a word or phrase. These can then be used as mnemonic devices by taking the first letters of words or names that need to be remembered and developing an acronym or acrostic. Take music class for instance. If you have to remember the order of notes so you can identify and play the correct one while reading music, you can remember the notes of the treble staff as EGBDF. The most common acrostic used for learning this is *Every Good Boy Does Fine.* The notes on the bass staff are ACEG, which is most commonly translated into the acrostic *All Cows Eat Grass.* An often-used acrostic in math class is *Please Excuse My Dear Aunt Sally*, which represents the order of operations in algebra and stands for parentheses, exponents, multiplication, division, addition, and subtraction.

Rhymes & Music

Rhyming words can be used as a mnemonic to help us learn and recall information. A rhyme is a saying that has a similar terminal sound at the end of each line. Rhymes are easier to remember because they can be stored by acoustic encoding in our brains. For example, *In fourteen hundred and ninety-two Columbus sailed the ocean blue.* The ability to memorize and remember these kinds of phrases is often due in part to repetition and in part to rhyming. Think of nursery rhymes you were brought up singing. You can rearrange words or substitute a different word with the same meaning to make them rhyme. Think of the familiar spelling rule, *i before e, except after c*. This phrase sticks in our memories because we've heard it multiple times (repetition), and also because of the rhyming within it. You can also use music to encode the information into your brain. Remember the ABC song you learned as a kid? Music has been proven to stick with us long-term, so search online and find there are plenty of songs that exist to help you learn certain information - anything from state capitals to the countries in Africa, and beyond!

Chunking & Organizing

Chunking information is a mnemonic strategy that works by organizing information into more easily learned groups, phrases, words or numbers. More simply, it is a way of breaking down larger pieces of information into smaller, organized chunks that are easier to manage. In the United States, our telephone numbers do this for us, so we can more easily recall them. If you have to memorize a long digit phone number, 1234567891011 12 (and it wasn't so easy to do because it's in order), it would likely take some effort to remember. However, if you break it down into more digestible pieces, such as 12345 6789 101112, it will be easier to recall. Chucking has also been studied as a means of helping those with early stages of Alzheimer's disease improve their verbal working memory.

In a similar vein, organizing information into either objective or subjective categories helps with memorization. Objective organization means you place information into well-recognized, logical categories. For example, trees and grass are plants, and a cricket is an insect. Subjective organization, on the other hand, is when you categorize what appears to be unrelated items in a way that helps you recall the items later by ascribing meaning to them, such as trees, grass, and crickets being things you might find in a meadow. This can be useful because it breaks down the amount of information to learn. If you can divide a list of items into a fewer number of categories, then all you have to remember is the categories that will then serve as memory cues in the future. An example of this is relating to how you ride a bike with learning how to drive a car.

Keywords

If you're studying a second - or even third or fourth - language, then using the keyword mnemonic method will significantly improve your learning and recall. A keyword mnemonic is an elaborative rehearsal strategy that helps encode information more effectively because it ascribes meaning to the content you're trying to memorize. A keyword mnemonic involves two steps. You first have to choose a keyword that sounds somewhat similar to the word you're trying to learn, and then you form a mental image of that keyword as being somehow connected to the new piece of information. Studies have shown that visualization and association trigger the recall of the correct word. Let's say you're learning French, and you want to memorize the word *parler*, which means to speak. Every time you think of this word, you associate it with a pearl coming out of your mouth. By visualizing it this way, when you see *parler*, you will think of the pearl in your mouth and recall what *parler* means in French.

Linking & Connecting

The linking method for mnemonics consists of developing a story or image that connects pieces of information together that you need to remember. Each item leads you to recall the next item. For instance, you know you need to bring your glasses, keys, notebook, lunch, and wallet with you to work every day, so you can think of a short story to help you remember everything. Jill's notebook needs special keys so it can open her glasses, which she needs to see her hungry wallet that holds her lunch. If you add humor to the story, it's even easier for you to recall this kind of information. A similar strategy involves making meaningful connections with something that you are already familiar with or know. Making this kind of connection is another kind of elaborative rehearsal, which I've mentioned above. An example of this is if you meet a man named Ned and you notice he is unusually friendly. To help you remember his name, you can think of him as Neighbor Ned or Neighborly Ned so that the next time you see him, you can more easily recall his name.

The more you can relate new concepts to ideas that you already understand, the faster you'll learn the new information. Memory plays a central role in our ability to carry out complex cognitive tasks, such as applying knowledge to problems we haven't encountered before and drawing inferences from facts we already know. By finding ways to fit new information with pre-existing knowledge, you'll find additional layers of meaning in the new material. This will help you fundamentally understand it better, and you'll be able to recall it more accurately. When you connect the new to the old, you give yourself mental hooks on which to hang new knowledge.

However, you go about using mnemonics to help you improve your memory, keep in mind that you want to incorporate imagination, association, and location. If you create images that are engaging and vivid, you will be more likely to recall that information. Likewise, your brain wants to link ideas; it's constantly looking for ways to associate pieces of information, so if you can, link concepts together as a means of remembering new information. Location is also a great way to integrate new material into your memory because you already have so much knowledge about the places you know.

You also want to remember the learning techniques I discussed from earlier chapters that will help speed up your learning as well as retain it for longer. Remember how images activate our learning so much more than information that is verbal or written? We are great at recognizing visuals and can easily invent our own to help guide our memories. If you need to remember a task that you have to do in the future, try creating a vivid mental image of it actually happening. When you meet someone new, spend a few seconds picturing something about them that might give you a visual reminder of their name. Whatever the case, ascribing images and meaning will be invaluable to you for your recall. Using mnemonic memory strategies can give you that boost in your memory that we all need, and it can likewise improve your efficiency in learning. Keep in mind that you may need to practice a few of these strategies before they come easily, but once you have them down, they should stay with you long-term.

Create Memory Palaces

A memory palace is taking the method of loci to a new level. This mnemonic is when you think of an imaginary location in your mind where you can store specific, meaningful images. The most common type of memory palace is when you make a journey or path through a place you know well, like a building, town, or route. Along that path, there are specific locations that you are used to always visiting that are also in the same order. Think of your memory palace as a place that you can easily visualize where you store new or important information. You will associate a memory journey or path with an actual journey or path.

You first want to choose a place you know very well, like your home or place of work. Reacquaint yourself with this place as needed.

You may need to walk around it several times, take pictures, and so on, so you feel like you really know it. Try to visualize the entire place. It doesn't have to be in incredible detail, all you need to be able to do is to orient yourself and move around the space in your mind. Visit the place as often as you need to in order to do this mentally. Once you have, you can begin to plan or map your route. It should have a starting point and an endpoint. For example: the bottom of the stairs, the top of the stairs, the closet, the hallway, shoes outside your bedroom door, bathroom, shower, and so on, until you find a logical endpoint. You will be able to revise your memory palace after you test it a few times, so don't worry if it's not perfect your first go at it. If you have a lot to learn, you will make many different memory palaces.

You'll next want to find a different place where you can relax and really visualize the place you chose for your route. Practice following your route a few times, first forwards, and then backward. Remember, you can always make changes to it if you find there are hiccups anywhere. When you have your route down, then you want to assign certain stations (or loci) where you will store new information in. Each locus should be unique and serve as a separate image that you don't want to confuse with other stations along your route. Go back along your route and make sure the places you have picked are unique. Again, practice doing this forwards and backwards, so you really know your route.

Now that you have your memory palace and route primed, and your stations selected, you want to begin to assign new learning to it. Take a list of something you want to memorize, like a shopping list or key vocabulary words you want to learn. Take one or two items at a time and place a mental image of them in each locus of your memory palace. Try doing a few at a time and practicing as you go, so you can really begin to associate your list with your route. You also may want to try exaggerating the images of the items to have them really interact with the location. For example, if the first item on your list to memorize is an apple, and the first locus in your memory palace is the front door, picture a giant apple walking through your front door.

Because we are such visual learners, making your mnemonic images come alive with your senses will improve your ability to remember them. Exaggeration of the images and humor will always help you recall them in the future. Keep in mind that you can also use spaced repetition to get this information into your long-term memory. Spaced repetition, also called the distributed study practice (which I discussed earlier on in this book) is a learning technique you can use that incorporates increasing intervals of time between when you review new material, so you can strengthen your recall ability.

A solid memory palace strategy is, without a doubt, the most effective way to study efficiently. Their use has been recorded in history for over a thousand years, and they have even, most likely, been used back during the hunter-gatherer times. Memory palaces are used by mental athletes during memory competitions (where people perform feats like memorizing a shuffled deck of cards and so on in only a few minutes), as well as for schoolwork and learning - even for memorizing an entire book. As a memory technique, it unlocks your spatial memory and spatial mapping. The more you create and use memory palaces, the more they unlock multiple levels and layers of memory that you can use in order to learn faster. These levels of memory include: autobiographical memory, episodic memory, semantic memory, procedural memory, figurative memory, and more. Each of these is unlocked through this memorization strategy that is devoted to improving your memory as you study. It will make your study sessions so much faster and more powerful.

Chapter Summary

Improving your memory begins with the most important element in learning a new skill: sleep. Sleep aids memory consolidation and improves our ability to remember what we learned during the day. It can strengthen our memories and is irreplaceable as a learning tool. If your current schedule doesn't allow you to get the recommended seven to eight hours of sleep every night, find a time when you can prioritize sleep. It's that important! Mnemonics are simple shortcuts that allow us to associate the information we want to remember with an image, a sentence, or a word. A memory palace is a specific kind of mnemonic device when you think of an imaginary location in your mind where you store specific, meaningful images to help you remember complex concepts. Both are memory tools you can use to help improve your memory. In the next chapter, I'll overview what you can do if you find yourself needing to cram.

CHAPTER NINE:

How To Cram (When You Have To)

Let's face it, we only pull all-nighters when we've fallen behind. Cognitive scientists have conducted study after study that demonstrates that cramming doesn't help us as long-term learners. Attempting to cram all of this new information into our brains uses (and over-uses) our short-term memory. Remember that with long-term learning what we need is our long-term memory to help us recall and retain most facts.

Short-term memory tends to fade rapidly, so if we don't reuse that information quickly, it will disappear within a period of a few minutes to a few hours. Cramming, in general, doesn't allow this new information to move from short-term to long-term memory, which is critical for performing well over time. Remember, the best study method is breaking it down in intervals, and it's always better to begin early - both early on in your learning and early on in the day. Studies show our body clocks tend to prepare us to perform better during the day and in the morning as opposed to later on in the day. Early in the morning studying is typically more recommended than late at night studying.

In this day and age, we will all encounter sleep deprivation at some point in our lives, whether willingly or unwillingly. There are the days when the responsibilities seem endless. Studies have shown that staying awake all night is not beneficial to your study habits. You will actually work better the next day if you have a good night's rest.

Our brains lose their efficiency with sleep deprivation, so instead of staying up all night and missing out on the recommended amount of sleep (experts suggest anywhere between seven to nine hours), it's much better to rest your brain and wake up early for a last-minute study session. Cramming, in general, makes us feel overwhelmed, frustrated, and keeps us asking questions we cannot typically answer under pressure. Where do you start? How do you begin? It will make you feel more overwhelmed than you need to feel, so try to avoid it.

All the same, we all find ourselves from time to time in a situation where we are trying to quickly catch up on information or a project - and time is running out. If the unthinkable happens, and you find yourself the night before an exam or a big presentation, faced with the prospect of having to pull an all-nighter, there are a few things you can still do to give yourself a higher chance of performing well.

To begin with, don't panic. If you are in a high-stress state of mind, your concentration will be shot, try to relax first and foremost. If it helps, try something like meditation or a short walk before beginning your cram session. Once you're in a good mental place, make sure you have all your notes and books with you. You'll only need your books to look something up - in general, you'll want to use your notes to stick to the core things you'll need to remember. Have your pencil or pen, a notebook or legal pad, and some colored highlighters nearby in case you need them. Most importantly, turn off your social media. This form of addiction will only serve to distract you and make your cram session ineffective. Take a break from Facebook, silence your phone, turn off the TV, and get ready to focus. You're going to need all of your energy directed towards the content you're trying to learn last minute.

Now work on breaking your study material down into more digestible pieces. If you have an exam coming up solely based on one book and you procrastinated all semester and didn't do the assigned readings, focus on what you really need to know. Look at the chapters and remember three things per chapter. Essentially what you're doing is focusing on the big ideas and key details. Because you're officially cramming now, your learning has a shelf life. You want to stick to the basics and parse out the main ideas because those are the most likely points to be on the test. You have limited energy, so you want to direct it to key headings, dates, chargers, passages, vocabulary, themes, motifs, and so on. Filter out all the rest.

You can use a study guide as the foundation for your cramming - and even better, if you don't have one, you can make one. This will help you filter the materials you have into information you can focus on. It doesn't have to be neat, or perfect. Write it out, read it out loud, and revise it where it makes sense to. You can even ask a peer to give you feedback on it, or use it as a guide for a study group. Teaching the material to others will help you retain the information better.

Cramming is about finding a good rhythm, so if it helps, set a timer to break it up into sections. Using a timer will help you find a good study rhythm. If you study for eight hours straight, you're more likely to fall asleep during your test than you are to ace it. I recommend a five to one split. For every five parts of study, give yourself one part of anything else. For example, if you study for fifty minutes, then take a ten-minute break to play soccer, listen to music, take a snack break, or something similar. Your choice, just give yourself a nice break - and then get back to it.

If you've ever worried that all the information you've crammed in during a study session might not stay in your memory, research suggests a quick bout of exercise may actually help solidify some of it. One study found that when students did moderate exercise - such as running - after a period of learning (including cramming for an exam), they actually performed better than if they only crammed.

The active nature of exercise helps the brain retain new information and recall it when desired, whereas a passive activity, such as playing a computer game, does not. The stress hormone, cortisol, is known to have an impact on our memory retention. In some circumstances, cortisol can help us remember things, and in others, it impairs our memory. There are two types of stress in this sense, psychological and physical. Researchers think chemicals are released by physical activity, like running, which then improves memory retention. Researchers also recommend talking out loud as you cram, so you involve your auditory memory as you re-learn (or just learn) salient content. Make hand motions, use funny voices, pace around your apartment - do whatever it takes to keep yourself in an active learning state.

As you cram for your exam, presentation, or whatever it is you are cramming for, you will want to set an end time to it so you have the motivation to finish, and also so you can prioritize sleep at some point. If you need extra motivation, give yourself a reward at the end of this stretch too. Maybe it's your favorite sushi dinner, or ice cream, or chocolate, or a glass of wine. The key is you can't have it until you're done studying. Deadlines and rewards will help you stay on track. If you're a dedicated dieter, use carrots and hummus instead. Whatever you need to do, set some kind of personal goal for yourself that will help you keep moving forward without stagnating or getting bogged down.

Chapter Summary

Cramming makes us feel overwhelmed and frustrated, and is generally not recommended. There are a few things you can do if you find yourself in this position, however, and it involves breaking your study material down into more digestible pieces. Focus only on what you really need to know. Look at key chapters, headings, or notes, and remember the main ideas and critical details. Stick with the basics. Exercise will also help your brain retain this new information and recall it more easily, so take a run in between cram sessions. Lastly, and most importantly - prioritize sleep. It is the single best thing you can do for your performance. In the final chapter, I will give you pointers on how you can train your brain to stay focused.

CHAPTER TEN

Train Your Brain to Stay Focused

If you're like me, you find yourself having days when you feel like everything is happening all at once. It's like you can't think straight, or even begin to make a plan because everything is coming at you constantly. The to-do list never seems to end. During such times, it's even more important for you to get organized and to slow down. Prioritizing this above your to-do list will help you get on track and in the long-run will actually help you work through things more quickly. Productive people will often spend a few minutes every morning organizing their day. They look at their calendars, make a prioritization list, set reminders for themselves throughout the day, and so on. In many cases, more productive people will also boost their productivity by resisting the temptation to be constantly accessible to others. So how can you be more like productive people? I have three key recommendations that I detail below that will help you train your brain to stay focused.

Beware of Digital Distractions

In today's world, we are increasingly bombarded with distractions to our work. Studies have shown that it can take more than twenty minutes to fully return our attention to an interrupted task. Constant phone calls, incoming emails, and colleagues stopping for a chat or with a "quick" question can seriously disrupt our train of thought and workflow. More productive people will set aside specific times for answering emails or returning calls and texts in order to build efficiency. It may take some adjustment for colleagues or clients, but with good communication these schedules are possible.

The internet itself has provided learners with a range of helpful search tools that give us so many positives in terms of learning and research; however, studies indicate teachers are concerned these kinds of technologies are creating more easily distracted generations of learners who have shorter attention spans. Some even think they distract more than they help students academically - that the negative outweighs the positive. Too many students today, "research" and "Google" are synonymous words. To these students, the process of doing research has shifted from a relatively slow method of intellectual curiosity and discovery to a much more fast-paced, short-term exercise with the end goal of locating just enough information to complete an assignment. Some teachers reported that, specifically, they are concerned their students will become over-dependent on search engines and will struggle with how to determine the quality of sources they discover, which will affect literacy rates as well as have lasting consequences on attention span, time management development, and critical thinking capacity. Many teachers also reported that, despite their students being raised in such a digital age, they are surprisingly lacking in their online search skills, such as having patience and determination in looking for information that is hard to find.

The repercussions of relying on digital learning are more critical for younger learners than adult learners, and yet are still important to note. Regardless of your age, overexposure to technology can result in a lack of focus and diminished ability to retain knowledge. For adult learners, these findings should primarily serve as a caveat to not get sucked into the digital realm too much when trying to learn something new. Because the internet and related technologies are so immediate, they work against our attentional control. Attentional control is our source of attention in our minds. It helps us maintain awareness (or alertness), process and orient information from sensory input, and resolve inconsistencies or conflicts in our learning. The effects of anxiety on attentional control are key to understanding the relationship between anxiety and performance. In general, studies have found anxiety inhibits our attentional control on a specific task by impairing our processing efficiency. Digital distractions work in much the same way.

If you're wondering what this has to do with your learning, the answer is: everything. How your brain can stay focused and on task ultimately determines how well you will learn something new. Only when you are able to fully concentrate will you be able to dedicate yourself to your learning endeavor. You will find that you can retain information much more easily when your brain isn't being constantly distracted. Having a clear head will make such a difference. You will have to come to see the blocks of time you set aside for learning as sacred to everything else (minus, of course, emergencies). You will want to set aside time in your day at some point where you can devote yourself purely to directing your focus to your learning. You have to really make yourself follow through on this because we tend to give in easily to distractions.

It can be tough to know where to begin when you sit down to learn. Something I've grown to be quite fond of is - depending on what the learning is, of course - pre-reading. I find that it's a great way to introduce your brain to new learning, get interested in the topic, and prime your brain for the learning ahead. Pre-reading is the process of skimming a text to find key ideas before you carefully read a text or a chapter of a text from start to finish. It's also called previewing or surveying, but either way, it's the same idea. It's a kind of inspectional reading where you can use certain clues like the table of contents or chapter headings as a roadmap for your learning. It will give you an overview that will increase your reading speed and efficiency. In general, you'll want to play an active part in your reading to help with your retention. Think as you read and pre-read. Look at titles, subtitles, chapter beginnings, introductions, chapter summaries, headings, study questions, and conclusions. You may even want to check the index if the book has one to see what range of topics will be covered, or read the publisher's blurb.

Pre-reading will help you see the big picture and the overall purpose for the reading ahead so you can direct your attention to the concepts that really matter. It will actually increase your capacity to understand the material you are studying. In many cases, taking only a few minutes to pre-read can help you with your overall comprehension and retention. Just think: if you build your understanding of the big picture before you even begin to read the text, you have a conceptual framework already in place. When you encounter a new detail or piece of evidence in your reading, your mind will know better what to do with it and how to organize it.

Ask yourself as you're pre-reading: what kind of clues is the text giving me for my future learning? How can I apply what I already know to what I'm going to be learning here? What is the author's purpose for telling me this? Generating these kinds of questions as you go will help you both identify and achieve your purpose in your learning. If for some reason you're short on time - say, if you're cramming for an upcoming exam or quiz - then you can prioritize the first and last paragraph of every chapter (or only the introduction and conclusion or chapter summaries), while keeping in mind each chapter heading. This method shouldn't be a substitute for actually reading the material (which you should do at a later point), but it will help give you a quick overview of the salient themes and concepts from the text. If you want to take pre-reading one step further, you can email yourself your pre-reading study guide and compare it to your notes once you've actually read the text. Emailing as a practice actually helps train your attention better, because for every non-topic related email you have in your inbox, you can help remind your brain of your earlier learning by periodically emailing yourself summaries of your notes. Just the act of doing more with the information will be helpful because you will be able to read back over it with fresh eyes.

Different people learn in different ways. For example, some people can learn and retain information better if they listen to background music or some kind of neutral noise. Even the general hustle and bustle of a coffee shop conversation or a busy shopping area can help some people direct their focus to their study. Other people prefer absolute stillness and silence. For either category of learner, headphones can be useful as a means to either provide sound or to cancel it and other distractions out. This is something you need to work out for yourself, where you fall on this spectrum. In terms of listening to music while you study, research suggests it depends on the content of the study. Music (mostly classical music) has been shown to provide mental boosts for clarity and focus when playing low in the background, specifically for tasks that don't require a lot of digesting of complex material. Tasks that require you to keep track of several pieces of information at one time while processing them as well place heavy demands on your working memory, and so may hinder your learning. Regardless, positive effects of background music have been found and it may certainly be worth trying out if you're struggling with focus.

Another key discovery by cognitive scientists is the importance of drinking water as you learn. Staying adequately hydrated has a number of other benefits: it's good for our skin and immune system, and it keeps our bodies functioning at optimum levels. Interestingly, staying hydrated is also critical for enhancing our cognitive abilities, and can actually make us smarter. One key study indicated that students who took (and drank) water with them into an examination room performed better than students who did not. Dehydration, on the other hand, can seriously affect how our brains are able to function. When you fail to drink water, you are basically making your brain work harder than usual to do the same tasks.

Use the Pomodoro Technique

I discussed the Pomodoro Technique in an earlier chapter, but in the context of information overload and concentration it takes on a new, improved meaning. Learners can use the Pomodoro Technique to help themselves focus throughout the workday and over time. This process involves taking timed breaks and having timed work sessions when working on a task so you can more easily restore your focus and reach your work goals. It will also help you avoid becoming overwhelmed or distracted in your learning. Especially if you are stressed or anxious, your brain will not be able to effectively store and process new information. The best way to prevent this kind of brain fatigue from happening to you during your learning is to give your brain a break in between using it for a specific learning or work task. This brain break is a state of rest, or redirecting your attention and shift to a new activity for a short time. Even a five-minute break can relieve brain fatigue so you are able to give your full attention back to your learning when you return to it.

People in several fields have used this technique in order to improve their productivity and concentration. Using the Pomodoro Technique will enable you to really stick with a task because it gives you both accountability and control over your work schedule in a way that organizes and motivates you. It will help you achieve better results in less overall time. How it works is you break your work into twenty-five-minute work sessions throughout the day. During these twenty-five minutes, you concentrate deeply on that particular task with as little distraction as possible. Then, you switch to something else during a quick break (usually around five minutes). You can repeat this as many times as you need throughout a workday. It may be best if you start with trying one or two of these sessions a day before trying to build up to three, four, or even five. I'd also recommend you start with a lower time slot (twenty-five minutes) before trying to work up to longer time slots (thirty-five or even forty-five minutes if you want to try it).

For your break, you can stand, walk around, have a snack, or scan an article in the news before you return your focus back to concentrating on your work. It's best if you keep these breaks to under ten minutes. Experts highly recommended you move around if you can during this break. Studies have shown how sitting (or even standing) for long periods of time can lead to increased risk for a number of health problems, including diabetes, heart disease, stroke, and decreases in brain function. In general, it's best for you to alternate sitting and standing at various points throughout the day, so you're not doing too much of either one. You can use your five minutes to stretch, grab a cup of coffee, or go on a quick walk outside around the building. Your brain will thank you for this!

If you're finding it difficult to begin a big task because you know it will take a long time, you're not alone. Most people do. What the Pomodoro Technique does for you, is it gets you to break this task down into blocks of work so that it's easier for you to digest over time. It can be tailored to your specific learning needs, so if you'd like, you can set a shorter time period for work, to help you gradually build up to the task. Likewise, you can make your breaks a little longer if you find that helps activate your work sessions better. On the official website, it's also recommended that learners try to estimate how many work periods are necessary to complete a particular project so you can better break it down by month, week, day, and perhaps even by a work session. This will inevitably help motivate you in reaching the finish line. Remember to block off your calendar and turn off your phone notifications to limit distractions so you can maintain your focus.

Try Meditation

Meditation is a simple practice that anyone can learn, at no cost, with no fancy equipment, and with no extensive training. It has been practiced for thousands of years by all kinds of people. One of the most common reasons people try meditation is to reduce stress and anxiety. Studies have shown meditation reduces levels of the stress hormone, cortisol. When we encounter something stressful, our cortisol levels increase. This was likely an adaptive reaction developed by our ancestors as a means of increasing their chances of survival during uncertain times. These days, our cortisol levels are influenced by other forms of mental stress that can have adverse physical effects on us, such as disrupting sleep, causing depression and anxiety, increasing blood pressure, and contributing to fatigue and demotivation. Research has shown over and over that meditation relieves these symptoms of stress and can even relieve a variety of other stress-related conditions, such as irritable bowel syndrome or post-traumatic stress disorder. Meditation can also reduce symptoms of anxiety disorders and anxiety-related mental health issues including panic attacks, obsessive or compulsive behaviors, and phobias. In turn, over time meditation will also help improve sleep patterns and reduce instances of insomnia, which is stress-induced as well. A related effect is reduced blood pressure, which decreases not only during the meditation practice, but also gradually in individuals who consistently meditate. Regular meditation can then reduce strain on the heart and arteries, which helps prevent heart disease.

The distractions our world presents to us make mindfulness activities like meditation critical to our ability to focus and stay focused on tasks. Some of these tools are essential for our work and social lives, so finding a balance in their usage is difficult yet necessary. Our ability to concentrate on tasks well determines our ability to create complete memories. Remember short-term and long-term memory? Complete memories are the product of deep and mindful learning. Our lack of attention to detail, or our tendency to want to rush through our learning, makes it difficult for us to remember crucial and important pieces of information. Having excellent concentration may not necessarily lead to better memory, but it is, however, essential to building a well-formed and useful ability to retain and recall information.

Unfortunately, there are more barriers to our concentration now than ever. The notification-saturated world of the internet constantly bombards our focus with bits of information that vary in their usefulness to us. You have to take an active role in creating that balance so you have an ideal work environment and so you achieve your goals. It's hard, too, because even merely thinking about your email or social media accounts will interrupt your concentration, so only going offline may be insufficient for your ability to focus.

If any of this sounds familiar to you, meditation could be the answer. Meditation has been found to help with increasing the strength and endurance of attention, memory retention, and problem-solving. Research has found consistent meditation practices can help people both reorient and maintain their attention for longer. This can help with creativity in solving problems as well as better task management and focus. Meditation has also been known to improve tendencies in mind-wandering, excessive or uncontrollable worry, and inability to stay focused or alert. Besides improvements in attention and clarity of thinking, meditation may also help keep your mind young and memory intact by reducing the chances of age-related memory loss. Some studies have even indicated the possibility of meditation to reverse or partially improve the effects of dementia. It is still relatively unclear to scientists the precise reason why meditation has the effects it does; however, there is more than enough evidence to indicate its usefulness in improving our cognition, memory, and focus. If you are just beginning, here are some quick tips to keep in mind.

Always find a quiet space to do your meditation practice, so that distractions are minimized. As you begin, your mind will likely wander and that will be distraction enough. You can set a timer for the amount of time you want to meditate. Similar to the Pomodoro Technique, start slow (about five minutes per session) and work up from there. You also don't have to meditate on the floor. You can do it in a chair, on your sofa, or even in bed. Just try not to fall asleep if you do so; meditation is about restful wakefulness. The key is you want to be comfortable as you're doing it. Remember to close your eyes and focus on your breath. Where do you feel your breath at its strongest? Let thoughts enter and depart your mind free from judgement. You don't have to reject thoughts or feel guilty if you have them; simply acknowledge them and let them go as you return your attention to your breath. If it helps, you can even think (or say out loud), "I am letting this thought go and returning to my practice." Do whatever you need to do to return your focus where it matters. This is key for training your brain. No matter what happens or comes up along your meditation journey, it's important not to judge yourself. All that matters is that you're dedicating yourself to this practice, and that is a good thing.

If meditating in silence or alone is too difficult for you, you can try one of the varieties of guided meditations. There are videos on Youtube, phone apps such as Headspace and Breathe, or a number of more in-depth guides you can search for at a local bookstore. Most research on meditation suggests that to get the most out of it, you should aim to meditate as consistently as you can at least four times a week. Don't worry, you can build to this consistency in your own practice, and you can take it slow. Even if you're only meditating for ten or fifteen minutes a day, your mind will thank you.

Some people will even opt to do walking meditations, especially if they're new to it. Like with other forms of meditation, the key here is to track your breath. For instance, every time you breathe in or out, you give the breath a number. Count to as high a number as you want, and take note of anything that distracts you or causes you to lose count. If you don't like the idea of counting your breath, you can also focus more on syncing your breath with your steps as you walk. Every time you inhale or exhale you also take a step. Then you can build to taking two steps per breath, then three, four, five, six, and so on until it feels too uncomfortable. The goal is for you to maintain focus on your practice, not to get to the highest number possible. You have to follow your instincts as you pay attention to what's happening in your body as you practice.

If you enjoy nature walks, you can also focus on syncing your breath to the sensory world around you in a way that prioritizes your connection to the natural world. The goal here is to focus intensely on your breath and body and how they interact with the world as you move through it. Begin with your feet and notice how each foot has contact with the ground. What does it feel like? What do you notice about this ground? Feel your weight engage with the air, your clothes, and so on. Feel the temperature outside, and notice any lingering sensations on your skin. You can zero in on different sounds, visuals, or smells in a similar manner. Again, the key is to focus on your breath while immersing yourself in your surroundings. In general, you'll find the world unbelievably peaceful when you take it as a physical reality around you without analyzing or judging it.

Once you grow some experience with your meditation practice, you can try using similar techniques of immersion and breathing principles while reading, eating, or even in social settings in conversation with others. It will help you be more involved with your life and more present, in the moment. Finding more of this presence is the primary function of meditation. Presence helps you concentrate, which helps you integrate more information into your memory. This process is intentional and purposeful. Meditation is a powerful tool for improving concentration and your overall cognitive abilities. Rather than waste your time on useless or negative thoughts and worries, you can focus on your physical being in the present moment. You'll be amazed at how much more you enjoy life when you do. As you begin your practice, don't overthink the process, and don't give in to analysis paralysis. Just focus on deepening your practice, and be patient with yourself. With regular sessions, you'll see notable improvements.

Chapter Summary

There is no secret to productivity - it's all about organizing your day in a way that works for you. Look at your calendar. Make a to-do list. Set reminders for yourself. Lastly - and most importantly - limit your use of technology. Training your brain is all about avoiding certain stimuli (including digital distractions) and prioritizing what will keep you on track. The Pomodoro Technique is your best friend in doing this, as are mindfulness practices such as meditation.

CONCLUSION

You have made it to the end of your reading journey, which may have felt like a lot to process at times. Don't worry. You don't have to remember everything, and you can always come back to revisit chapters as you put these lessons into motion.

While this book gives you a roadmap to accelerated learning, it's up to you to put in the work, study, practice, and get feedback. No matter what topic you're learning, begin by understanding these principles so you don't get stuck in the details. Learning those come later. Be sure to connect new knowledge with what you already know in order to help with memory, and use the Pomodoro Technique to train your brain and retain your focus. You can keep this handbook close by for whenever you want to re-read or remember techniques along the way to rapidly acquire your new skills.

Now think of a topic or skill you've been meaning to learn. Write it down and put it somewhere you will see it every day! It's time to get started. We tend to get in our own way by overthinking something or by not taking action. Remember: you hold yourself back more than anyone else in the world, which means, on the other hand, you alone have the power to hold yourself up and help yourself achieve and learn what you've always wanted to.

As human beings, we can grow and change and learn to an infinite degree, and it is this sentiment I want to leave you with. You have so much power and potential. Each day you spend not believing that statement is a day you are wasting. It may be the end of the book, but it's really only the beginning of your life-long learning adventure. All it takes is making that first step. Believe in yourself, and believe that you can achieve greatness - and you will!

Eating for Cognitive Power

Super Foods, Recipes, Snacks and Tips to
Boost Your Brain Health, Focus and Memory

John Torrance, Productivity Coach

TABLE OF CONTENTS

INTRODUCTION

You know that annoying friend who just seems to get everything done? You know who I mean, because the minute you read that first sentence, a face popped into your head. Yes, I'm talking about the person who seems laser sharp *all the time* and who never skips a beat. As much as that person drives you nuts, deep down inside you'd like to be just a teensy bit more like that, wouldn't you? Okay, admit it. Maybe a whole lot more like that. A little more success wouldn't do you any harm, or your wallet, either! Am I right? (I'm paid to know these things.)

Well, your old grandma was right all along: *You are what you eat*. Mounting research is proving her true. After years of too many drive-through orders on jam-packed days, too many snacks consumed while binge watching your favorite TV episodes, and too many salads skipped in favor of mac n cheese, you're definitely feeling the effects. What is more, you're a walking showcase of what you're eating. The muffin top and love handles bear ample testimony of your lifestyle. Personally, I'm not interested in the shape of your body. I'm more interested in the shape of your brain--your body just tips you off about having become an accident looking for a place to happen.

You feel bloated much of the time. Your work is suffering. Your relationships are suffering as well. You just don't feel like going dancing or engaging in that game of touch football. You skip breakfast most days and opt for a pastry you scarf down during your commute. What lunch? Mid-mornings and mid-afternoons you crash and need a *Snickers* to keep your productivity humming. You are tired in the morning and tired in the evening, but when you go to bed, your brain isn't switching over to the *off* position. This is no way to live. Literally.

Your brain is a ticking time bomb, and one day it will result in a cerebral incident (stroke) or, just as bad, permanent fog (dementia). Those kinds of life-changing incidents are actually years in the making and offer no quick fix. The fix is now. Today. Tomorrow.

Let's face it. You need to engage. Your relationships need you to be all in. Your kids beg for attention and if they don't get it, they act out in unacceptable ways. Your work requires more and more time, more and more effort. You need to be increasingly productive to stay competitive. Whatever the demands you're juggling, you need to be at your absolute best, and I can relate.

Not so long ago I was in your shoes. Every one of those symptoms described my daily life, and I knew I had to do something to pull myself up by the bootstraps and make a change. I simply couldn't juggle all the balls in my life, and, all too often, the one I dropped caused serious consequences. It took some research. I did a lot of experimenting. What I learned knocked my socks off. Every symptom I described related directly to what I was eating...or not eating! In this world of way too much information, I had not been getting the information I needed. There is a connection between food and the brain, and when I discovered that connection, my world shifted.

All of a sudden, something I'd known all my life got spun around in just a little different perspective, and it changed the way I thought, the way I acted. For me it was seeing a colleague my age succumb to a stroke, his life permanently changed in the blink of an eye. The once vital friend I enjoyed on adventures was confined to a wheelchair and communication became a whole lot more difficult. His mind didn't seize the words he wanted to say. His filter was gone, and what came out of his mouth alienated many of his friends. He became lonely and bitter.

And I vowed to change. Just like that. I began to change. Not in a day. Not drastically. I started reading my way to better health. I started experimenting with what I read. I started changing the way I ordered food on a menu at my favorite restaurant. I started making grocery lists based on what was good for me, rather than impulsively picking things off the shelf that looked good on the spur of the moment. Slowly but surely, I changed. You can as well.

What you eat must supply the raw energy your brain needs for optimal function. That does *not* include a diet of cheeseburgers and soft drinks. Eating the right foods increases the cognitive power of your brain, the thinking power. It reduces the risk of Alzheimer's disease, one of the newest plagues of our generation. It removes brain fog leaving you in a slump at your desk. It improves your memory. The *right* food = less brain fog, more brain function. The *right* food = less dementia, more focus. Food = brain function (or lack thereof)..

When I made just a few changes in the way I looked at food and its intake, an elemental shift took place. I ate better. I performed better. I slept better. I decided I needed to make this information available to others. I began with friends and family. When they raved over what I discovered, I tried to branch out, but my circle of influence was not wide enough. How should I change that? I first looked at the wonderful world wide web.

Here's what I discovered: Too many gurus want to charge you megabucks for an online course. There's a whole lot of talk, and who has time for that? It's certainly not what *I* had in mind. I wanted to put together an easy to follow, life-changing program, for just the cost of a book, making it enjoyable to read, and easy to follow. Here's my plan for you: Read the information so you understand why you've been feeling low. Study my findings on superfoods, and how easy it is to incorporate them into your life. Try my recipes. Then turn around and teach this information to your family. Chart your progress. You will be amazed.

The **benefits** of this program are hard to beat. You will find easy to digest information and enjoy reading it! You will feel better. You will probably look better...you're not opposed to dropping a few pounds, are you? You will earn kudos from clients and your boss, who will be impressed with your soaring productivity.

Here's my promise to you: I *will not* make claims I cannot prove. I *will not* bore you with too much background information...though I will provide a lot of detailed research in a glossary at the back of the book. I will coach you to better health. That's a keyword. Did you catch it? *Coach?*

- A coach inspires, never drives.
- A coach causes you to want to change, not forces you to change.
- A coach stays right there with you when the going gets tough.

I want to be all these things for you. Coaching is my life. I want to take all those skills I use every day to help CEOs and top executives improve their careers, then mix it with the research I've discovered, and roll it up into an easy program for you to follow. I want to walk with you to a state of better health with increased productivity. Are you with me?

It all begins with you, my friend. You were drawn to this book for a reason, and it just takes turning the page to Chapter One and then diving in. Start reading, and then eating a new way to improve your brain. Think better. Think smarter. Act better. Act smarter. See where I'm going with this? You'll find in the next few pages everything I've promised and more. What's *the more*, you ask? It's my tips and tricks, starred information to help you get every last drop of benefit from this book. It's the in-depth information you'd hear, and never absorb, in a fancy high falutin online course. And those little nuggets are where you'll find the gold.

So I'm asking again. Are you with me? It all starts with page one. Let's start learning about superfoods and super powers. Let's do this!

CHAPTER ONE:

How Food Affects Your Brain

If you're normal, you've probably been eating with an eye on your waistline, not with a focus on your brain. But what has your waistline done for you lately? Your brain, on the other hand, works tirelessly to control each breath and each beat of your heart, perception of each sight in your field of vision, each sound around you. It's called the **Autonomic Nervous System.** It's where a lot of your body's work takes place, and while you're not supervising each transaction directly, your brain requires high-performance nutrients to do this well. This is Coach John telling you: *To be a brainiac you need to eat brain food.* It's true. There are certain foods good for your brain, and certain foods your brain would rather you avoid. You're going to be learning some new concepts, and that's good. I don't expect you to know it all ahead of time. I had to research this for myself, and my goal is to feed you these bits of knowledge in easily digestible portions.

★ Each time you see a term in **bold,** you'll know it's a term covered in your glossary. My promise is to make this engaging and readable, with lots of information you can read if it triggers a desire to learn more. That means some of the heavy lifting is in the back of the book. I suggest you read it once, go through the glossary, and then read it again, pencil and paper in hand, ready to really begin this adventure of discovering better health.

★ Eating for brain health may sound radical, but research studies have proven that the foods you eat are an important part of not just your health, but your brain function and the prevention of cognitive problems. Certain superfoods are now known to improve cognitive function--which includes boosting your memory, improving your decision-making abilities, decreasing response time, and get this, even boosting your mood. These foods are the basis of clean eating. It's a way of eating that may not only save you hours in the kitchen, but give you more hours of a meaningful life, so pay attention. Read the next sentence two or three times, it's just that important:

What you eat has a far-reaching impact on your brain.

- The food you eat is the source of brain energy. What you eat affects how much energy your brain has to work with, in both its autonomic function and its cognitive or thinking function.
- The food you eat is the source of the transmission of nerve impulses. Your brain needs to send messages, and it needs a chemical to pass the message along from one nerve to the next nerve to ensure it happens.
- The food you eat is the basis of sustained mental health. As of 2018, researchers have connected the dots of serotonin and gut health, and the role it plays in Alzheimer's progression. They predict that dementia will affect more than 65 million people worldwide by 2030. It is the plague of our generation and you, in your choice of what to eat, can make a difference.

Let's cover a little of the new research hitting the medical journals. I can save you some time and energy by narrowing down the plethora of information into the best articles. I'm providing a detailed list of them; you can dive in for some more intensive study if you've got the time. For our purposes, though, let me do the heavy lifting for you.

Serotonin: Nothing But the Facts

First of all, let's look at **serotonin**. Your body produces serotonin, which is a neurotransmitter regulating sleep, appetite, pain receptors and moods. Of course, the building blocks for its manufacture must be present for your body to do its job. Did you know 95% of the serotonin your body produces is made in your gastrointestinal tract (GI)? I didn't. Your bowels are lined with millions of nerve cells called neurons. Every moment of every day, a war is waged in this small arena, a war with far-reaching implications. Good bacteria protect the intestinal lining, and form a barrier against bad bacteria who march to battle, leaving toxins and inflammation in their wake. Your diet needs to give your body a fighting chance at producing serotonin by harboring good bacteria.

Remember I said it helps regulate sleep, appetite, pain, and moods? These are the very basic building blocks of a happy, well life. I experienced a time in my life when I routinely awakened each night at 2:30 am. After a while, I was running myself ragged. Upon examination, my doctor correctly diagnosed an imbalance in my system and recognized that the serotonin keeping me asleep was getting taken up too soon by a hyperactive spool in my brain. I was prescribed very low doses of a medication blocking its uptake, and voila! I started sleeping through the night again.

Too often we run the gamut of self-help through melatonin or valerian root and then jump straight to sleeping pills. This sets us on a course of either dependence on medications to put us to sleep, or a teeter-totter of sleep and no sleep, depending on when we're taking sleeping pills and when we're off them. That's not the answer. Eating foods that help in serotonin production, getting diagnosed if your brain is in a state of imbalance and replenishing your serotonin, is a much healthier reaction to the problem.

Read the extended information on serotonin in the glossary and look at regulating your levels in a healthy way.

Probiotics? Say, What?

We refer to a diet fostering good bacteria as being rich in **probiotics**. If you're like I was, it sounded like a lot of New Age mumbo jumbo, a fad that would quickly pass away. I couldn't have been more wrong! Probiotics are live organisms you consume, either by purchasing an expensive supplement or by tweaking your intake to include yogurt or other fermented foods. Most commonly you're looking for Lactobacillus and Bifidobacterium. These good bacteria limit inflammation, improve the absorption of nutrients and activate neural pathways traveling constantly between your gut and your brain. I'll bet you didn't see that one coming. Neither did I. The relationship between my stomach and my brain required some research on my part. Let me give you the *Reader's Digest* version.

Startling discoveries linking a healthy gut to dementia offer even more incentive to change your diet. Some gut bacteria actually accentuate the buildup of brain proteins, significant since amyloid and tau proteins comprise the plaque in Alzheimer's disease. Research on mice suggests that simply changing your diet may reduce these amyloid plaques and decrease inflammation. What do you suppose happens next? Exactly. Your memory improves. I don't know about you, but I found that pretty compelling evidence for needing to mend my ways.

Some diets affect the presence of these probiotics. The Mediterranean or the Japanese diets, both stand in stark contrast to the typical Western diet of processed foods, unhealthy amounts of salt, way too much sugar, and lots of red meat. The **Mediterranean Diet** stems, naturally, from countries like Greece and Italy along the Mediterranean Sea. It is recommended by both the World Health Organization and the Mayo Clinic. It is characterized by a lifestyle of more vegetables and fruits, whole grains, beans, nuts and seeds, and olive oil, as opposed to other processed oils. Many of these unprocessed foods are fermented, packed with natural probiotics.

The **Japanese Diet** includes more fish, vegetables, and fruit. It involves eating mindfully and slowly. Japanese recipes emphasize simple seasonings as opposed to heavy sauces. Food is served in smaller dishes. Well, that makes portion control a whole lot easier, doesn't it? The secret to satiation lies in utilizing more variety. A staple food is combined with a soup, a main dish, and a few sides. The staples are rice or noodles. The soup is typically a miso soup with seaweed, shellfish or tofu and vegetables in a fermented soybean stock. The main dish would be comprised of fish, seafood, or tofu with small amounts of meat, poultry, and eggs. Sides consist of vegetables, seaweed, and raw or pickled fruit. I couldn't see myself eating like this and I, for sure, couldn't see my wife cooking all this.

See what's missing here? Both of these diets eschew the same staples of the Western diet: red meat, lots of dairy, processed foods, lots of salt and sugar. Both diets require a fundamental shifting of the taste buds, and while they may seem like radical departures from your regular household menus, you don't have to jump into this with both feet. The good news is that some very basic tweaks in your current diet will do the trick. We'll get into more of that later.

Antioxidants

When I first heard this word, the analytical side of my brain took it apart. Anti meaning against. Oxidants. Was that oxygen? Why would I want to do anything against oxygen? Silly me. The word was *oxidant,* like oxidizing metal into rust. I was a little slow on the uptake here. Of course, I'm all against rusting out my brain. Millions upon millions of chemical reactions are taking place in your body every single day. In the process, some compounds become unstable, with a free, or extra electron. (Think back to your ancient class on organic chemistry with the descriptions of protons and electrons in each element.) That tiny free electron is known as a *free radical.*

Oxidants containing free radicals are the leftover sludge when your body metabolizes and interacts with a rich stew of building blocks, creating all new chemicals from the food you eat. The antioxidants balance the oxidants in your bloodstream. Let me break this down: Your body is a complex machine with all kinds of checks and balances, moves and counter moves. The antioxidants are warrior compounds your body ingests, like ascorbic acid (vitamin C), or synthesizes to keep that nasty oxidation in check. One body-synthesized **antioxidant** is glutathione, made from three amino acids: glutamine, glycine, and cysteine.

Not only does your body produce oxidants in everyday living, you are also exposed to more in smoking, radiation, and other pollutants. You acquire even more as a result of stress and alcohol consumption. When the balance of antioxidants and free radicals gets out of whack, **oxidative stress** results. The stress weakens cell membranes. It damages connective tissue and collagen (think your knees!). It is a precursor to cancer and cardiovascular disease. It is a culprit in autoimmune diseases like arthritis and psoriasis. It affects diabetes. It doesn't take a genius to realize this is bad.

This is why we make the effort to include foods rich in antioxidants into your diet. These antioxidants are loaded with essential fatty acids that stimulate and strengthen brain cells. Some people flock to health food stores and buy supplements.

★ Here's a clue, though. You don't need them. Eat a diet rich in antioxidants, and save that money.

What exactly is on your healthy menu? I'm glad you asked. Read on to Chapter Two. As your coach, it's my job to feed you small bites of information, lure you into appropriate action, and slowly win you over. Unfortunately, you aren't meeting me face to face, and I'm not speaking with you directly. This book is your lifeline. It's a lot cheaper than individual counseling sessions, and you can digest the information at the convenience of your schedule. The danger is one you know all too well.

How many times have you tried to change before? How many other self-help books mock your efforts and line your bookshelves? To be successful this time around requires a meeting of our minds. I'm writing to you, gentle reader, so read this out loud if it makes it easier to imagine my presence. Think of me as your new best friend, someone who sits on your right shoulder as time moves forward, but who speaks with you as we work our way through this process of change to a healthier you.

Chapter Summary

The food you eat affects your brain.

- Serotonin is a neurotransmitter required for optimal brain functioning.
- Probiotics are essential for gut health, and that's good news when it comes to producing serotonin.
- Antioxidants, rich in essential fatty acids, combat the free radicals of oxidation.

In the next chapter, you will learn what foods to feed your brain for optimal function.

CHAPTER TWO:

Eating for Better Cognitive Power

The key to eating for optimal brain health isn't a hog-wild change into a whole new way of eating. It's changing things, a little here, a little there. As you incorporate these small changes into your life, you will see the benefit, and feel encouraged to another step toward better eating, better cognitive functioning. Remember. Baby steps.

In order to defend against a variety of age-related conditions impairing your memory and the general function of your brain. a good first step is to concentrate on incorporating just three nutrients into your diet. They may be new to you, and you will be wondering just what strange things you have to eat. Seaweed? Stinky tofu? Relax, my friend. I didn't go there either.

Let's begin by looking at omega-3 fatty acids, antioxidants, and **flavonoids**. We touched on some of this very briefly in the last chapter, but it's time to dive a little deeper and get serious. This is your coach saying, try it. Take a chance. Give it a week and see what a difference it makes. You'll never look back.

Omega-3 Fatty Acids

As you age, your brain experiences some normal degeneration. The old maxim of being over the hill need not apply, however, if you pay attention here. Yes, your nerve cells shrink, and nutrient-rich blood supplies in the brain are diminished over time. Inflammation complicates the situation. In response, your brain produces fewer neurotransmitters and the result is poor or patchy communication between the cells. Your memory suffers. It is just that simple. Don't be afraid, because there is a solution for that.

What if I told you that a diet rich in **omega-3 fatty acids** would make a difference? A 2014 study, published in Neurology, submitted evidence that postmenopausal women who have higher levels of omega-3 fatty acids (EPA and DHA) in their blood had increased brain volumes. Remember, smaller brain volume is linked to Alzheimer's disease. They documented a difference of one to two years of healthy functioning which their counterparts lacked. Think about what you might look forward to with an extra two years of just being there, your brain running on all four cylinders. I don't know about you, but I want to be mentally aware and able to enjoy the birth of grandchildren, and perhaps see them grow up as well. Let's get down to facts.

When scientists talk about these as being essential fatty acids, they mean that while your body can synthesize much of what it needs, it cannot make these. They must be ingested. Fish are one of the best sources, but one caveat is the danger of mercury and other heavy metal contaminants in swordfish and bluefish. Perhaps you're not fond of fish? That's okay. There are other non-fish foods rich in this brain protector. Foods rich in omega-3 fatty acids include:

- Oily cold-water fish: anchovies, tuna, bluefish, herring, sardines, mackerel, salmon, halibut, and, lake trout.
- Leafy greens: Brussel sprouts, spinach, arugula, mint, kale, and watercress.
- Oils: flaxseed oil, chia seed oil, cod liver oil, and krill oil.
- Eggs.
- Walnuts.

Antioxidants

As touched on in the last chapter, antioxidants protect your brain against free radicals. If the balance between oxidants and antioxidants in your body gets out of whack, a condition known as **oxidative stress** can result, with ensuing damage to your brain.

This becomes more important as you age. When you were young your brain shrugged off the rogue compounds known as free radicals like brushing away ants from your blanket at a picnic. Time changes things. With age, it's not so easy. Your body produces thousands of these unstable oxygen molecules every day. Add in pollutants and ultraviolet radiation, and your brain finds it more and more difficult to protect itself from the constant barrage.

If ignored, free radicals harm the body. It's a process called oxidative stress, and it leads to mental decline and a series of debilitating illnesses. The good news is your body can defend against oxidative stress by ingesting antioxidants. These substances shield the brain and its nerve cells from destruction. The goal is to keep a large supply in stock. Eat foods rich in antioxidants:

- Vitamin C--We all think we know how to ingest Vitamin C. But do we? Here are some things you may not have known:
    - Strawberries are an unexpected source. One serving of strawberries can give you 20 mg, one half of your daily requirement.
    - Citrus fruits (no brainers). One orange gives you 70 mg, meeting your daily requirement. A glass of orange juice can offer up to 90 mg.
    - Chili peppers. A half-cup of chopped peppers offers almost 110 mg of Vitamin C.
    - Red bell peppers. One cup is 200 mg of Vitamin C.
    - Papayas. One serving meets all your required Vitamin C for the day.

- ○ Kiwis. Surprisingly, a kiwi contains more Vitamin C than an orange.
- ○ Brussel sprouts. Another surprise. One cooked serving is worth 50 mg of Vitamin C.
- Beta-carotene--Traditionally we think of carrots, but three foods that weight for weight will beat them are sweet potatoes, grape leaves, and microgreens.
- Selenium--This is a tricky one. The amount of selenium you get from your food depends on the soil in which it was grown. Brazil nuts, almonds, seeds and fish are the three top sources.

Another source of antioxidants is in **flavonoids**, and they deserve a heading all of their own. A great many fruits, vegetables, and herbs contain flavonoids that serve to reduce inflammation, reduce the risk of heart disease, and decrease symptoms of eczema. As it turns out, flavonoids are also good for the aging brain.

Researchers in 2012 at Brigham and Women's Hospital found that older women who ate large amounts of berries, experienced significantly less memory decline when contrasted with another control group. The difference, the researchers believed, was because berries are rich in flavonoids. Continuing research broadened that claim. The Foundational Medicine Review published a 2018 paper stating that flavonoids interfere with key enzymes triggering cell death. Most importantly, they protect the brain against neurotoxins and suppress inflammation of the brain.

The research is replete with raves over the role of flavonoids. The most recent research suggests they improve many cognitive skills, including memory, learning and decision making. It's also suggested these foods may prevent age-related mental decline. In the UK, 2% of the population aged 65-69 have dementia. This figure rises to one in five, or 20%, for those aged 85-89. Most centenarian studies report dementia in the very old at 45 to 65%. Flip these statistics, and you realize that dementia is not natural or inevitable. 80% of people in their eighties and nearly half of all centenarians enjoy life dementia-free.

The significance hit me squarely between the eyes. I didn't have to end my life in the years of mental fog we call debilitating dementia. The choice was mine. I could enjoy a healthy diet, or reap the consequences later. I've chosen to improve my diet. My advice to you is simply this: let's do this together. When you hit the grocery store and start making dinner tonight, realize I'm doing the same thing. If it's Monday, it's fish. We'll cook alongside each other, and you'll feel the weight of my support.

Me? I'm eating all the foods rich in flavonoids that I can. These foods include:

- Green tea.
- Leafy greens--spinach, kale, and watercress.
- Berries--blueberries, strawberries, and blackberries.
- Cocoa.
- Coffee.
- Dark chocolate.
- Red wine.

Vitamin E is another antioxidant worthy of its own section. It's a well-known fighter of free radicals, preventing cell damage. I grew up well aware of this lifesaver. My mother had a heart attack in early adulthood and turned to Dr. Shute, who focused on natural healing. He pioneered much of the research on this antioxidant back in the 1950s. Her prescribed regimen included large amounts of Vitamin E, and within months, her cardiologist found no trace of the previous damage. His groundbreaking research led me to appreciate the wonders of Vitamin E.

Dr. Shute lists twelve benefits of Vitamin E:

- It reduces the oxygen requirement of tissues.
- It melts fresh clots and prevents embolism.

- It improves collateral circulation.
- It's a vasodilator.
- It is known to lyse scar tissue.
- It prevents scar contraction as wounds heal.
- It increases low platelet counts.
- It decreases the insulin requirement in about ¼ of diabetics.
- It is one of the regulators of fat and protein metabolism.
- It stimulates muscle power.
- It preserves capillary walls.
- It prevents hemolysis of red blood cells.

I often wondered if his groundbreaking work has ever been verified. Current researchers are honing in on how it plays a part in brain health. A 2014 study published in the American Heart Association's journal discussed one type of Vitamin E, tocotrienol. This is found in palm oil, and it appears to have a beneficial effect in decreasing both Alzheimer's, and Parkinson's disease. It also seems to reduce the likelihood of strokes.

Vitamin E is actually a conglomerate of eight different compounds, four tocopherols, and four tocotrienols. The daily recommended dose is 15 mg or 22.5 IU and researchers prefer you get it from food as opposed to supplements. The benefits of **supplementation** are a source of contention among researchers, and initial studies of its efficacy have been disappointing.

Dr. Axe concurs and notes that Vitamin E deficiencies affect the young and the old more severely. He recommends eating two or three foods rich in Vitamin E each day:

- Sunflower seeds: 1 cup contains 33.41 mg.
- Almonds: 1 cup is 32.98 mg.
- Hazelnuts: 1 cup is 20.29 mg.
- Wheat germ: 1 cup, plain and uncooked is 18 mg.
- Mango: 1 whole raw piece of fruit is 3.02 mg.
- Avocado: 1 whole raw is 2.68 mg.

- Butternut squash: 1 cup cooked and cubed is 2.64 mg.
- Broccoli: 1 cup cooked is 2.4 mg.
- Spinach: ½ cp cooked or 2 cups uncooked is 1.9 mg.
- Kiwi: 1 medium piece of fruit is 1.1 mg
- Tomato: 1 raw sliced tomato is 0.7 mg.

Other researchers added to the list:

- Nuts and seeds: almonds, pecans, peanut butter, peanuts, hazelnuts, pine nuts, sunflower seeds.
- Oils: wheat germ oil, sunflower oil, safflower oil, corn oil, and soybean oil
- Leafy greens: spinach, dandelion greens, swiss chard, and turnip greens.

Let's take just a moment and talk about clean eating. It's a term that may be new to you, but it's a hot topic at our house. It means you eat your food fresh and raw as much as possible. You can find a whole website dedicated to the concept. They describe it as eating the way nature intended. Dr. Bowden is even more explicit. "It stands for eating real food made without a lot of unnecessary processed ingredients and additives. Eating foods as close to their natural state as possible. Eating foods that you could hunt, fish, gather or pluck. Eating foods your great-grandmother would have recognized. Eating food that spoils. Eating food that doesn't have a bunch of unpronounceable ingredients, whether it's labeled 'natural' or otherwise."

Don't start hyperventilating. Remember, we're taking baby steps here. Begin by choosing one favorite food on the above lists, and eat it naturally. Visit the Clean Eating online magazine. Try out one of the recipes I've included to help you along your way. Your trip to optimal health is a journey, not a destination. Don't beat yourself up, but please do let me coach you to more productivity. If I can make these changes one little step at a time, so can you. What's on your grocery list this week?

Chapter Summary

We've been taking a deep dive into the three tops things you can include in your diet for brain health and higher levels of productivity.

- Omega-3 fatty acids are your friends. They are heart-healthy fats.
- Antioxidants are found in foods rich in Vitamins C and E.
- Eat a colorful diet.
- Dip your toe into the world of clean eating.

In the next chapter, you will learn how to incorporate these healthy foods in a painless way. Still with me? Good for you!

CHAPTER THREE:

Brain Foods Neuroscientists Want You to Eat Daily

Dr. Lisa Mosconi, Ph.D., says, "To function best, the brain requires around 45 nutrients that are as distinct as the molecules, cells, and tissues they shape. The brain, being radically efficient, makes many of these nutrients itself, and only 'accepts' whatever else it needs from our diets. Put simply: Everything in the brain that isn't made by the brain itself is 'imported' from the food we eat." She advocates eating your way to better brain health. She is not alone.

Mounting evidence suggests that simple math can change your future. It's all about adding more of the good and subtracting more of the bad. Let's start with the good. We've looked at the whole subject as eating from the viewpoint of what *types* of nutrients we need to be eating, but we haven't really gone through each of these essential foods, and how to incorporate them into your diet.

- As you read this chapter, get out a pad of paper and a pencil. Begin jotting down next week's grocery list, and let's add a few new items and put a few clean eating items into practice, shall we?

Fatty Fish

You already know by now that not all fat is bad fat. Coldwater fatty fish like Alaskan salmon, mackerel, bluefish, or anchovies, are all high in those omega-3 oils your brain needs each and every day. Adult women need about 1.1 grams of omega-3s daily, according to the National Institute of Health. That means that a 3-oz salmon filet will meet your daily requirement, offering about 1.24 of the two most important fatty acids, DHA and EPA. To offer a little context, your brain is about 60% fat. Studies show that DHA may help boost memory and cognition skills and that it possesses anti-inflammatory properties which are just as valuable. But what if you don't like fish?

It's time to readjust those taste buds. Rub the salmon in a mix of spices and make a lovely sauce. It won't be the healthiest salmon you've ever eaten, but it will start recontouring your taste buds for better eating. Most of the recipes are in the back of the book, but I'm including one with each of the super-foods here, just to get you used to the idea of working them into your diet.

Even my non-fish lovers like this, adapted from Real Simple:

No Way, But Well, Okay Salmon

- Turn on and preheat your oven at 500°.
- Line a baking pan with foil and drizzle it with extra virgin olive oil.
- Lay the salmon fillets in the pan and turn them to coat them with the oil.

For the rub, combine 1 tsp chili powder, ½ tsp cumin, ½ tsp smoked paprika, 1 tbsp honey. Add salt and pepper. Rub this all over the salmon, and then place the pan of salmon in the oven.

Roast the salmon until it's opaque on the outside and just translucent on the inside, about 5 minutes. If you want it well-done, roast it for an additional 3 to 5 minutes.

While it's in the oven, prepare your sauce, which will serve as a double for salad dressing for your spinach salad. Chop two small handfuls of flat-leaf parsley or chives or mint. Place them in a small bowl, and add enough extra virgin olive oil so it pools around the herbs. Grate a clove of garlic into the bowl. Add a few splashes of red or white wine vinegar, salt, and freshly ground pepper. Stir and sample. If it's sour, add salt. If it's salty, try adding another splash of vinegar.

Plate the salmon and drizzle on your sauce.

I've included other recipes in the back of the book, but try this one and see what you think. Remember; be flexible. You can take any recipe and adapt it for your own use. Be creative.

Dark Leafy Greens

If you're not already incorporating brain greens like spinach, kale and Swiss chard into your diet, it's time to start. They're full of vitamins, minerals, fiber, and disease-fighting nutrients. Your brain will thank you. An easy way to adapt is to make fresh salads, increasing the ratio of spinach or kale to leafy red lettuce each day. Gradually you'll get used to the change and adapt.

If you're making the salmon above, try a fresh salad of spinach leaves, red leaf lettuce, walnuts, craisins, green onions, and mung bean sprouts. Drizzle on the dressing you used for the salmon, and you have a quick side that complements your meal.

If you are wrinkling up your nose and just *don't* want to eat fresh greens, try cooking the kale or spinach. Trust me, you'll like it. This isn't an especially healthy recipe, but it's a good first step for people who detest everything green.

Wilted Greens

- Clean a handful of dark leafy greens. I use a salad spinner for rinsing and then draining water from the leaves.
- Fry up a slice of bacon, and remove it from the pan. (I know. I didn't promise this was the best recipe...just one to train you to eat your greens.) Break away the fat so you have a few little morsels of bacon remaining.
- Toss your clean spinach into the pan and saute it, adding salt and pepper. Add the bacon bits and even the pickiest eater will chow down happily.

Extra Virgin Olive Oil and Flaxseed Oil

Of all the cooking oils you can stock in your cabinet, and there are a lot, try a new one. If you watch Rachael Ray, you are familiar with EVOO. You may not be so conversant with flaxseed oil. Get some and try using it. Both of these oils are loaded with anti-aging nutrients, rich in omega-3's and vitamin E.

You already know I'm a proponent of eating your way to good health, so let's add this oil without using a supplement. If you are bringing home your first bottle of flaxseed oil, this is what you need to know. You may see it labeled as linseed oil, and it's okay under either label. It is extracted from dried and pressed flax seeds. If the bottle says it is virgin, it means it was done by mechanical means only, without the use of any chemical solvents. It lasts a long time, so I recommend springing for the organic or virgin brand and just pay a little more for the better processing.

It has a crisp, almost nutty flavor when used directly on your food. It is volatile and has a very low smoke point (225°), which means it isn't easy to use on the stovetop searing meat or vegetables. Rather, drizzle it over roasted veggies and eat it directly rather than cooked.

Cacao

Do you need an excuse to eat chocolate all the time? Here's your reason to rejoice! You heard me right. Dark chocolate definitely has a place in your brain diet. Look for varieties with 80% or higher cacao content, indicating it is rich in theobromine, a powerful antioxidant. The award-winning Kim Smith, director of the Brain Healthy Cooking Program, asks, "How much chocolate a day will keep dementia at bay?" Her answer may surprise you.

Here's her lowdown on chocolate:

- The darker, the better. Look for brands advertising 60-70% cacao.
- 1.0 to 1.6 oz per day is recommended. Beware of that candy bar, typically 3.5 oz in size. Split it into thirds.
- Keep a calorie count. A full candy bar each day can add 600 calories to your diet, and extra weight is not brain-healthy. You may end up eating less of other brain-healthy foods.
- Some like it hot. It's okay to enjoy a mug or two a day.

One eight-day limited study focused on the consumption of 70% cacao, with the added controls of receiving no antioxidants 48 hours before the study began, as well as during the study. Results did indicate an anti-inflammatory response signaled by increased cytokines. Another study involved EEG measurements after ingestion of 48 grams of 70% cacao dark chocolate and reported increased brain hyperplasticity. Take that as a good thing.

One thing they all agreed on: eat more dark chocolate.

Complex Carbohydrates

Despite the unstoppable rise of the keto diet, many nutritional experts still love complex carbohydrates. At first, I was pleased because I never met a potato I didn't love. Unfortunately, that doesn't include potatoes. Complex carbs are foods like legumes, which include beans and lentils, sweet potatoes and whole grains.

These foods feed your brain with a steady supply of glucose for a longer period of time, as opposed to peaking quickly and then fading away. Note, when I say beans, I'm not referring to green beans as much as navy, pinto, kidney or garbanzo beans. I add them to salads and soups, but a favorite in our household is chili. This is a version of our favorite white chicken chili:

Smoked Chicken Chili Warm Up

1. Do yourself a favor and get a smoked rotisserie chicken when it's on sale at your supermarket. Debone it and cut it into chunks.
2. Chop and saute one onion
3. Add small cans of green chilis and diced jalapenos. (Remember you can't take out the heat once you've put it in, but you can always add more.) Let them simmer a bit with the onion.
4. Add 4 cans of rinsed white beans and 2 cans of chicken broth. (I know. Rinsing the beans removes the B vitamins, but it also removes the gas, and I'm all for that.)
5. Let it simmer for a while, and just before serving, add a can of evaporated milk.

In the recipe section in the back I'll add other recipes with legumes, but for now, just get used to the idea of eating more of them.

Berries

A great source of both fiber and glucose, berries also have a very low glycemic index, which means they help regulate glucose levels in your blood. I pick them up whenever they're on sale, and freeze what we don't eat immediately. Eat them for dessert and toss them in salads.

Blueberries are often referred to as the brain berry and are exceptionally high in antioxidants. This fruit, native to North America, offers brain benefits whether you eat them fresh, frozen, canned, or as an extract.

1. Blueberries lower the risk of acquiring dementia. One recent study found that seniors who drank 30 ml of *concentrated berry juice* (the equivalent of 230 grams of berries) exhibited a significant increase in brain activity, blood flow, and memory compared to the placebo group.
2. They reduce the effects of Alzheimer's disease once it is diagnosed. The University of Cincinnati conducted tests in which participants ingested either a placebo powder or a *freeze-dried blueberry powder* (equivalent to one cup of berries) once a day. The adults eating the blueberry powder demonstrated improved scores in cognition and word retrieval with increased brain activity

Any way you ingest them, it is almost universally accepted that berries, and specifically, blueberries, improve memory, brain cognition, and brain health.

Water

★ If you remember nothing else you read here, commit this to memory: Water consumption is incredibly important for brain health.

Avocado

The monounsaturated fats in avocados help improve blood flow, which then contributes to a happy and healthy brain. The problem is they aren't that cheap and they turn in the blink of an eye. The key to enjoying avocados lies not in using them in the nanosecond when they are ripe and still good, but in buying the best produce in the first place.

These are my top tips in choosing the best fruit:

1. Pay attention to color. The darker the color, the sooner you must use it. Get a green one if you're not using it for several days, or a black one if you're making guacamole today.
2. Give it a gentle squeeze. A firm one isn't ready. A soft, mushy one is probably riddled with black spots. You want one that yields just a bit to gentle pressure with no soft spots.
3. Check the skin. It should not have any indentations, symptomatic of bruising.
4. Examine its stem. Peel back the little end cap and look at the color underneath. If it's green, it's ready for you to use, if it's brown it's probably over-ripe.

Now that you know how to find the best fruit, bring on the guacamole!

Pumpkin Seeds

Roasted pumpkin seeds are a favorite in our household after Halloween. We scrape and save those seeds, washing away most of the remaining strands of pumpkin. Let them dry. Drizzle them with extra virgin olive oil and a shake or two of salt. Roast them at 350° until they are slightly browned. Yum!

Nuts

Be a squirrel and graze on nuts throughout the day, but dieters are smart to be concerned. A handful of nuts can be up to 10% of the suggested caloric intake for a man, much less a woman. Nuts are worth the risk if you eat them the healthy way: as a garnish on salads or side dishes. Eat nuts instead of other snacks, not in addition to them. The following table will help you scale this valuable addition of brain food to healthy portions.

1 oz Nuts	Calories	Fat grams	Protein grams
Almond	168	15	6.2
Brazil nuts	184	18.6	4
Cashews	161	13	4.3
Hazelnuts	184	17.5	4.2
Macadamia	201	21.4	2.2
Pecans	200	20.1	2.6
Pistachios	160	13	6
Walnuts	184	18.3	4.3

Did you notice the one ounce serving size? That's not settling onto the couch with a large package of cashews, eating half the bag and feeling smug about how good they were for you. One ounce is a handful.

Broccoli

Tell the kiddos they're eating brain food the next time you serve broccoli for dinner. This veggie is filled with antioxidants and plant compounds called carotenoids that are highly protective of the brain. I find even the pickiest eater likes it roasted.

Roasted Florets

1. Heat the oven to 425°.
2. Cut the florets from a stalk or two of broccoli and place them on a sheet pan protected with foil. Drizzle them with extra

virgin olive oil, and sprinkle them with salt and pepper. Generously sprinkle on some garlic powder.

3. Place them on an upper rack in the oven, and let them roast until they are slightly burned around the edges.

Coffee

Don't ditch your java juice prematurely. Research confirms that coffee drinkers reduce their odds of developing Alzheimer's disease later in life. If what I just told you makes your heart beat with relief and joy, you may not be overthinking the issue. One of you is wondering, though, *just how does it do that*?

It is a stimulant and the notion that it keeps you up at night is true. Its molecular structure mimics adenosine, a neurotransmitter slowing your brain down at night. When caffeine binds with those same receptors, it doesn't slow down your brain, so you have more trouble falling asleep. I must confess that I love coffee so much, that I even enjoy a cup before bedtime with no ill effects at all. I must also admit that it's probably a matter of conditioning since I've enjoyed the habit for many years, but I love any diet that lets me drink all the coffee I want.

The bugaboo for me was not just the coffee flavors, but the creamer that made my coffee luscious. Flavored coffees are simply laboratory-derived additives included in the roasting process, so that burst my bubble right off the bat. Worse, I've never acquired the taste for strong black coffee. The sugar, corn syrup and dairy adds up and isn't part of a MIND diet, however, so I had to learn other ways to flavor my coffee, I went to the Coffee Detective. I began getting fresh beans, adding vanilla or ground pods of cinnamon to them before grinding them. For creamer, I learned to enjoy fat-free milk with a dash of vanilla and a touch of maple flavoring. Before long my taste buds caught up with my brain and all was well.

Aside from stimulation of the central nervous system and thus increasing alertness, does it really make for a healthier brain? The answer is, yes! Coffee contains antioxidants and its regular consumption is linked with a reduced rate of neurological diseases like Parkinson's and Alzheimer's. The evidence in your mind should be piling up. Antioxidants are vitally important to your brain.

Chapter Summary

We covered thirteen great brain foods. You got your first recipes for a happy, healthy brain.

- One of the most important things we covered is the importance of eating the right portions of these superfoods.
- Another important lesson was that there are ways to sneak these foods into the diets of picky eaters.
- A brain-healthy diet is multifaceted and contains a balance of these foods. Learn to like them all.

In the next chapter, you will learn which foods to subtract from your diet for better brain health. Don't let yourself have that reflex knee jerk reaction. It's not going to be that hard. I promise you, we'll get through this change together.

CHAPTER FOUR:

Foods Your Brain is Addicted To

Scientists rightfully classify heroin and opium as addictions, but they have been hesitant to add important new addictions to that category. One is **sugar**. According to Psychology Today, the average American eats 156 pounds of *added* sugar a year. About half comes from soft drinks, sporting energy drinks, and fruit drinks. That sugar triggers dopamine release in the brain's nucleus accumbens, the area associated with motivation, novelty, and reward. This is the same brain area that responds to cocaine and heroin. Think sugar cravings aren't an addictive response to your pleasure center? Think again.

These food addictions play a catch-22 with your brain, and ultimately with your life. Your brain's health requires removing them from your diet, but at the same time, your brain has become used to them and their addictive responses. It just keeps signaling for more. That's the power of an addiction. I replaced sugar for nine months with stevia-based substitutes and alcohol sugars. I not only saw the benefits in my waistline and joint health, (who knew sugar was such an inflammatory agent?), but I was more mentally alert. I became a believer in not just the present value of eating sugar-free but in the life-giving benefit of postponing a fate of dementia.

Mounting evidence suggests that diet plays a starring role in your brain health, and, no matter how overwhelmed you may be feeling about the topic right now, you can make these changes. Your goal is to stay away from anything that gives you brain fog and slows down the rhythm of brain productivity.

Research shows we can adapt to new lifestyles. You may have learned poor health habits growing up. You may have a lifetime of poor food choices behind you. That's okay. You *can* change. Found in the National Institute for the Clinical Application of Behavioral Medicine: "New research in neuroscience is showing that while our brains may have developed in a less than ideal manner, we can apply neuroplastic principles to help re-develop our brains." What does that mean in real language? It means you can train your brain to like and joyfully anticipate new foods.

What are the worst eight foods and how can you replace them with something brain healthy? Let me show you. If you just take favorites away you create a vacuum, and sooner or later your bad habits will return. The secret to change is in taking baby steps and then replacing an old favorite with a *new* favorite. My trek into the land of no sugar produced surprising health benefits, and I managed to keep cravings to a minimum. I'm not saying you can never enjoy special treats on special occasions. I'm encouraging you to find healthy replacements and occasionally treat yourself. I fall off the wagon during the holidays. I yield to temptation since I love pumpkin pie and Christmas cookies. Not just any pumpkin pie, but the old standby my mum used to make. Don't give me some doctored version when it's a holiday. *Don't mess with my holiday!* I want iced sugar cookies cut into Santas and stars, pumpkin pie with whipped cream, and all my favorite trimmings. After the holiday I climb back on the wagon and get back into the routine of charming my brain with clean eating all over again. See what I mean? It's not a life sentence. It's a matter of making peace with yourself as you make changes, give yourself grace, and putting lifelines into place.

That digression through the holidays takes place because I eat brain-healthy foods as a regular habit. It can only be a digression if you have a habit in the first place. How do you develop that habit?

Unsurprisingly, the trek into better eating habits begins with staying away from the middle shelves of the grocery aisles. Look at the top and bottom shelves. Many supermarkets now stock healthy alternatives in the same vicinity as the store: I find sugar free Lily baking chocolate in the same aisle as Hershey's. Learn to read labels. Begin a file of good-for-you recipes and a shopping list of items to replace your old standbys.

1 No-No: Commercial Muffins

Commercial bakeries still use hydrogenated oils, high fructose corn syrup, soybean oil, and trans fats. A study conducted in Montreal found that mice fed these substances displayed withdrawal symptoms when given a healthier diet. It's no secret that a muffin will probably give you a muffin top. A typical blueberry muffin (and blueberries are good for you, right?!) carries nearly 400 calories and a third of the day's fat. Yikes!

Remember we talked about eating clean? That means *eat the blueberries, not the muffin.* When you skip breakfast and find yourself tempted by a pastry at the coffee counter, opt for taking your coffee to your desk, where you've stashed some healthier options.

If you're at a meeting at Starbucks, that may not be an option. Just remember that a muffin with 500+ calories may be packing 25 grams of fat and 56 grams of **sugar** and 500 mg of sodium in the form of **salt**. A better alternative is a cheese Danish. It's still not perfect, but it's better, at half the levels of the muffin.

#2 No-No: Sugary Drinks, Including Sodas

There is absolutely nothing worthwhile about sodas or other sugary drinks. Aside from the quick sugar rush (followed by the inevitable sugar crash), you don't gain anything but added calories. Soda isn't the only culprit. Avoid energy drinks, sports drinks, and juices. *But orange juice is healthy, right?* Read the label and be sure there's no *added* sugar.

This is a hard habit to break, and some of you are already protesting that a zero-calorie soft drink can't be that bad for you. I'm sorry, but the research is not on your side. Forbes reported a study in the journal *Stroke,* which demonstrated a correlation between diet soda and both stroke and dementia. Those drinking at least one diet soda a day were three times as likely to develop dementia or suffer a stroke.

The best remedy is stopping soda cold turkey with a replacement of water. I know, it sounds harsh. A good step down might be having soda just with certain meals. When you splurge and have pizza, indulge in a soda. The rest of the time, refrain.

Focus on the healthy benefits of water. Did you know your body is 70% water and it needs up to 125 ounces a day, depending on who you read? What scientists do know is that the old advice of 64 fluid ounces is not the correct number. It's higher. Your brain needs a minimum of seven to eight *glasses, not cups,* a day for optimal brain health. Consider something as simple as sleeping through the night. You haven't lost sweat with exercise, but you are still waking up dehydrated. With each breath, water vapor is expired and your reserves are depleted.

Your inability to focus may be as simple as brain dehydration. You don't suspect dehydration when you're not crawling through the desert, but your brain needs water to concentrate. When you go into a fog it may be as simple as your brain conserving its resources.

The water you drink serves as a way to remove toxins from your brain. Your cerebral vessels need hydration to make those important cell transfers. The water you drink produces less concentrated blood, and thus it has more room for those toxins which built up when you were dehydrated when there was no room to transfer them out of the loading zone.

Obviously, water is good for you, but what if you just don't like it? Begin with adding infusions. They aren't expensive and they alter the flavor. You can also purchase powdery or liquid flavor enhancers, but be sure to read labels and avoid the ones with added sugar. Set a goal of how much water you want to drink per day or hour. Keep a water bottle handy. Get used to it. Water is your new best friend. Gradually decrease your need for flavorings and just drink the real deal. Your skin, your body, and your brain will thank you.

3 No-No: Canned Tuna

It's true that the American Heart Association recommends eating fatty fish like tuna at least twice a week, and sticking to their recommendation will be doing your brain a favor. Put canned tuna on the menu too often, however, and you could end up doing more harm than good. Why? Bigeye, ahi, albacore and yellowfin tuna are all high in mercury. Ingesting too much creates another set of concerns. Too much of the heavy metal can cause cognitive decline.

To stay on the safe side, incorporate other varieties of seafood like anchovies, wild salmon or trout. They offer the same benefits but don't carry the risk of excess mercury exposure. That's a little intimidating, isn't it? Salmon is very expensive and who likes anchovies?

I went on a rampage to learn to like them, and I discovered that sauteeing them in extra virgin olive oil, and then including just a few in other recipes changed my whole perspective. Pasta, spaghetti and pizza sauce all survived a little kick of anchovies without a storm of protests from my diners. I didn't simply eat anchovies or expect my family to. I started by using just the butter derived from searing them in olive oil and not the fish itself. I gradually added bits of fish as palates (mine included) got initiated to them. Not so bad! Better yet, they disappear into thin air when chopped up, so once you get used to the flavor, you'll never find them in a recipe where you've added them.

#4 No-No: Alcohol

Yes, some studies do promote one glass of wine per day, but overdoing it leads to lower cognitive function and lower overall brain health. A recent study of more than one million dementia patients in France found that one of the most preventable causes of dementia is alcohol consumption. In particular, the majority of early-onset dementia patients suffered from alcoholism or heavy drinking.

Learn to enjoy just a bit of wine paired with the entree of the meal. Resist the urge to indulge in mixed drinks or heavier forms of alcohol away from the dinner table.

#5 No-No: Refined Bread and Pasta

Refined bread and pastas have been stripped of their nutrients, so there remains no fiber to slow down metabolizing their nutrients. Instead, these processed carbohydrates rush through your system and cause a spike in blood sugar. A diet full of refined carbohydrates has been linked to impaired memory in both adults and children. This can be a hard one for bread lovers. (I particularly suffer when bread is removed from the diet.)

I'm not a fan of many of the whole grain alternatives, either. My transition to healthier eating was the implementation of a step-down program. I was strict with myself and kept track of meals. In the first week, for every five meals of yummy pasta or crusty french bread, I ate one with whole grains. In the second week, I dropped it to 4:1, and then 3:1, etc. I held at a 2:1 ratio. For every two meals with refined carbohydrates, I substitute one with whole grains *in the same food*.

For example, I like wild rice. I also like white french bread. Wild rice isn't my substitute for refined bread. Wild rice is a substitute for refined white rice. Homemade whole-grain biscuits are my substitute for French bread. See what I mean? Whenever possible I substitute brown or wild rice for white rice. I keep whole wheat flour on hand as well.

My Doctored Whole Wheat Biscuit Recipe

- Preheat the oven to 450°.
- Combine 2 cups whole wheat flour with some special seasonings: ½ tsp salt, ½ tsp ground mustard, ½ tsp sage, and ½ tsp celery seed. Add 4 teaspoons of baking powder.
- Cut in a half stick of hard butter. Work it gently and just to pea-sized pieces.
- Pour in 1 cup of sour milk. (I add a dash of lemon juice or apple cider vinegar to fresh milk to make it sour.)
- Work your dough and form it on a floured surface into a slab about an inch thick. Cut out biscuits and bake for ten to twelve minutes.
- These savory biscuits are crowd-pleasers, and I sometimes have to make four or five batches when there's a holiday full house.

#5 No-No: Soy Sauce

It doesn't seem like a big deal sprinkled on your sushi, but just one tablespoon has nearly 40% of your daily **salt** recommendation. What has salt got to do with a foggy brain? A lot, actually. According to a Hypertension journal study, highly concentrated sodium-packed foods can restrict blood vessels and thereby impair focus, organizational skills, and memory. High salt intake can also cause an electrolyte imbalance with resultant dehydration, making it difficult to keep your head in the game.

The next time you order sushi, opt for a low-sodium soy sauce or eel sauce (which tastes a lot like teriyaki) and keep the serving size small. Making this simple swap can cut your sodium intake in half, keeping your focus laser-sharp.

#6 No-No: Vegetable Oils

It only *sounds* like they're healthy. You might be thinking vegetable oils have got to be better for you than butter, but don't bet on it. You'd be wrong. Certain oils, like sunflower, soybean and canola oil do have higher levels of omega-6 antioxidants. But this fatty acid causes inflammation in the brain. What you want are omega-3 fatty acids.

A better choice is extra virgin olive oil. You can use it anywhere when you would have used butter, including over vegetables, in baked goods, and even on popcorn!

#7 No-No: Too Much Red Meat

Some red meat is good for you, but if that sounds like permission to have beef every other night, you'd be wrong. Studies have shown a correlation between populations that eat diets high in red meat and the increased incidence of Alzheimer's disease. One plausible theory is that it raises iron levels in the bloodstream, and iron causes oxidative damage. The sad result of cell deterioration and brain damage doesn't make that burger or steak quite as palatable, does it?

★ When you do buy meat at the supermarket, look for grass-fed cuts, and limit the nights you serve beef.

Chapter Summary

Are you still with me? Remember, it's baby steps with all of these treasured favorites. Reduce the no-nos and slowly implement changes. You can do this. Find friends with similar values and start a supper club. You'll learn new recipes and get a lot of moral support.

- You learned the fallacy of canned tuna as a primary way to increase fatty fish consumption.
- You learned a dynamite new recipe for whole-grain biscuits. That's a win!
- You learned the one thing that sounds the hardest. It's different for every person, but you know what you dread losing from your line up. That's your challenge. Begin chipping away at bad habits. Coach John says, "Baby steps," right?

In the next chapter, you will learn just how easy it is to craft a brain-healthy menu.

CHAPTER FIVE:

The MIND Diet Improves Brain Health

We eat for all kinds of reasons, don't we? Some people eat for bodybuilding. They want to enter competitions where they grease their bodies and lift weights. By eating certain foods in certain ways, they optimize their program. Some people eat for their waistlines. They want to look a certain way, so they diet and watch their food intake. Some people eat for their hearts. They've been scared by a cardiac incident, and they change the way they eat for heart health. Watching what you eat is not a new thing in any way, shape or form.

But eating brain food, a diet specifically designed to enhance your thinking and cognitive function, may still seem radical to you. Let me remind you why you're doing this: you want to improve your function. That means you must feed your brain what *it wants to eat*. Yup, my friend, it's that simple. Your brain functions at peak levels when it receives the nourishment it craves, and that means tweaking your diet.

I referred to dietary studies earlier in this book and demonstrated the data and the statistics behind their efficacy. As your coach, I want to encourage you to take this next step. Hopefully, you practiced the recipes in the last chapter. They are meant to whet your whistle, so to speak, to show you that you *can happily* make these changes. Let's make a pact with one another, shall we?

Try this plan for sixty days. *Whoa! That's quite a commitment!* I can hear what you're thinking and you're coming in loud and clear.

The twenty-one days to form a new habit is an urban legend. You heard me right. It's a myth. Not true. A lie.

It stems from an audiobook written by a plastic surgeon who looked at the way patients became accustomed to a new appearance after reconstructive surgery. He found it took them about twenty-one days to get accustomed to their new appearances. From that, it became popular to assume it took twenty-one days to form a new habit. It's easy. Anyone can try something for twenty-one days, right? Sadly, it left many unhappy with the outcome and feeling rather inadequate. They tried. The new habit just didn't stick.

New research explains just why. A study published in the European Journal of Social Psychology demonstrated that it took an average of sixty-six days to form a new habit. For many, it took three months. The study was based on a twelve-week longitudinal study of self-reporting behaviors and illustrated the reason why a longer trial is needed than three weeks. *We all slip off the wagon upon occasion.* During the eighty-four days of the study, missing one day had no effect on the outcome of the trial. New habits were formed. Expanding the effort compensated for the off day we normally experience upon occasion. Make no mistake. It takes time to change. and then keep the change.

It's true. Therapists and coaches across all disciplines now forecast ninety days to ameliorate an addictive behavior, and there's nothing more addictive than food. None of us can live without it, and it's a behavior we indulge in regularly. I'm not going to sugarcoat the facts. Remember, I promised *not to lie to you!*

So here's Coach John talking. Create a chart or purchase a planner with a calendar in it. I'm not asking you to measure calories or record your diet, though you may find it beneficial. *I am asking you to track your progress. Self-evaluate each day if you followed the plan.* Do this for three months. Then look back over the experiment and evaluate your performance. I am providing you with both recipes and meal plans in the back of this book. If you want to do this the easy way, just follow my ninety days of meal plans. If you are the creative or adventurous sort, take the recipes you love and create your own.

Most of my successful partners begin with the meal plan, and soon cross over to planning their own diets. They get the knack of what is being suggested and find it easy to adapt. I think you'll be like most of my partners. That's why I'm describing the plan in detail for you. Understand it. Follow my suggestions for a week or two, and then leap out on your own. Don't worry right now about digression from the plan. I'll cover how to eat at a restaurant or party without derailing your success as we go along. For right now, just understand the science behind the MIND dietary regimen and don't freak out, okay? Still with me?

Let's begin. Eating certain foods (and avoiding others) has been shown to slow brain aging by 7.5 years, and lessen the chances of developing Alzheimer's disease. It's called the MIND diet, derived from a study funded by the National Institute on Aging and conducted at the Rush University Medical Center. Nutritional epidemiologist Martha Clare Morris, Ph.D., blended the popular DASH (Dietary Approaches to Stop Hypertension) diet, and the Mediterranean diet, into a hybrid regimen emphasizing foods proven to impact brain health.

Why is it so helpful? Because it removes the necessity to prepare full menus by a meal plan. True, I'm providing the meticulous-of-mind an outline to follow, but here's the key point: *You don't need to make it hard. It's meant to be an easy guideline for healthy living.* Say *yes* to some things. Say *No* to others. Yup. It's just that simple.

Here's what it looks like, pared down to essentials. You're going to love how easy it is to eat a brain-healthy diet!

Load your plate with certain vegetables

As it turns out, your mother was right all along. Clean your plate and eat your veggies. Dark green leafy vegetables are specifically shown to lower the risk of dementia and cognitive decline. I know some of you are dying to ask: Why?

I'll tell you. Greens are packed with nutrients linked to better brain health, nutrients like folate, vitamin E, carotenoids and flavonoids. Just one serving a day has been shown to slow brain aging. That's *one serving*. Expand that for optimal success. To jazz up your diet, aim to eat at least six servings a week of greens. Then round it out with at least one serving of another vegetable each day.

Eat berries for dessert

I suppose you're familiar with the saying, *An apple a day keeps the doctor away*. I try to eat one each day, myself. But when scientists reviewed the studies on diet and brain health, one type of fruit proved more significant than all the rest. In a twenty-year study of over 16,000 older adults, those who ate the most blueberries and strawberries had the slowest rates of cognitive decline. Researchers credit the high levels of flavonoids in berries with the benefit.

Treat yourself to two or more berry servings a week for peak brain health. Remember we talked about clean eating earlier in the book? Yes. Just eat berries. Cut down your time in the kitchen and *just eat the berries.* The USDA sets serving portions for most fruits and vegetables, and you may be wondering by now, what constitutes a serving? It's easier to picture a serving size of kale or spinach prepared in a salad or side dish, but berries standing alone as your dessert are a little harder to fathom. They suggest one cup, but really? That's eight large strawberries. Just 2.6 ounces of blueberries is about half a cup. So figure on half a pint of blueberries.

Snack on nuts (and pass on the Oreos)

Nuts, as we have discussed, are high in calories and fat, but they are also loaded with fat-soluble vitamin E. We've talked about vitamin E more than once, so by now you recognize how much your brain appreciates its stellar qualities. It's a good trade-off. Grab a handful of brain-healthy nuts at least five times a week. Skip the processed snacks like chips or pastries, and that means foregoing the Oreos. Be a label reader. Check the list of ingredients, and opt for dry-roasted or raw, unsalted varieties to avoid the extra sodium sweeteners or oils. Just as a caveat, be aware that no-stir peanut butter usually have stuff added in. You can find healthy varieties, but *read the labels*!

Cook much of the time with extra virgin olive oil

Another Mediterranean diet staple you'll see in the MIND diet is extra virgin olive oil. Researchers recommend avoiding butter and margarine. Use more olive oil. That was a steep change for our household. We were among the original Mrs. Buttertons, and that was a hard habit to break. Here's what we discovered: Cooking with olive oil and seasoning with fresh herbs made our favorite dishes just as palatable. Growing windowsill herbs was a treat for both the eye and the stomach.

New to olive oil? Rachael Ray coined the popular EVOO, extra-virgin olive oil, and that's exactly what you're looking for on the label. If you'll remember from earlier in the book, extra virgin relates to the way it has been processed, without chemicals. Further, purchase a bottle in opaque or darkened glass to preserve its integrity and freshness.

Learn to enjoy meat-free meals

Brain-healthy eating encourages means you will start to eat less meat. Count on eating red meat less than four times a week in the ideal MIND diet. Beans, lentils and soybeans, all rich in protein and fiber, make a worthy substitute. They offer satiety, and, as an added benefit, are rich in B vitamins, also very important in brain health. I have not one, but two dog-eared copies of *Diet for a Small Planet*. Lappe offers evidence and recipes on how to begin changing out meat-laden menus for healthier alternatives.

I eventually lost or loaned out my first copy and had to purchase a second. Naturally, I found my original, so now I have two, and I'm able to loan one out at will. Ms. Lappe talks a lot about complementary proteins, and I'll share how I've adapted some of the recipes and created my favorites in the back of the book. For now, just roll the concept over and over in your brain. Get used to the sound of it. I promise you, it's not as painful as it sounds.

Plan on fish once a week

Do you have trouble remembering the names of people you just met? It's common as we age...or is it? Adults (over the age of 65) who reported eating fish once a week earned higher scores on memory tests than their counterparts who didn't like fish. That's right. They remembered facts better and did better in number games than the non-fish eaters. If you are not a fan of fish, take heart: there is no evidence than eating it more than once a week offers any extra benefit for your brain.

That's once a week for peak performance. You got this, right?

It's okay to drink wine

Obviously, I'm not talking about over-indulgence. Too much alcohol is bad for your body on so many levels. However, studies do suggest that a glass of wine in moderation may lower your risk of dementia. I mean, it may delay the onset of Alzheimer's disease by one to two years. That's pretty significant.

Look back through your planners for the last two years. What significant events would you have missed if your brain checked out too early? Weddings, holidays, promotions, graduations, many special events dot your life. They are significant for you, and also significant for your family and friends. Be good to yourself and your loved ones. Guard your brain so you can continue to enjoy those events!

Chapter Summary

We covered a lot of key foods in this chapter, foods you need to include in your diet.

- Eat more green, leafy vegetables.
- Try clean eating your sweet treats.
- Be a nut (by eating more nuts).
- Opt for extra virgin olive oil.
- Eat less meat.
- Eat more fish.
- Have a cup of wine with your dinner.

In the next chapter, we are going to roll up our sleeves and deep dive into the meal plans that will optimize your brain health. I'm excited!

CHAPTER SIX:

What's On Your Grocery List?

Theory alone doesn't get it done. If you really want to protect your brain, it's time to put it into practice. We can learn all we want and say all the right buzzwords. Until we dig in and make it happen, it's just that. Talk. It's time to get down to business and go from dabbling with the idea to seeing what a day on the MIND diet looks like. You'll want to read through it, try it and get used to it. We talked about trying it for three months, and this is your first taste of what a day in the MIND diet looks and tastes and feels like...I hope you enjoy it!

Let's review. The MIND diet means:

- Six servings a week of green, leafy veggies, and one serving a day of other vegetables
- Five servings of nuts a week.
- Two servings of berries each week.
- Three servings of beans and legumes a week.
- Down with the red meat, up with the white--two servings of poultry a week.
- Get fishy with your menu once a week.
- Ditch the butter, cook with olive oil.
- Enjoy one glass of wine a day.

Being specific, your no-nos include cutting red meat to less than four servings a week, cutting butter to less than one tablespoon a day, reducing cheese to less than one serving a week, holding pastries and sweets down to less than five servings a week, and indulging in fast food less than once a week. These are your starting parameters. Work at reducing them as your ninety-day trial moves forward.

Breakfast

No one questions the role of breakfast for good health, so it's a no-brainer than your brain loves breakfast as well. This was a tricky one for me. My usual hunger alarm sounds off around 10:00 am, despite my need to be out the door by 7:30 in the morning. My formerly bad habit of staying up late, and sleeping until the last possible minute, further complicated the process of eating a healthy and nutritious breakfast.

Making the switch to a MIND breakfast required a complete paradigm shift for me and by extension, my family. We talked about it. We mapped out what a week of MIND breakfasts looked like, and then hit the grocery store. We started with the goal of having a MIND breakfast twice that first week, and then broadened our menus and gradually increased it. Here's our first effort in making that transition.

Start your day with a brain-boosting breakfast. Eat a whole-grain cereal, and we found we appreciated steel-cut oats, topping them with nuts and berries. It was easier for us to start it the night before in a crockpot, and then we added the toppings in the morning. This was our first effort. It's a great dump recipe, and it's easy to make.

Apple Pie Oatmeal

Serves two.

- Dump two sliced apples into a crockpot.
- Add ⅓ cup stevia sugar. We used brown sugar.
- 1 tsp cinnamon
- Dump two cups of steel-cut oats on top.
- Pour 4 cups of water over the top.

Do not stir. Cook overnight for eight to nine hours. In the morning, top each bowl with a handful of nuts and ½ to 1 cup of blueberries. We dribbled a little fat-free milk on top and chowed down.

It helped that we started in the fall when crisp mornings began the order of the day. It was warm, rib-sticking and such a delight. Before long it became a weekly staple the whole family enjoyed.

Lunch

Lunch for me was often a desk affair. I developed the bad habit of grabbing fast food and dashing back to my desk to eat it while I worked. It's no wonder my brain got sluggish by mid-afternoon, leading to a Snickers to get me through the rest of the day. This meal was pivotal for me in changing over to a brain-healthy way of eating.

★ The key was in making a great evening meal in portions large enough to allow for leftovers to bring to work. The break room microwave heated my meal and I ate at the desk as I worked, the same as always.

More importantly, I no longer experienced the usual 3:00 pm slump. I was a working machine all afternoon.

Mid-Afternoon Snack

At first, I kept containers of nuts and trail mix (minus the M & Ms) at my desk to nibble on and ease cravings on the days when I *didn't* have a brain-healthy lunch. Since I love nuts, this was easy. I eventually developed a pattern for my snack foods, but more on that in the next chapter!

Dinner

The majority of my calories and fats were traditionally eaten during dinner. I needed dementia-fighting recipes, and, at first, shunned the idea of trying new foods like quinoa. I grew up as a meat and potatoes kind of guy, suspicious of new ingredients. My adventurous spirit was a developing thing, once I got used to feeling good and wanting to put some variety into my life.

Swashbuckling Clucker

Serves 6

We had to be creative to bring the whole family along on this endeavor, and it meant adapting recipes and coming up with more attractive names for the meals. Don't ask me how we arrived at this moniker for a Mediterranean style of pasta. I think our children were into pirates and we used sabers (long knives) to slice ingredients. But do you see how easy it is to lure little minds (mine included!) into the adventure of exploring a whole new way of eating? This was our first foray into the world of healthy, brain-loving MIND dinners.

Boil lightly salted water and cook a package of whole-grain pasta al dente. Rinse it.

Prepare for stir fry:

- 2 chicken breasts, sliced thin or cubed
- 1 onion, minced
- 4 cups washed spinach, sliced into narrow ribbons the younguns' can't pick out
- 1 package mushrooms, cleaned with a damp paper towel, sliced
- 1 clove of minced garlic
- 1 cup of sliced almonds
- a handful of minced herbs

Sautee the stir fry ingredients in extra-virgin olive oil in the order given. When they are ready, add your bow-tie pasta. We topped it with chopped fresh herbs since we had window sill pots of sage, basil, rosemary, and flat-leaf parsley. Our favorite on this was the flat-leaf parsley. Then we dribbled on a little more olive oil to make sure it was moist.

This became a favorite of everyone in the family. Our household heartily recommends it.

Your Shopping List

For week one, pick up these items at the grocery store:

From the fresh aisle:
- 1 container of steel-cut oats
- 2 pints of blueberries
- a bag of apples
- 1 eight-ounce container of fresh mushrooms
- 1 large bag of fresh spinach
- 1 small onion
- 1 bulb of garlic
- 1 small bundle of fresh herbs if you're ready to pack some flavor into your meal

From the grocery aisles:
- 1 tub of steel-cut oats
- a sugar substitute. We use both stevia and sugar alcohol substitutes.
- a large sack of sliced almonds from the bulk canisters
- one package of whole-grain bow tie pasta
- one bottle of extra-virgin olive oil

From the meat counter:
- 2 chicken breasts

From the dairy aisle:
- 1 gallon fat-free milk

Are you ready? Be brave. Give it a try. You are armed with all the facts, and you know the benefits. Now you have a plan to try out. This is where the rubber meets the road. This is where you invest some effort and get ready to chart your progress.

★ Remember we talked about that chart? Put a star or checkmark on each square where you inserted a MIND meal into your daily routine. Snacks count, of course. Your goal by day 90 is to have three or four marks of valor in each square. This is how you measure your progress in a visual way that reinforces your efforts.

Chapter Summary

Reading about brain health does little good when you aren't *eating* brain-healthy foods. It's time to invest a little effort and money into learning how to live for a dementia-free future.

- Remember, we're only trying it out this week. It's one day. Twenty-four hours.
- These are baby steps. Trying too much too soon is a form of self-sabotage.
- You have everything you need to be successful at this, all you need is to show up at the table.

In the next chapter, you will learn how to snack healthy. This is just as important as your first-day trial run.

CHAPTER SEVEN:

The Best Brain Foods for Snacking. Period.

Let's face it. Sometimes you're going to snack. Whether it's the big game, cramming for a test, finishing a project, or just vegging with friends, you're going to snack. Some of your current snacks aren't helping. Sugary snacks lead to a sugar crash followed by an emergency nap. Salty chips and artery-clogging dips are just downright unhealthy. The right snacks will make you more productive. Eat things to sharpen your focus. Nibble on brain foods.

Let's focus on good snacks. Good appetizers. Foods you, your family, your guests will enjoy. I'll start with snacks you can use to stock the pantry, ever available for a quick pick-me-up, and then add recipes for items you'll want to prepare for that special event.

❖ Go nuts for nuts. Almonds are healthy and enjoyable. If you're not a fan, try peanuts, cashews, walnuts or pistachios.

★ The trick here is to purchase the unsalted varieties and sprinkle on just the amount you want.

❖ Unseeded grapes. Pick up a bunch when they're on sale, pop them into a ziplock bag and toss them into the freezer.

★ If you have children, you may need to hide them. Ours found the stash and grabbed some to take outside. Let's face it. They grabbed the whole baggie and absconded with their loot!

❖ Dark chocolate. You'll no doubt remember all of the benefits (antioxidants and natural stimulants) for your brain. Think about the endorphins and happy thoughts you're providing at the same time. Also, remember the calories. This is a nibbling snack, not a grazing commodity.

❖ Air-popped popcorn. Make a healthy version, dribbling on some extra virgin olive oil, and then sprinkling on some salt. Keep a shaker of cinnamon sugar handy if you've got sweets on the brain. Make it healthy and enjoy it because it's a snack.

★ Ditch those microwave bags and get used to popping your own.

❖ Veggies and hummus. You know you like it, but did you know it's good for you? Made with chickpeas, it's high in B vitamins and the fiber is rib-sticking.

★ When you buy your veggies, don't just plop them in your fridge as you put your groceries away. Take a few moments to wash and slice them for easy snacking. You'll find it much easier to turn to a healthy snack if it's ready and waiting.

❖ Greek Yogurt. Not only is it higher in protein (twice as much per serving), it's chock-full of bone-building nutrients and gut-happy probiotics as well.

★ Ditch those sugary varieties and season your own. Drizzle in honey or add some leftover fruit salad.

★ Jazz it up for company as a fruit parfait. I use clear plastic cups to appreciate its full effect. Alternate layers of yogurt with layers of fresh fruits and top it off with a few flakes of oatmeal. This is company-ready to impress guests or treat your family on a sleepy Saturday morning.

❖ Trail mix. Keep it in an air-tight container for up to a month, so it's always available in a pinch. Be wary of store-bought varieties, made with hydrogenated oil, salt, and sugar.

★ Make your own. Use pumpkin seeds, cashews, sunflower seeds, pecans, almonds, dried cranberries, raisins...but skip the candy. Replace it with luxuries like dried pineapple or other favorite yummies.

❖ Fruit salad. Make a big batch and use it for breakfast as well as snacks. Use all your favorite fruits, like apples, oranges, grapes, strawberries, blueberries, kiwi, unsweetened pineapple chunks and bananas. Besides satisfying the taste buds, you'll be filling your body with good energy, natural fiber and a host of vitamins and minerals.

★ We love a handful of chopped mint in ours. Keep some on your windowsill and it will always be in season.

❖ If you can't resist the urge to dip, dip apples in peanut butter. Yum!

★ If you're making them for a party, fashion those delightful little sandwiches you can find on Pinterest.

❖ Roasted chickpeas. If you need to find the perfect alternative to chips or crackers, you've found it. It's full of fiber and protein.

★ Roast them in the oven at 200° for 45 minutes to an hour. Season them with chili powder and a dash of salt. For a variety, add garlic and parmesan or honey and cinnamon.

❖ Avocado anything. We love to mash it up and spread it on toast. Make guacamole and please everyone!

❖ Banana ice yum. Treat yourself to your daily dose of potassium by buying bunches on sale. Peel and freeze them for smoothies, or just whip them in your food processor for a creamy ice cream substitute.

❖ Kale chips. Yup. Roast them like chickpeas and nosh on them in place of potato chips.

No chapter like this would be complete without a section on smoothies. These are the ultimate go-tos for our family. Most of our creations begin with ice. Toss in your fruit. Add your seasonings. I generally toss in a handful of frozen kale. (They never notice it.) Pour in a little almond milk or water or juice. Set your blender to smoothie and get those taste buds ready. You may need to stop it if frozen fruit gets lodged in the bottom. (You'll know it needs a nudge because your blender will start groaning and ultimately smoking.) I use a wooden spoon handle to smoosh it around and add a dash more liquid. Then it's humming on all four cylinders. I add one or two packets of stevia if it taste tests on the tart side. I always have some non-sugary protein powder on hand if my jeans feel tight and I need a keto snack. I have a tall glass that's always brimming with straws for any occasion. These are our favorite versions! You'll notice I seldom measure anything. Let's make this simple and easy.

- ❖ Chocolate Yum. A few ice cubes, frozen bananas, a couple of tablespoons of peanut butter, frozen kale, a quarter cup of oatmeal flakes and a heaping spoonful of cocoa. Sometimes I throw in a smidge of almond milk.

- ❖ Blueberry Delight. Start with a few ice cubes, add some frozen bananas, of course. Add one of those sacks of frozen blueberries you got on sale and stashed away for future use. I usually add some almond milk.

- ❖ Choco-Avi-Shake. Half an avocado, a few tablespoons cocoa, one or two packets of stevia, a teaspoon of vanilla, a cup of ice and some coconut milk. Yum! Deeply satisfying and keto to boot!

- ❖ Aloha Smoothie. Oranges and pineapple pieces with fruit juice.

- ❖ Sunshine Shake. Strawberries and bananas, vanilla protein powder with almond milk.

- ❖ Choco-Berry. A few ice cubes, fresh or frozen strawberries, a couple of tablespoons of cocoa, some frozen kale and almond milk.

- ❖ Tummy Trimmer. A banana, a handful of oats, a handful of frozen strawberries, and a cup or so of water.

❖ Chocolate Frostie. Ice cubes, a couple of tablespoons of cocoa powder, a small frozen banana, a half teaspoon of vanilla, a pint of almond milk. (Frozen kale just makes it look more chocolatey.)

❖ It's a Date. I use almond butter instead of peanut butter. Chop up a couple of pitted dates, add a banana, and a cup of almond milk.

❖ Green, Green, Green. Of course, it's almost pure spinach. I add either a sliced apple or pieces of pineapple. I always have a frozen banana in the freezer. Sometimes I toss in some leftover cucumber. I include a couple of tablespoons of plain greek yogurt. Top it off with some orange juice. This is a detoxifying smoothie that won't hurt your tastebuds.

Dress up your smoothies with a garnish of fruit, or line a ring of some sliced bananas around a clear glass. Sprinkle some oats on the top. These are worthy of any occasion from a weekend breakfast to a summer afternoon pick-me-up. They make a great breakfast on the go, rinsing out your plastic glass once you hit the office.

Appetizers occupy a fair amount of my attention. From company parties to neighborhood socials to having a crowd over for the game, sometimes I just need something fancier than Ants on a Log (celery with peanut butter topped with raisins). The worst part is I always seem to need an appetizer on my busiest day of the week when I am the least prepared and most frazzled. That's why you need a few go-to ideas, so you're never tempted to relapse into the chips and dip mode (Gasp! Don't do it!) These appetizers are sure to please, and I've only included those recipes of things you can make from a well-stocked cupboard or freezer.

★ There's a grocery list at the end of this chapter. Stock up. Prepare the veggies or fruits as directed as you unpack and store them. It will make life easier, and you'll never be scratching your head feeling like a dunce.

Being prepared is the antidote to serving your friends and family something that looks good, but is filled with unwanted, artery-clogging fat. They don't have to be fried or topped with mounds of cheese. Adapt to a healthier style of entertaining and don't sacrifice class in the process. I promise you, these are pleasing to the eye, mouth-watering, and dare I say it? Let me whisper it. *Healthy*. Opt for quality. Always. Here are a few of our favorites.

Poseidon's Spear

These are incredibly simple, glamorous. They join crunch with savory yumminess. And yes, you can prepare them in minutes.

1. Score the skin on an English cucumber, leaving a few pieces for color. Slice the cucumber.
2. Top each slice with a dollop of Greek yogurt seasoned with dill and horseradish. (I use a ratio of 3:1 when mixing it up. One cup of yogurt with three tablespoons of dill and one tablespoon of horseradish.
3. Lay some bite-sized pieces of smoked salmon on top.
4. Now spear it all with a fancy cocktail pick.
5. Lay some leftover dill sprigs in the tray and voila! It's ready for sampling.

Plated Apples

These are certain winners (if you're competitive, which I'm not, laughing hard here). Pairing the sweet crunch of apple with the savory flavor of chicken salad is genius! Pure genius.

1. I always buy a couple of rotisserie chickens when they are on sale. I debone them, chop the chicken, and freeze them in labeled ziplock bags. The messy step is done when it's time to make an appetizer. Pull one out of the freezer and zap it in the microwave for a minute, and you're good to go.
2. Turn that thawed chicken into a bowl. Add dried cranberries, roasted chopped pecans, thin-sliced celery, halved grapes, small bits of pineapple, etc. If you haven't figured it out yet, I

just empty the refrigerator of whatever I have on hand. You can't mess this up. Seriously.

3. Create a dressing. I start with Greek yogurt, and add some lemon juice, salt and pepper, a dash of curry powder.
4. Slice a whole apple into thin little plates. If you aren't using this immediately, splash the apple in a slurry of lemon juice so it doesn't turn brown.
5. Put a spoon of chicken salad on each of the plates. Boom!
6. Pair them with a white wine and you've just taken it from game food to parlor foot in one easy step.

Pinwheels

I don't care what day of the week it is, there's always a bag of tortillas in my fridge. We love tacos and burritos, and these take the place of bread in sandwiches. What great vehicles for getting the filling to the mouth with clean fingers and happy tummies for the score! These plate up nicely and make a great presentation.

1. Start with any flavored tortilla you have on hand.
2. Create the spread by mixing in a bowl hummus, chopped spinach, chopped basil, some sun-dried tomatoes, and stir in a few toasted pine nuts.
3. Slather each tortilla with a layer of your mix, and roll them up.
4. Slice and plate them. Add a sprig of fresh herbs for a garnish to make the dish extra fancy.

Not Your Mother's Stuffed Mushrooms

These are pretty fancy-shmancy! The best part is, you won't need to sacrifice flavor for empty calories. This taking brain food to a whole new level. Think of it this way: Start with fiber and lots of vitamins and minerals. Add a whole lot of antioxidants. Season with sprinkles of flavor. Pop them in the oven, and, in minutes, you have something fabulous to serve at even the fanciest of occasions. They are perfectly sized, super cute, and oh so good for you.

1. Preheat your oven to 350°.
2. Wipe fresh mushrooms with a damp cloth. Remove the stems. I make a couple of dozen because they disappear so quickly. Lay them on a baking sheet.
3. Mix up a bowl of yummy stuffing:
   a. I use a base of leftover quinoa, about a half cup.
   b. Add two or three minced cloves of garlic. If your family likes it, add a quarter cup of chopped onion. Saute this in some extra virgin olive oil.
   c. Use a couple of handfuls of chopped spinach, and add it to the pan. I usually add my leftover quinoa here, to warm it up.
   d. Throw in some chopped pecans.
   e. Chop up the mushroom stems and add them. Let's not waste anything.
   f. I often season the mix with a couple of tablespoons of parmesan cheese from the fridge,
4. Fill the mushrooms, mounding up your luscious stuffing.
5. Bake them for fifteen or twenty minutes.
6. Plate them and pair your appetizer with a glass of white wine to make it a black-tie affair.

Mama Mia Sweet Peppers

These sweet peppers come in several colors rich in antioxidants, Vitamin B_6, Vitamins C and A. They are full of fiber, and you never even need to slice or dice them and you may ignore the mess with their seeds. There's nothing easier than this! Marinate the peppers and serve them. Did I mention this was a speedy appetizer? Keep them in a sealed canning jar for a lovely presentation, and you'll have the kiddos begging to fish them out.

1. Buy sweet peppers in those two pound bags.

2. Wash and dry them.

3. Coat them with some extra virgin olive oil, and char them in an oven set to about 325°; turn them after about five minutes, charring both sides. Let them cool.

4. Chop equal amounts of herbs. I usually use dill and parsley because I always have some in the windowsill. Dice them up and get them ready.

5. Prepare the marinade:

    a. Add about six packets of stevia.

    b. You'll need to put in a crazy amount of salt. Don't flinch. Just add two tablespoons of salt. Remember, they will be sitting in it, and you aren't drinking it.

    c. Stir in a cup of white vinegar and water.

6. Put herbs in the bottom of a sealing jar. Pack in the roasted peppers, Pour on the marinade. Let the peppers soak up the flavor overnight, and serve them straight from the jar with a long fork for spearing them and pulling them out.

Buffalo Bites (aka Not Your Normal Chicken Wings)

Sometimes you just need them. No judging here. We make these minus the chicken, and calorie-conscious guests never complain. They are fiber-filled and great for dipping. You'll need napkins. These are crazy good and if you can live without the chicken, much better for you.

1. Preheat the oven to a hot 450°. Spray it with a non-stick coating and have it ready.

2. Break up cauliflower florets and toss them into this coating mixture:

    a. ½ cup flour

    b. Add your favorite seasonings. We like a teaspoon of garlic powder, salt and pepper. Stir them together.

    c. Add ½ cup water.

3. Place your coated cauliflower onto your prepared baking sheet and give them about fifteen minutes. You will probably need to flip them once in the process.

4. Remove them when they are ready, but leave the oven on for the next step. Drizzle on some extra virgin olive oil and toss the cauliflower florets to coat them. Put them back on the baking sheet and continue baking them for another half hour. You want them crispy.

5. When you take them from the oven, allow them a resting period of ten or fifteen minutes.

6. Serve them with a dipping sauce of plain Greek yogurt mixed with garlic powder and chopped dill.

Salsa Addiction

We can't get enough of this, and we make an enormous batch. Serve it with baked pita rounds for a healthier version of chips and salsa. It's good on any grilled chicken or fish. It dressed up celery sticks. You can't go wrong with it in any combination. It's the perfect date for any party. I use mostly fresh ingredients, mix it up in the bowl and it's done.

1. 4 chopped tomatoes. You can get fussy and use Romas, but I use what I have.

2. 1 medium mango, peeled and chopped. I usually chop them on the pit.

3. 1 ripe, chopped avocado

4. ¾ to one cup of thawed frozen corn

5. 1 can of drained, washed black beans

6. 1 small red onion, diced finely

7. 2 or 3 diced cloves of garlic

8. Diced jalapenos. If I take the seeds out, I use four. I leave the seeds in, I use two. Wear gloves for this process and for heaven's sake, don't rub your eye. (Been there, done that.)

9. 1 bunch of diced cilantro

10. 3 tablespoons lime juice

11. 1 tablespoon extra virgin olive oil

Grocery List

Did you see what was missing from all these appetizers and smoothies and people pleasers? Red meat. I used one rotisserie chicken from my freezer. You're going to start revising the way you buy groceries, and instead of spending way too much money on red meat, allocate a few of those saved dollars to the fresh produce aisle. I'm giving you a list of items I keep on stock. Some I use as appetizers, and whatever isn't in a recipe or salad gets included on a plate of fresh veggies.

I also deal with my produce when I bring it into the kitchen. Life gets hectic and having the prep work done makes a huge difference. I know, it's a matter of switching one time slot to another, but trust me. When your fresh produce is prepped and ready for use, it won't go to waste. You will use it.

Produce

- apples, 1 bag
- oranges, 1 bag
- red onions
- sweet baby peppers
- celery--break apart stalks, clean them, cut them into sections you will use
- carrots--peel them, cut them into strips
- bananas--buy 4 or 5 bunches, peel, and freeze most of them in sandwich baggies stowed inside freezer bags.
- fresh spinach--I wash and bag portions. If I can't use it fast enough, I freeze it for smoothies to replace ice cubes.)
- nuts and seeds (We typically buy them in bulk at the produce section.)
- garlic, 1 head or bulb
- avocados if you will be using them

- English cucumber (with an edible skin)--slice them
- head of cauliflower (or 2)--Remove the florets and keep them in a baggie in the fridge
- blueberries, 1 or 2 pints. Clean and freeze ½ cup to a sandwich baggie stored in freezer bags
- strawberries--unless you're using them the next day, process them. Clean, cut off the stems, slice and freeze in portioned sandwich baggies, stowing several in larger freezer bags
- seedless grapes, whatever's on sale
- mango if you're making salsa
- jalapenos if you're making salsa
- tomatoes
- pineapple if it's on sale--peel, cut and freeze bite-sized sections
- mushrooms if they are on sale and you are stuffing them this week
- dried cranberries, and other dried fruits if you're making trail mix
- fresh herbs if you don't have a windowsill garden

Grocery Goods

- cans of black beans when they are on sale
- quinoa
- spices
- 75-80% dark cocoa
- cans of sun-dried tomatoes
- pita bites if you're needing a vehicle for carrying a yummy morsel
- peanut butter (I usually look for a natural variety without sugar)
- tortilla wraps
- extra virgin olive oil, vinegar, lemon juice, and lime juice

Deli Section

- rotisserie chicken (I buy several when they are on sale. I immediately debone them and store half of each chicken in separate freezer bags for later meals.
- smoked salmon if you're making cucumber bites
- hummus

Dairy Section

- almond milk
- Greek yogurt
- Freezer Section
- frozen corn

Chapter Summary

I hope you're listening to Coach John and revising your grocery habits. Once you begin clean eating, having tapas for supper, cutting back on red meat and sugar, you'll never look back.

- Spend your money on foods your grandma would recognize.
- Buy fresh, eat fresh.
- Get lots of whatever is on sale if you can freeze it or use it later.
- Eat lighter meals.

In the next chapter, you will learn a whole lot of new entree recipes for those dinner meals. Look for things your family will learn to love and get used to a couple of stunning recipes for company.

CHAPTER EIGHT

A Week of Super Brain Food Recipes

You may find this the most valuable chapter in the book. These recipes are your lifeline to a fully functioning mind, a brain working on all four cylinders. I'm excited for you!

Breakfast Recipes for a week of super brain functioning:

Sunday Morning Breakfast Casserole (serves 6)

Ingredients:

- 2 tablespoons fat of choice (extra virgin olive oil or ghee) melted
- 1 large sweet potato or yam, diced
- ½ teaspoon of fine sea salt
- 1 pepper, diced
- ½ yellow onion, diced
- 2 cups chopped spinach
- 10 eggs, whisked
- ½ teaspoon garlic powder
- ½ teaspoon salt

Directions:

1. Preheat your oven to 400°. Grease a 9x12 baking dish with sprayed olive oil.
2. Toss the diced sweet potatoes in olive oil and sprinkle with salt.
3. Place the sweet potatoes on a baking sheet and bake for 20-25 minutes, until soft.
4. While the sweet potatoes are baking, place a large sauté pan over medium heat. Add the onion and pepper. Cook until the onions are translucent and the peppers are soft.
5. Place your vegetable mix in the bottom of your baking dish. Add the sweet potatoes and spinach. Then add the eggs along with the garlic powder and second salt. Mix until well combined.
6. Place in the oven and bake for 25-30 minutes, until eggs are set in the middle.

Ezekiel French Toast (serves 1 or 2)

Ingredients:

- 2 slices of Ezekiel bread
- 2 eggs
- 2 tablespoons almond milk
- 1 tablespoon cinnamon
- 1 teaspoon raw honey (optional)
- 1 teaspoon coconut oil
- toppings of choice (I recommend pure maple syrup, and sliced strawberries, and bananas)

Instructions:

1. Heat a non-stick pan over a low to medium heat. Grease the pan with coconut oil.

2. Whisk the eggs, milk, cinnamon, and honey in a medium bowl. Transfer the egg mixture to a pie dish or low-set bowl.
3. Dunk the Ezekiel bread in the egg mixture for 15 seconds on each side.
4. Cook the Ezekiel bread for 2-3 minutes on each side, until golden brown.
5. Serve warm with toppings of choice.

Omelet Olé (serves 2)

Ingredients:

- extra virgin olive oil
- 4 eggs
- 1 tablespoon almond milk
- diced veggies of choice (peppers, onion, leftover sliced baked potato, etc.)
- 2 ounces crumbled fresh goat cheese (or grated cheese of choice)
- 2 cups baby spinach leaves
- diced cilantro
- sliced avocado
- ¼ cup Salsa Addiction

Instructions:

1. Drizzle extra virgin olive oil into a medium sauté pan on medium heat, add veggies and cook until soft.
2. Meanwhile, beat the eggs and milk in a small bowl.
3. Add the beaten eggs to the pan, then stir once, leave the vegetables mixed into the eggs. Reduce the heat to low for three minutes. Lift the edges of the egg mixture as it cooks and tilt the pan, letting the uncooked eggs fill the bottom. When it is slightly firm, add the goat cheese and fold the omelet onto its side. Cover the pan with foil and leave it on low heat for another few minutes until the eggs are cooked

through. Turn the stove off and leave the pan covered, letting the residual heat "bake" it until the center is fully cooked.

4. Serve with avocado slices and salsa. You won't even miss the hash browns and toast!

Egg in a Basket (serves 2)

Ingredients:

- 2 eggs
- 1 tablespoon extra virgin olive oil
- 1 avocado halved
- salt and pepper
- Salsa Addiction

Directions:

1. Drizzle the olive oil in your sauté pan over medium heat.
2. When it is warm, crack your eggs into the pan, frying them as you prefer.
3. Slide each egg into half an avocado.
4. Top with salsa. Yum!

Busy Morning Oatmeal Buttermilk Pancakes (serves 4)

Ingredients:

- ½ cup water
- ½ cup instant dry milk
- 1 tablespoon honey
- 2 cups buttermilk
- 1 ½ cups rolled oats
- 1 cup whole wheat flour
- 1 teaspoon baking soda
- 1 to 2 beaten eggs
- 1 tablespoon coconut oil

- Fresh fruits and honey for toppings or Luscious Berry Syrup

Directions:

1. Mix the water, milk, and honey. Stir in the buttermilk. Add the rolled oats. Let the mixture refrigerate overnight to soften the oats.
2. Beat in the remaining ingredients.
3. Fry the pancakes on a hot griddle coated with melted coconut oil. Keep your heat low. When the pancakes are covered with bubbles, flip them and let them cook through.
4. Serve with toppings.
5. Luscious Berry Syrup: Puree a defrosted 16 ounce bag of frozen berries in your blender. Add 1 teaspoon cornstarch and boil over medium heat, stirring frequently. Cook until the mixture thickens. Serve warm over pancakes.

Granola (makes 12+ cups)

Ingredients:

- 7 cups rolled oats
- 1 cup wheat germ
- 1 cup bran flakes
- 1 ¼ cup sesame seeds
- ½ cup sunflower seeds
- ½ cup whole millet
- 2 tablespoons brewer's yeast
- 2 cups shredded coconut
- 2 cups pumpkin seeds
- 2 cups sliced almonds
- 1 cup chopped walnuts
- 3 cups dried fruits
- 1 cup honey
- 1 teaspoon vanilla
- ½ cup coconut oil

Instructions:

1. Heat your oven to 400°.
2. Put the oats in a baking pan or Dutch oven, and let them toast, shaking frequently.
3. Add the rest of the dry ingredients. Toast for another 5 minutes.
4. Add the coconut oil and honey and vanilla. Stir well. Toast 5 minutes more.
5. Store in an airtight container

Sunny Morning Wrap (serves 4)

Ingredients:

- 4 eggs
- ¼ teaspoon pepper, sprinkle of salt
- 1 cup of leftover rice
- 1 red pepper, diced
- coconut oil
- 4 six inch tortillas
- 4 ounces grated smoked cheese
- Salsa Addiction

Instructions:

1. Preheat the oven to 350°.
2. Drizzle coconut oil in a pan over medium heat. Cook the pepper until soft.
3. Reheat the rice in a microwave.
4. Whisk the eggs with salt and pepper.
5. Add the eggs to the vegetable mix, and cook, stirring to scramble the eggs.
6. Wrap the tortillas in foil and warm them in the oven for a few minutes.

7. To assemble, layer the egg and vegetable mix with rice, grated cheese, and salsa in the middle of a tortilla. Fold the left third to the center. Roll the bottom edge to the top.

8. Serve immediately, topping with more salsa. You can store them in an airtight container and reheat one or two wraps at a time in a microwave oven for 1 to 2 minutes.

Breakfast Rice Pudding (sort of) (serves 4)

Ingredients:

- Equal amounts brown rice and liquid in an instant pot. I use half water, half almond milk.
- Dried fruit.
- Cook on the rice setting.
- Serve with blueberries and almond milk.

Lunch Recipes

Warming Carrot, Ginger and Tumeric Soup (Serves 2)

Ingredients:

- 3 carrots, sliced
- 1 white onion, diced
- 3 cloves garlic, minced
- 1 inch piece of grated fresh ginger
- 2 inch piece of grated fresh turmeric
- 4 cups vegetable stock
- 1 tablespoon lemon juice
- Canned coconut milk (for topping)
- Sesame seeds (for topping)

Instructions:

1. Dice the onion and carrot into small chunks. (There is no need to be precise, as everything will be blended at the end.) Grate the ginger and turmeric finely.
2. Heat a small amount of extra virgin olive oil in the bottom of a large stock pot and saute the onion for 3 minutes until translucent. Add the garlic, turmeric and ginger. Sauté another minute.
3. Add the diced carrot and sauté another two or three minutes.
4. Add the vegetable stock and simmer for 20 to 25 minutes, until the carrots are cooked through and soft.
5. Transfer the soup into a standing blender and give it a spin to process the ingredients smoothly.
6. Stir in the lemon juice.
7. Serve with a swirl of coconut milk and top with some sesame seeds.

Good Medicine Chicken Vegetable Soup (serves 12-15)

Ingredients:

- A 3 or 4 pound chicken (stewing, broiler-fryer, thighs, drumsticks, breasts, etc. to equal poundage)
- 6 - 8 cups water
- 1 medium onion, diced
- 4 cloves garlic, minced
- 3-4 carrots, sliced
- 4 stalks celery with leaves, sliced
- 1 cup brown rice
- 16 oz frozen corn or 15 oz canned whole corn, drained
- 16 oz frozen green beans or 15 oz canned green beans, drained
- 4 large diced potatoes
- 1 pound of pasta (unless rice is used). Rotini, corkscrew, bowtie, ribbons, wagon wheel, orzo, any flavor
- ½ cup fresh flat-leaf parsley, chopped or ¼ cup dried parsley

- ½ fresh thyme, chopped or ¼ cup dried thyme
- 1 cup green or red cabbage, sliced

Instructions:

1. Prepare chicken and stock: Place chicken in a large Dutch oven and add enough water to cover. Leave the lid ajar for steam to escape, bring to boiling. Simmer until the chicken is tender, about one hour. Remove the chicken, strain the broth. When the chicken is cool enough to handle, remove meat from the bone. Discard the skin and bones. Use as directed below or save for another day.
2. Sauté the onion and garlic in a small drizzle of extra virgin olive oil. Add to the broth.
3. Add the carrots, celery, rice, frozen vegetables to the broth. Simmer until the carrots are soft.
4. Add the potatoes and pasta.
5. Add herbs, cabbage, and cook just until the cabbage is starting to soften, but still a tad crispy.

Taco Verdes (serves 2)

Ingredients:

- 4 tortillas
- 8 ounces tofu
- 1 ripe avocado
- 2 tablespoons lemon juice
- ¼ cup coconut oil
- 1 teaspoon fresh dill, minced
- ½ teaspoon salt
- ¼ cup water
- 1 can drained black beans
- 1 small onion, diced
- 2 cups lettuce and sprouts
- Salsa Addiction

Instructions:

1. In a blender; pureé tofu, avocado, lemon juice, oil, seasonings, and water.
2. Sauteé the onion until translucent. Add the black beans and heat through.
3. Make tacos with the black beans, blended mix, veggies and salsa in each tortilla.

Extreme Salad Bowl (serves 8)

Ingredients:

- Red lettuce, 1 head
- Romaine lettuce, 1 head
- Fresh spinach, 1 bag baby leaves
- 1 teaspoon lemon pepper
- 1 can drained garbanzo beans
- 1 can drained black beans
- 1 head broccoli
- 1 head cauliflower
- 2 peppers, one green and one red, cut into thin strips.
- ½ cup sliced almonds
- ½ cup dried cranberries
- 1 cup blueberries
- ¼ cup sunflower seeds
- ¼ cup pumpkin seeds
- ½ cup plain Greek yogurt
- 2 tablespoons dill, minced

Instructions:

1. Break the greens into bite-sized pieces
2. Generously sprinkle the greens with lemon pepper, toss.
3. Add the drained beans.
4. Cut broccoli and cauliflower florets and add.

5. Add the pepper strips.
6. Add all the nuts and seeds and fruits.
7. Mix the dressing of yogurt and dill, add, and toss well.

Egg Salad in a Bowl (serves 4)

Ingredients:

- 6 hard boiled, peeled eggs
- Mayonnaise and mustard
- Salt and pepper
- Two large tomatoes

Instructions:

1. Dice the hard boiled eggs.
2. Add mayonnaise and mustard and stir to moisten and hold the eggs together.
3. Season with salt and pepper.
4. Halve the tomatoes and dig out the pulp.
5. Serve with the egg salad in the hollowed tomatoes.

Tabouleh in a Jar (serves 2)

Ingredients:

- 2 cups water
- 2 bouillon cubes
- 2 cups bulgur wheat or cracked wheat
- 1 cup chopped fresh flat-leaf parsley
- ½ cup chopped onions
- 2 fresh tomatoes, chopped
- 2 T minced fresh mint
- ¾ cup lemon juice (approximately juice of 4 lemons)
- ½ cup extra virgin olive oil

- Surprise additions: broccoli florets, chopped zucchini, cauliflower florets

Instructions:

1. Soak the water, bouillon, and wheat in warm water for at least an hour, or until the liquid is absorbed.
2. Add to the wheat the parsley, onions, tomatoes, lemon juice and oil.
3. Add favorite extras.
4. Toss it all together lightly and parcel it into pint canning jars. Stash them in the fridge to grab on the way out the door to work in the morning.

Sunday Dinner and Night Time Suppers

Chicken Piccata

Ingredients:

- 2 boneless chicken breasts butterflied and patted dry
- ⅓ cup almond flour
- 5 tablespoons extra virgin olive oil
- 6 tablespoons coconut oil
- ⅓ cup fresh lemon juice (two to three lemons)
- ¼ cup capers
- ⅓ cup fresh flat-leaf parsley chopped
- salt and pepper to taste
- 5 ounces baby portabella mushrooms, sliced
- 2 cups chicken broth
- 2 cups brown rice

Instructions:

1. Place the chicken broth and brown rice with appropriate seasonings in your instant pot. Set for rice and ignore it.

2. Season the chicken with salt and pepper. Pour almond flour in a bowl and dredge both sides, shaking off the excess.

3. In a large skillet over medium-high heat, melt 2 tablespoons of coconut oil with 3 tablespoons of olive oil. When it starts to sizzle, add 2 pieces of chicken and cook for three minutes, or until browned. Flip and cook the other side. Remove and transfer to a plate. If you are cooking for more people, replenish the coconut and olive oil in the pan and continue to cook more chicken.

4. With one tablespoon coconut oil, sauté the mushrooms. Remove with the chicken.

5. Return the pan to the stovetop and add the lemon juice, stock, and capers. Bring to a boil, scraping up the brown bits from the pan for extra flavor. Taste to check the seasoning, then return the chicken and mushrooms to the pan for five minutes.

6. Plate the chicken over the bed of rice. Add remaining coconut oil to the sauce and whisk it thoroughly. Pour the sauce over the chicken and garnish with parsley.

Baked Chicken and Orzo (serves 2)

Ingredients:

- 1 cup orzo
- 1 cup chicken broth
- 2 four or five-ounce white fish fillets (cod, haddock or other fresh fish from your local supermarket)
- 2 cloves of garlic, crushed
- 1 tablespoon extra virgin olive oil
- 1 pint of cherry or grape tomatoes, halved
- 1 tablespoon white wine
- ¼ cup of black or kalamata olives, pitted
- handful of fresh basil, finely chopped

Instructions:

1. Put the orzo and broth into your instant pot and set to rice. Ignore it.
2. Pour the olive oil into a large oven-safe skillet set over medium heat. When shimmering, add the garlic. Cook, stirring it often. Burnt garlic turns bitter. It should be fragrant but not brown. One to two minutes.
3. Add the tomatoes. Stir in the white wine. Remove from heat.
4. Season the fish fillets. Place them into the pan so they touch the bottom of the pan. Top the two fillets with olives and basil leaves. Spoon some of the tomatoes and pan juice over the tops of the filets.
5. Transfer the skillet to the oven and bake until the fish is done, ten to fifteen minutes.
6. Serve with orzo and sauteéd zucchini or summer squash.

Coconut Curry Roasted Sweet Potatoes (serves 2)

Ingredients:

- 2 large sweet potatoes, rinsed, scrubbed and dried. Cut off any bruised spots. Cut into 2-inch chunks
- 2 tablespoons coconut oil, melted
- 1 tablespoon curry powder
- 1 teaspoon Himalayan sea salt to taste

Instructions:

1. Preheat the oven to 415°.
2. In a large mixing bowl, toss the sweet potato cubes with the melted coconut oil, curry powder and sea salt until the potatoes are thoroughly coated with both the oil and the spices.
3. Spread the seasoned potatoes in a large baking dish, and place them on the middle rack of the oven.

4. Set the timer for forty-five minutes. Flip the potatoes every fifteen minutes to avoid burning.

Seafood Chowder (serves 4)

Ingredients:

Fish broth:

- 3 to 4 pounds of fish heads. Be sure the skin, bones, fins, and tails are removed.
- Salt
- 2 tablespoons coconut oil
- 1 chopped onion
- 2 chopped carrots
- 2 stalks of chopped celery, including leaves
- 1 cup white wine
- 1 handful of dried mushrooms, preferably matsutake
- 2 bay leaves

Chowder:

- 1 tablespoon coconut oil
- 1 cup chopped yellow or white onion
- 2 celery stalks chopped. Use the leaves.
- 1 ½ pounds peeled and diced potatoes
- 5 to 6 cups fish broth or 4 cups chicken broth plus one to two cups water
- 1 to 2 pounds of fish cut into chunks
- 1 cup of corn, fresh or thawed
- ⅔ cup of cream
- black pepper to taste
- 2 tablespoons chopped fresh dill or chives for garnish

Instructions:

1. To make the broth, bring a large pot of water to a boil and salt it well. Add the fish heads. When the water returns to a boil, cook 1 minute. Remove bits of fish and save them, but discard the water. Blanching this way will give you a cleaner-tasting broth when you are done.

2. Wipe out the pot. Add the oil and turn the heat to medium-high. When the oil is hot, add the onion, carrot, and celery, stirring often. The onion should be cooked in four to five minutes. Add the white wine to deglaze the pan. Use a wooden spoon to scrape up any browned bits from the bottom. Add the bay leaves and dried mushrooms. Let the wine boil for a minute or two, then add the blanched fish. Cover with enough cool water to cover everything by about ½ inch. Bring to a very gentle simmer (barely bubbling) and cook for forty-five minutes.

3. Get a large bowl for the broth and set a strainer over it. Line the strainer with a plain paper towel or cheesecloth. Turn off the heat under the broth and ladle it through the strainer and into the bowl. Don't bother trying to get the last bits of broth from the pan, because it will be full of debris. Discard the contents of the pan and the strainer, but retain the broth.

4. To make the chowder, melt the coconut oil over medium heat. Add the onion and celery and sauté until soft. Add the potatoes and fish or chicken broth and bring to a simmer. Add salt to taste. Cook until the potatoes are tender, about fifteen to twenty minutes

5. Add the corn and chunks of fish. Cook gently until the fish is just cooked through, about five minutes. Turn off the heat and stir in the herbs, heavy cream and black pepper.

Pesto Pasta (serves 5-6)

Ingredients:

- one 16-oz package pasta of choice (rotini, corkscrew, bowtie, ribbons, etc. Any flavor)
- 2 cups fresh basil leaves
- 1 cup pine nuts
- 1 clove minced garlic
- ½ Parmesan cheese
- 1 tablespoon grated cheese
- ½ almond milk
- 8 oz unflavored Greek yogurt
- ½ teaspoon salt
- pinch cayenne pepper

Instructions:

1. Cook pasta following the package instructions.
2. In a blender or food processor, blend the basil leaves, pine nuts, garlic, cheese, lemon juice, and almond milk until nicely chopped. Add yogurt, salt, and pepper and process the pesto until smooth, stopping to scrape the sides as necessary.
3. Drain the pasta well. Return it to the same pan. Add the pesto and mix well to coat evenly. Transfer to a serving dish and garnish with basil leaves if desired.

Spanish Bulgur Wheat (serves 2)

Ingredients:

- two tablespoons coconut oil
- 1 clove minced garlic
- ½ cup chopped green onions
- ½ green pepper, diced
- 1 ¼ cups bulgur wheat

- 1 cup cooked kidney or pinto beans
- 1 teaspoon paprika
- salt to taste
- ¼ teaspoon black pepper
- eight to ten tomatoes

Instructions:

1. Heat the oil in a skillet and sauté the garlic, green onions, green pepper, and bulgur until the bulgur is coated with oil and the onions are translucent.
2. Add the beans, paprika, and seasonings.
3. Blanch the tomatoes to remove the skins, chop and add.
4. Cover and bring to a boil, then reduce the heat and simmer until the liquid is absorbed and the bulgur is tender, about fifteen minutes. Add chicken broth or water if more liquid is needed.

Lasagne Swirls (serves 4-6)

Ingredients:

- eight lasagne noodles
- 2 pounds fresh spinach
- 2 tablespoons Parmesan cheese
- 1 cup ricotta cheese
- ¼ teaspoon nutmeg
- 2 tablespoons coconut oil
- 2 cloves minced garlic
- ½ cup chopped onion
- 2 cups tomato sauce
- ½ teaspoon basil
- ½ teaspoon oregano

Instructions:

1. Cook and drain the noodles until al dente. Set aside. Preheat the oven to 350°.
2. Wash the spinach, put it in a pan with a tight-fitting lid, and wilt it about seven minutes over medium heat.
3. Drain the spinach and squeeze it in cheesecloth or paper towels to remove any excess moisture. Mix it with the cheeses, nutmeg. Season the mixture with salt and pepper.
4. Coat each noodle with the mixture and roll them up. Place in a shallow baking pan with the open side down.
5. Heat the coconut oil and sauté the garlic and onion until the onion is translucent. Add the tomato sauce and herbs. simmer, season to taste.
6. Pour the sauce over the noodles and bake for twenty minutes in the heated oven.

What about those times when a sugar craving just knocks your socks off? When you need to binge watch something and munching is in order? Well, I have a few healthy recipes for just those situations. You can only eat berries or dessert so many times before you just naturally rebel, and remember, I emphasized baby steps!

High Protein Chocolate Chip Cookies

Preheat the oven to 375°. I use parchment paper on the cookie sheets because I don't like to wash the pans, so if you're like me, line those baking sheets before you begin mixing. This isn't a purist version of cookies, it's the kind that allows you to fudge while still stocking up on protein.

Ingredients:

- 1 cup of butter (two sticks)
- ¾ cup of stevia or erythritol brown sugar (alright, use the regular if you must!)

- ¾ cup of stevia or erythritol (or white sugar if you're suffering)
- 2 eggs
- ⅓ cup powdered milk
- 1 teaspoon baking soda
- 2 cups whole wheat flour
- 1 teaspoon salt
- 1 package chocolate chips (I recommend the Lily sugar-free chips, but I've thrown up my hands, here.)
- ½ cup chopped nuts (unsalted peanuts or cashews or walnuts
- ½ cup of unsalted sunflower seeds or pumpkin seeds

Directions:

1. Cream the butter until it's soft.
2. Add the sugars and blend until it's well mixed.
3. Add the eggs.
4. I'm lazy and add all of my dry ingredients in a well on the side of the bowl at one time. Then I mix them in completely.
5. Add the chips, nuts, and seeds.
6. Drop onto the parchment-lined baking sheets in spoonfuls according to how big you want your want your cookies. Bake 8-10 minutes. If they spread out too much, you need more flour. If they are too poofy you added too much flour.

Wine

Remember I told you that a glass of wine is actually good for you? I grew up in a teetotal household and had to learn how to pair wines for satisfying results. Here are some tips you may find helpful:

- Your wine should be both more acidic and sweeter than your food.
- Your wine should be as intense as the food on your menu.
- A white wine pairs better with chicken and seafood.

Gourmands will describe twenty different flavors in food. I found that pretty amazing. These include the usual sweet and sour, and proceed into much more eclectic sensations. To pair wine, you just need to know three things. How sweet is the wine? How bitter is the wine? How acidic is the wine?

I go by two basic principles: Do I like it? Is it for dinner or dessert? See how easy that was? For dinner wines, I get a basic white or red (if I'm serving beef). For dessert, I like a Moscato or sparkling wine. One glass a day. Remember wine is high in calories, so it's just like dark chocolate. One serving. Be honest and don't fudge on this!

Chapter Summary

By now you should be feeling comfortable with the recipes that nourish your brain. You will need to compile your own grocery list this time because I have to way of knowing how soon and how fast you'll dive into this world of brain-boosting menus. Are you adding your checkmarks to your calendar? If you are still with me, you are within a couple of months of living with a super-charged brain. I'm proud of you!

- What you've noticed in this chapter is how easy it is to find and fix brain foods.
- Did you notice the lack of red meat? I specifically offered you recipes to complement the ones you already know.
- Remember to add these new dishes into your regimen slowly. You don't have to divorce yourself from a good steak. A cordial separation with visiting rights will do.

In the next chapter, you will learn how to detox your brain. That sounds scary, doesn't it? It's okay, I promise.

CHAPTER NINE:

How to Detox to Improve Brain Health

We hear a lot about detoxing, but let's be sure we're all on the same page here. Physiologically, it's a cellular function your body labors at incessantly. As your cells detoxify, they package the leftover debris in the form of food and secretions being excreted from the body. Obviously, the food exits via the alimentary tract. But you also excrete toxins via the respiratory tract, through sweat, and via the genitourinary tract. To accomplish this task, your liver, lungs, gallbladder, skin, kidneys and yes, your brain, all get involved.

Of all the organs in your body, your brain suffers the most when toxins circulate through your system. You hear about assaults like tobacco, medications, inflammatory foods, alcohol, drugs, heavy metals, microorganisms, chemicals, and environmental pollutants all the time, but the natural assumption is that they affect specific organs and the bloodstream. Few stop to consider what happens when they cross the blood-brain barrier and invade the inner sanctum of thought and function.

This happens as your natural defenses get overwhelmed. Unhealthy metabolites trigger mitochondrial dysfunction and rogue cells get reproduced. Metabolic deficiencies, immunotoxicity, and neuroinflammation (inflammation of the brain) begin to affect your system. As a result, your body's energy is diverted to hot spots, like the brain. The heart and muscles suffer, and you experience fatigue, mental fog, cognitive difficulties.

You're starting your program of clean eating, learning to follow the MIND protocols, but there are still toxins lurking in your brain, and you need to get rid of that nastiness as soon as possible. If you're ready to turn over a new leaf, let's detoxify!

I'm going to suggest you embark on a comprehensive elimination diet. For some of you, this will look different than for others. Some of you aren't diabetic, but you are sensitive to sugar. Some of you are sensitive to salt and bloat when you indulge in salty snacks. Some of you are thinking, *I don't have problems like that, I don't need this!* Here's the thing. You don't have problems like that *yet*. You still need to detoxify.

Begin by focusing on what you're eating. Eat as many colors as you can in an array of different fruits and vegetables. All these colors contain vitamins and nutrients essential to the process. Include ginger, turmeric, garlic, beets, broccoli seed sprouts, and herbs like thyme and rosemary in your diet each day. Eat dark leafy vegetables and cruciferous vegetables like cabbage. Eat nuts, legumes and fatty foods like avocados and bananas. Does this sound familiar? You're already on the right track, aren't you?

Add to it interval eating. It's called **intermittent fasting**. Allow your body to take a break from constantly digesting, letting your divert energy from the GI tract to the organs your body uses for detoxification. Consult your doctor, but realize you don't have to go overboard. A simple intermittent fasting pattern allows your body to focus its energy on those organs that detoxify rather than the alimentary tract eating yet another meal.

This may be a new concept for you, but in reality, its roots lie in ancient times. Many religions fast to draw closer to the Almighty, and there are those who recommend "fasting" as a form of dieting, but it's time to look at what fasting is and is not. Fasting is not starving yourself to lose weight. It is the voluntary control of your food intake apart from the societal norms of three meals a day. Look at the process of your normal day.

You rise and "break the fast" of a night's rest. When you eat, your body spikes insulin to cover the expected influx of nutrients. Of course, you're probably eating more than you need for the moment, so your body processes the extra into glycogen (stored sugar deposited in the liver). As the day progresses the storage space for all that glycogen gets overloaded and your body begins to transfer that glycogen into fat (also stored in the liver, though I find a lot around my waistline). In the course of all these meals, your body doesn't have time to deal with increasing levels of toxins and it's like an accident looking for a place to happen.

When you fast, the opposite takes place. Your body changes its reservoir of fat into glycogen. That glycogen is then metabolized into glucose. Your body "feasts" on the fat of the land. See a doctor and be safe. Begin with a simple goal in mind. Fast one meal, and see how your body reacts to the experiment. Then expand your efforts. Design a plan, like twice a week eating for eight hours and fasting for sixteen. Some fast twenty-fours twice a week.

Remember that the goal is detoxification. You don't need to go overboard. Just give your body a rest from its normal job of processing too much food, and it will begin its clean up and internal regimen. These are the known physiological benefits of intermittent fasting:

- reduction of oxidative stress (that overload of too many free radicals we talked about)
- detoxification of your system
- resetting your insulin levels
- putting your body into ketosis (burning fat for sugar to provide energy)
- anti-aging benefits
- higher levels of human growth hormone
- reducing blood levels of triglycerides

During your detox, try to minimize toxins and food contaminants. Look for organic produce to minimize exposure to pesticides and farm chemical residues. Use eco-friendly cosmetics, personal care products, and cleaning agents. Paying attention to what you eat and use opens your eyes to how widespread the level of contamination is in our environment.

At the same time, increase your level of exercise. Run, walk, enroll in a yoga class, dance or bike. Just get your body moving and start sweating. That's right. Eliminate those toxins!

Don't forget to watch your water intake. Fill up your water bottle several times a day. Your body needs to flush out the toxins, but how can it if it's dehydrated? We're talking about water here, not counting that guilty indulgence of soda at lunch or your morning coffee. Drink water to detoxify.

Chapter Summary

Everyone wants to detox these days, but they usually want to do it for all the wrong reasons. The most important organ in your body is your brain. Let's expunge those pesky toxins to remain vital and alert.

- Detoxing your brain isn't difficult. Watch what you eat. Drink lots of water. Exercise.
- Intermittent fasting is great for detoxing, and a healthy lifestyle to adopt.
- We're talking about a way of living, not a one-time fix.

In the next chapter, you will learn how to be healthy, stay healthy. It's all about your immune system and revving it up to full potential.

CHAPTER TEN:

Boost your Immune System

We talk about our immune systems in terms of disease prevention, and rightfully so. Remember that event you went to the other night? The one where that poor soul hacked halfway through the event? Walking germs spread disease, true, but do you have to be the next victim?

When we talk about your ability to ward off disease, we talk about several basic factors. How virulent is the organism causing disease? Is this a bug that's been running its course over several days, or is this some superbug causing a worldwide plague? That answer depends a lot on you. How well rested are you? How strong is your immune system? Your body can fight off most infections if it is armed to the teeth with the right systemic warriors and if you are functioning at peak performance. Obviously, all of this affects your ability to think, process information, work at top efficiency. Let's look at what comprises your **immune system** and how you can improve it.

You may be surprised to learn that a small war has been going on for all of your life in the backstreets of your body. Your skin is your first line of defense. The bronchi in your lungs try to breathe out gaseous toxins, and your stomach acid labors to neutralize those ingested toxins. Some toxins leak through these defense mechanisms. Once a pathogen enters your system, the war is on.

Your lymph system, spleen, tonsils, and thymus are major players in producing agents to fight invading pathogens. You may be surprised to learn that your bowel plays an important part in this process as well. I know, right? Over and over again, you're learning that what you eat and how it is digested is a much bigger deal than you ever imagined. Listen to Coach Josh once again. The complex network of cells and systems keeping you healthy rely heavily on your gut. They rely on a healthy gut.

As many as seventy percent of your immune cells reside along the pathways of your intestinal tract. The lining of your intestines secrete antibodies that identify and destroy harmful bacteria. Your alimentary tract also synthesizes vitamins and compounds that either work for you or against you. When the body wages war upon itself, we call it an autoimmune disease. These take the form of chronic and often debilitating diseases that may plague you your entire life. If you know anyone with lupus, rheumatoid arthritis, fibromyalgia, you already know you want to avoid contracting these ailments.

Let's reinforce what we've already learned:

- for optimal gut health, you need probiotics
- processed foods have their innate goodness processed right out of them
- cooking from scratch with real ingredients helps
- clean eating means you're ingesting real food
- organic meats and produce mean you're cutting out the pesticides you don't want to eat

Talk with your doctor or a holistic health provider about potential food sensitivities. You may want to remove gluten, dairy, or soy from your diet. Stool tests can assess gut bacterial levels and identify imbalances. The foods you eat and the way your body handles them matter, and it's your job to become the detective ferreting out information for your optimal health and brain function.

Another area to look into is your vitamin levels. What is circulating through your bloodstream? What basic ingredients does your brain have to work with in getting you through the day? Vitamin

D is probably the single most important vitamin when we talk about your immune system. Many folks who are diagnosed with chronic ailments, like those autoimmune diseases, are walking around with low levels of vitamin D. Many doctors and holistic therapists recommend supplementation of 2,000 to 5,000 IU of vitamin D daily. Ask your doctor to check your level to determine the amount you need.

Another vitamin affecting your immune system is vitamin C. People under increased physical and especially emotional stress, find themselves at risk of the common cold. Remember we talked about the virility or strength of an organism in relation to how prepared you are to fight it off? When your body is stressed, it's not able to fight as well. Increase your levels of vitamin C to decrease your incidences of the common cold. Healthcare providers suggest taking supplements of 1,000 mg to 5,000 mg daily. If you're not eating your vitamin C, you may need supplementation.

Your immune system loves a balanced diet of whole, unprocessed foods with plenty of antioxidants. Does that sound familiar? What you're learning is the importance of the food you eat and how it affects not just your present health, but how you'll feel tomorrow, the next day, and ten years from now. Two superfoods affect your immune system. One is eating four or five servings a day of greens. Lettuce, mustard greens, collard greens, spinach, kale...you should know these by heart at this point! The other superfood may surprise you. Mushrooms. Did you know mushrooms are packed with vitamin D? Some studies suggest that various mushrooms offer much more. Maitake and reishi seem to boost white blood cell activity as well.

In addition, put more garlic into your menu. When it is crushed, garlic releases allicin, a compound that fights microbes causing infection.

Last but not least, you boost your immunity when you get adequate **sleep** at night. Healers recommend seven to eight hours a night, a luxury for most adults, but necessary nonetheless. Insufficient sleep lowers your ability to ward off disease. If you have trouble falling asleep or staying asleep throughout the night, speak with your physician. Chemical or hormonal imbalances may be the culprit. Try taking melatonin or valerian root prior to bedtime to improve the quality of your sleep.

Chapter Summary

To have a strong immune system, you need to protect and nourish your brain.

- Eat foods rich in Vitamins C and D.
- Eat a well-balanced diet with greens in every meal. Eat more fresh mushrooms.
- Sleep like your life depends on it. It does.

FINAL WORDS

Thank you for inviting me into your home, for taking the time to read and digest this material, for allowing me to be your motivational coach. If you have kept your intake records and been adjusting your eating habits, you are noticing a visible difference in both how you look and how you feel. If you've been slow to get on board, it's not too late. That's the beauty of having this book. You can jump back on the wagon when you feel the effects of too much indulging and recalibrate your system.

As your coach, I've tried to identify the issues underlying why you bought this book. I've tried to provide you a framework for understanding why you need to make a change, and I've offered you recipes to help you make those changes. Coaching is much more than that, however. As your coach, it's important that I've motivated you to see yourself for both where you are and where you want to be.

Take a moment, and list what you see in yourself right now. List the good habits, the indulgences, evidence of too much binging and not enough exercise.

Now list where you want to be. How would you change yourself if you could? If time and money were not an obstacle? List those changes, no matter how unattainable you deem them to be.

That space between the two lists is where motivation comes into play. To continue to make changes and become more healthy, you must remain motivated. Here are ways to pay yourself the richest of dividends: a newer, healthier you.

- Find an accountability partner and make a pact, set a goal.

- Continue to track your progress.
- Establish a notebook, or filing system, for healthy recipes
- Develop a meal plan your family will follow.
- Put together a master grocery list for weekly shopping.
- Keep taking baby steps. Don't make it too hard, and don't settle at what feels comfortable.
- Find the kind of exercise you enjoy and will do on a regular basis.
- Get a water bottle you like and keep it filled.
- Learn to cook from scratch.

You've read the book once and reached the very end. Now, go back and dog-ear the pages that were most helpful. Highlight those concepts you want to learn more about. Read the book again, more slowly, taking notes. This is where you find the gold. I know a few of you were speed readers. You scanned each chapter. You turned up your nose at some of the recipes. You shrugged and thought, huh! Now you're reading the Final Words to see if you really want to dive into the process of changing yourself. Let me promise you this: If you do, you will look back in three months, and be amazed at the change it has made in your life, your job, your relationships.

Your health is the one thing you may own without the intervening control of others. You can choose what to eat. You can choose to put down that soda and get a glass of cool, refreshing water. You can choose to eat less steak or fewer hamburgers, and eat more fish. You can choose to eat your greens. You can choose to walk more. No government, no boss, no friend is stopping you. It's all you. Ask yourself what your health is worth. These are not changes that will break the bank...but a major disease will. Try paying for a heart attack or dialysis. The time to make those changes is before it's too late to keep yourself healthy.

I know you want to make these changes because you picked up the book and came this far. Now go all the way. Go back and pick up those things that made you turn up your nose and find a way to work through them. Sometimes it takes a tragedy to make us willing to change, and I pray that's not true for you. Sometimes it's just a matter of picking yourself up by the collar and shaking yourself into caring and doing what needs to be done. Since I don't live near you, and we can't meet in weekly sessions, my pages must do the work for me. So go back. Reread the book. Do your homework. Control your destiny.

Learn as much as you can. I've given you a full list of resources, and you will learn a lot by reading other sources you find. This reading reinforces what you've learned and offers compounding interest in the object of increasing your motivation to become healthy, eat better, exercise more. In addition to reading more, follow good counsel. The world is full of peddlers selling easy cures to anything and everything that ails you.

Your health is too precious to try to self-medicate or to follow the wrong advice. Learn as much as you can, and get more than one opinion before making sweeping changes. Look critically at fad diets. Learn to recognize the credentials of the healthcare providers you trust, and look at their patients. Get recommendations. My biggest concern as your coach is that you may learn just enough to be a danger to yourself or become prey to someone who uses the right verbiage but who lacks the expertise to care for you. It's a dangerous world out there, my friends. Be smart, be vigilant.

Remember that good health comes from clean eating and lots of colors. I am not recommending pills or supplements or powders. I am not selling products of any kind. Instead, I want to sell you on health. Optimal health. Radiant health. Let me save you a fortune and a lot of time. Look at food as your friend, and let its colors heal you. Look at water as the source of life. Drink it. Look at exercise as the dance of life. Put some into your daily routine. This is Coach John signing off. Until we meet again, be happy. Be well. Be good to yourself.

GLOSSARY

Antioxidants--These are chemicals derived from the food we eat, and their main job lies in balancing the oxidants in your bloodstream. Let me break this down: Your body is a complex machine with all kinds of checks and balances, moves and counter moves. Oxidants are the leftover sludge when your body creates new chemicals metabolized from the food you eat.

The antioxidants are warrior compounds your body synthesizes to keep that nasty oxidation in check. One is glutathione, made from three amino acids: glutamine, glycine, and cysteine. Millions upon millions of chemical reactions are taking place in your body every single day. In the process, some compounds become unstable, with a free, or extra electron. (Think back to your ancient class on organic chemistry with the descriptions of protons and electrons in each element.) That tiny free electron is known as a *free radical*.

Your body produces some of these free radicals just in everyday living. It is exposed to some in smoking. radiation, and other pollutants. It acquires some as the result of stress and alcohol consumption. When the balance of antioxidants and free radicals gets out of whack, oxidative stress results. The stress weakens cell membranes. It damages connective tissue and collagen (think your knees!). It is a precursor to cancer and cardiovascular disease. It is a culprit in autoimmune diseases like arthritis and psoriasis. It affects diabetes. You cannot afford to ignore this all-important part of your dietary regimen.

The Autonomic Nervous System--It's often called the involuntary nervous system because it works while you sleep and without any self-direction. Losing control of muscles is the loss of

471

personal autonomy, perhaps loss of a particular line of work, loss of cherished activities. Loss of your autonomic functions is disastrous. Your brain's function and heart's life depends on the body's ability to serve as the most efficient workhorse mankind has ever encountered.

It functions from your medulla, at the back of the brain, and is divided into two separate centers: the sympathetic and parasympathetic. These two control centers perform different functions, often turning on and turning off various switches. What does your dinner have to do with all of this? More than you think.

Let's look at just one of many examples. You get up in the morning and want to get that adrenaline flowing, signaling the sympathetic nervous system to get to work. It does its fight or flight thing all day long. It requires a neurotransmitter to pass along all these messages throughout your body. What happens when you want to go to bed at night? The parasympathetic works in direct opposition, using acetylcholine to signal for chemicals like serotonin to let you relax and go to sleep. Think of a little wheel in a hamster cage. The hamster runs and runs, spinning it in one direction. Then all of a sudden it stops, maybe nibbles a bite of food, and starts spinning the wheel in the opposite direction. Your brain is like that hamster's spinning wheel, and which way it spins depends on the neurotransmitters activating those nerve transmissions.

The neurotransmitters are chemicals your body makes and stores at nerve endings, ready to be activated upon command so different events may take place. They all use the same brain, the same nerves, the same junctions, but each neurotransmitter sets off a different kind of chemical reaction with a different kind of result. Your body synthesizes these neurotransmitters from the food you eat.

That sobering reality is often lost on us when we binge on chips and soda in front of the TV, isn't it? No wonder we function poorly! The supply chain for manufacturing these nerve conductions gets interrupted. Do that often and long enough, and biological mayhem takes place. If you want to avoid such a tragedy, eat your fruits, and vegetables, and whole grains. Those are the sources for the building blocks you need.

Clean Eating--There is a plethora of experts wanting to sell you on the concept of clean eating. Literally. *Enroll in my program (for a monthly fee),* or *buy my magazine.* You may want to do either or both, but realize what clean eating is. Then try it. Then see if you need to pay to be in a program, or want to purchase a magazine subscription.

Researchers describe clean eating in simple to understand terms:

- Eat real foods. We talked about that, right? Avoid processed foods, and eat things your grandmother would recognize.
- Eat to be healthy, not to feel pleasure.
- Eat more plants.

What is the opposite of clean eating? Food additives, for one thing. Avoid sugar substitutes like aspartame, a known neurotoxin. Monosodium glutamate (MSG) stimulates nerve cells, ultimately wearing them out. Some believe it blocks your sensation of feeling satisfied, leading you to eat more. Other people are just plain sensitive to it, experiencing headaches, nausea, flushing, or even palpitations upon ingesting it. Trans fats are additives to extend the shelf life of processed foods.

You can find them in the labels under monikers like lauric acid, myristic acid, variations of linoleic acid, and arachidonic acid. Food colorings are added to processed foods because their natural colorings have either been stripped away in processing or to entice the buyer into picking up an attractive package. Every colored additive is linked to research on various carcinomas or diseases. Sodium sulfite, sodium nitrates, and sodium nitrites are other preservatives to avoid. BHA and BHT are added to processed foods to prevent them from changing color and to keep them from becoming rancid. Sulfur dioxide is a preservative that destroys your body's vitamin E. Potassium bromate is added to bakery products.

Are you seeing the pattern here? When you look at labels and have trouble reading some of the words, put the food down. Those hard-to-read additives are the opposite of clean eating. Eat the food. Not the way manufacturers have processed the food.

Flavonoids--These powerful derivatives of the foods you eat interact with enzymes for peak performance. One study describes their ability to increase interactions with neuroproteins and facilitate vascular connections with increased blood supply. Many of the preliminary studies suggest a vital connection between your brain health and these basic building blocks.

In plants, they are a part of basic processes of using ultraviolet rays in photosynthesis and utilizing nitrogen in healthy plant life. The Linus Pauling Institute describe six different varieties of these micronutrients: anthocyanidins (berries, grapes and wine), flavan-3-oils (tea, cocoa, berries, grapes, and apples), flavanones (onions, broccoli, berries, apples, and teas), flavones (citrus fruits and juices), and isoflavones (soy and legumes). The most common of these are the flavonols. They benefit the plants, and when you eat them, they continue to benefit you as well.

When you eat these colorful fruits and vegetables, enjoy chocolate, drink wine or oolong tea, you ingest these compounds and they are metabolized or transformed into chemicals that signal your body to undertake anti-inflammatory, antidiabetic, and anticancer actions. The clinical trials are promising enough to suggest you take notice. At this point the evidence is sketchy, but researchers are hopeful they can prove their value in neuroprotective mechanisms. This would herald a change in the way we treat dementia by preventing it altogether. I am expecting evidence to prove this true and recommending we eat as if it will be true. It will only make you healthier, and if it prevents Alzheimer's disease, what a great plus!

Immune system--Your immune system is a much larger part of your body than you may recognize. We talked about your skin being your first line of defense, but what you may not realize is that epithelial cells (like skin) are warriors that line every surface of your body exposed to the outside world. Your throat, intestines, blood vessels, and all your organs, have an epithelial lining. Look in an old biology book for a review: Some are flat (squamous epithelial cells lining blood vessels and lungs), cuboidal (in your kidneys and other glands), columnar (in your intestines, nose, and throat), and ciliated (lined with small hairs that push mucus around).

If your body isn't successful in warding off a microbe, it goes to war internally. If you review further, you'll remember a chapter about humoral immunity, which is where your body forms a second line of defense. The two most common are the blood-brain barrier and the blood-cerebrospinal fluid barrier. Each tries to filter out microbes before they can infect the brain or your nervous system, which controls the entire body.

If they get past the first line of defense, it's war. Your white blood cells only comprise about 1% of your blood, yet they work tirelessly. There are five types:

- monocytes--these break down the cell wall of bacteria
- leukocytes--these cells create antibodies to fight bacteria and viruses
- neutrophils--these cells hemolyze and digest bacteria
- eosinophils--attack cancer cells and allergens
- basophils--signal the release of histamine and other chemicals fighting allergic reactions

Once you're infected with a disease, your white blood cells and their support systems come into play. They produce interferon, which tries to disrupt viruses, and macrophages to carry away dead material. If the disease microbes enter your cells, phagocytosis (by way of leukocytes) begins, trying to surround the invading cells and overpower them. Granulocytes (neutrophils. eosinophils and basophils) attack the proteins of the bacteria and neutralize them.

When you get sick and visit your doctor, you may have blood drawn to analyze your white blood cells. A normal result is 5000-10,000 wbc. If a differential count is ordered, you'll see a lot of numbers that may seem meaningless to you at first glance. This chart shows what a healthy blood count would look like.

White Blood Cell by Type	Percentage in the Blood Count
neutrophil	55 to 73%
lymphocyte	20-40%
eosinophil	1-4%
monocyte	2-8%
basophil	0.5-1%

Determining which cells are present, if they are high or low, helps determine the kind of infection your body is fighting.

Seriously, this reads like an epic saga of good and evil, with heroic forces fighting against overwhelming odds at times, all in an effort to keep you alive. Everything you can do to boost your immune system provides these white blood cells with the energy and resources to wage that war. When you deprive them of what they need through a poor diet, through staying up late, etc., you leave yourself vulnerable to disease.

What happens when your immune systems run amok? If your body goes overboard and produces too many white blood cells, you are diagnosed with leukemia or lymphoma. Another problem occurs if your system produces too many cells and they never mature. That is a myeloproliferative disorder and is diagnosed upon finding an imbalance of cells. If your body goes overboard in waging war and begins to mistake your cells as the enemy, you develop an autoimmune disease like lupus, fibromyalgia, arthritis, psoriasis, etc. The body begins to attack itself.

All of this indicates the importance of keeping a healthy immune system in peak condition.

Intermittent fasting--Research is replete with the evidence: we eat too much too often. Giving your body a break from its incessant need to digest more and more food yields many benefits. The benefits revolve around four basic changes that occur while your body is resting:

- Insulin levels drop significantly, and as a result, you start burning fat.
- Your blood levels of growth hormone increase. A lot. That also facilitates burning fat while boosting muscle growth.
- Your body initiates important repair processes, like transporting waste to excretion depots.
- This is a big one. Your body engages several genes and molecules related to your immune system and longevity.

This all takes place when you participate in an intermittent fasting cycle. We're not talking about crash diets. It's more like scheduled retreats from food. Two or three days a week you adapt to a program of 8 hours of meals with 16 hours of no food or water. Some fast from food and water twenty-four hours twice a week. Talk to your doctor. Take a trial run. Figure out what works for you. These are some of the other benefits you'll enjoy.

1. Of course, you'll lose that stubborn belly fat. Expect a slimmer waistline.
2. Unless you're binge eating during your other hours, you'll also lose weight.
3. You'll lower your risk of Type 2 diabetes.
4. You'll decrease the inflammation and oxidative stress in your body.
5. There is no conclusive proof, but there is some promising evidence that fasting reduces the risk of cancer.

The benefits to your brain are what we are most concerned about here. Intermittent fasting increases levels of a brain hormone called *brain-derived neurotrophic factor (BDNF)*. Scientists believe a deficiency of this hormone is responsible for depression and other mental health issues. It is thought that fasting reduces the risk of a stroke, though that may be a result of healthier eating at the same time. Researchers think it may delay the onset of Alzheimer's disease, or at least reduce its severity. This lifestyle change improved Alzheimer's symptoms in nine out of ten patients.

One of the most common methods of intermittent fasting involves restricting meals to a short window of eight hours out of twenty-four. I find it easier to fast through my day of work. I'm able to accomplish more and my mind is sharper. I eat a meal in the evening and graze on nuts or dried fruit when I veg out to unwind.

The evidence is compelling, while not conclusive. It is compelling enough to make me change my patterns, and recommend it to my clients. Your heart will thank you. You will experience a decreased risk of cancer. Your body will have the energy to engage in gene repair. You'll probably live longer.

The Japanese Diet--Based on "washoku," traditional Japanese cuisine, those who adopt this diet eat smaller servings in dishes made with simple, fresh ingredients. Think about dining out at an oriental restaurant. No one gets a dinner plate the size of a wok. Rather, delicacies are served on dainty little dishes and tempt the palate without putting it to sleep with way too much heavy food. A great emphasis is put on making it pleasing to the eye, making part of the feast visual rather than palate sensitive.

The foods in the Japanese diet center around fish, various noodles, tofu, steamed rice, seaweed, and freshly cooked fruits, and vegetables. Some pickled or fermented ingredients balance the flavors and add probiotics to the mix. What you don't see is a lot of eggs, dairy or meat. Those occur in very small, complementary amounts. These meals are characterized by a fifth kind of taste bud sensation, a rich umami flavor, as it is called. Much of it centers around sushi rice, which is prepared with vinegar to make it sticky. That vinegar; does it make a difference?

According to research accepted by the World Health Organization, women eating this diet typically live to 87 years of age, and the men live to an average of 80 years. Studied subjects not only live longer, they exhibit less hypertension, less cardiac disease, fewer strokes, and enjoy better joint health. You don't have to eat raw fish to put some of their practices into effect. Eat smaller portions on tinier dishes. Use more vegetables and fruits. Eat less meat. Make your meals aesthetically pleasing. Live longer and better.

The Mediterranean Diet--Scientists noticed longevity and healthier lifestyles among those living along the Mediterranean Sea. It wasn't their doctors or their pharmacies. It was their dinner plates. It is regarded as heart-healthy. It includes a daily inclusion of vegetables, fruits, whole grains, and healthy fats. Each week there are fish, poultry, beans, and eggs. There are moderate dairy and less red meat. It includes sharing the meal with family or friends, enjoying a glass of red wine and lots of talks. It is plant-based, not meat-based.

This diet incorporates healthy fats as a mainstay, with fewer saturated and trans fats known to cause coronary disease. Olive oil is a monounsaturated fat lowering cholesterol and low-density lipoproteins (LDL) levels. Nuts and seeds, also prominent in their recipes, also contain monounsaturated fats. So are fatty fish such as mackerel, herring, sardines, albacore tuna, salmon. All are rich in omega-3 fatty acids, which are known to reduce inflammation. Omega-3 fatty acids provide other benefits, like reducing the risk of heart failure and stroke.

Typical health benefits are lower cardiovascular disease, less diabetes, lower blood pressure, less dementia, and a longer lifespan. The better health of people on this diet was first noted back in the 1950s and study after study since then has confirmed it. By contrast, the typical American diet of meat and potatoes, skip the green, please, is a killer.

Omega-3 Fatty Acids--Basically, there are two essential fatty acids: Alpha-linolenic acid (one of many omega-3 fatty acids) and linoleic acid (an omega-6 fatty acid). Theoretically, your body can manufacture everything you need from just these two substances.

Notice I said, "theoretically." The truth is, sometimes it doesn't and that's where diet comes into play. The good fat is essential. Two are critical: EPA (eicosapentaenoic acid) and DHA (docosahexaenoic acid). Don't ask me who named them. Why would anyone give something essential such a jawbreaker of a name? They are found in certain fish. ALA (alpha-linolenic acid) is found in plant sources like nuts and seeds.

The list of maladies affected by not having enough omega-3 fatty acids reads like a program at a conference of the AMA. Rheumatoid arthritis, depression, Alzheimer's disease, fetal development, ADHD, and asthma all point to deficient omega-3s as co-conspirators in disease processes. The old quack doctors selling serum that would cure everything from snake bite to palsy were not so far off base as once thought. It is true that some very basic building blocks form the basis of health, and the absence of them will wreak havoc on your body.

Probiotics--I'll bet you didn't know that bacteria outnumber your body's cells on a ratio of ten to one. It's true. Your gut-healthy intestinal bacteria and a few friendly yeasts are all-stars, assisting players in synthesizing important chemicals for your brain, In addition to synthesizing serotonin, they perform a number of other healthy functions within your body, and scientists are still struggling to ascertain all the facts.

That hasn't stopped the public from jumping on the probiotic bandwagon. In 2012 the National Institute of Health reported that four million United States adults reported taking probiotic supplements.

Even more revealing, 300,000 children had been given probiotics by their parents or caregivers. These health-conscious people read the emerging research and were quick to jump on the bandwagon.

According to Wang and Shurtleff, "The community of microorganisms that lives on us and in us is called the "microbiome," and it's a hot topic for research. The Human Microbiome Project, supported by the National Institutes of Health (NIH) from 2007 to 2016, played a key role in this research by mapping the normal bacteria that live in and on the healthy human body. With this understanding of a normal microbiome as the basis, researchers around the world, including many supported by NIH, are now exploring the links between changes in the microbiome and various diseases. They're also developing new therapeutic approaches designed to modify the microbiome to treat disease and support health."

Here is what the NIH has to say: They *may* support the cultivation of healthy bacteria in the body. They *may* influence your body's immune response. They *may* help relieve chronic pelvic pain. In other words, too little is known to make any veritable claims. But it's not too soon to eat more foods rich in probiotics, foods like Greek yogurt, dark chocolate, and pickles. Several, not so surprising, foods from abroad are included: miso, kefir, and kimchi.

Salt--Even the ancients recognized the value of salt. Early Roman soldiers were paid in salt, and hence the term 'worth one's salt' came into being. Salt was known as a preservative, and foods were salted to preserve them for another season.

Your body needs salt, but in reality, you're probably eating way too much. Processed foods are saturated with salt, and the average person consumes 77% of their daily salt intake in things like bread and chips. In addition, we've grown accustomed to salting our food as a matter of course. What happens when you ingest too much salt?

- Hypernatremia--in medicalese, this is too much sodium in the bloodstream, and it's seen when a person is severely dehydrated or has consumed too much salt. Symptoms include feeling irritable, having muscle cramps, acting confused, experiencing depression, and vomiting. Intravenous fluids are needed to rehydrate the body as quickly as possible.
- Bloating, which we all experience when we over-indulge in salty foods.
- Thirst

Here's what happens when you get too much salt in your system. Upon digestion, it moves into your bloodstream, and cells try to offload the excess into cells throughout the body. To keep your system in balance, you have to retain water, hence the bloating. All that extra fluid is hard on the lining of your blood vessels, and they become more rigid as time progresses, leading to high blood pressure. You've been eating your way blithely along and one day it will catch up with you in some rather serious consequences.

All of this shuffling of the unwanted sodium (from the salt, a compound of sodium chloride) is designed to keep you alive, my friend. Your body maintains a very delicate dance called homeostasis. You must have sodium and potassium for normal transport of materials in and out of each cell, and your bloodstream carries fluid to help in the process. To maintain this delicate balance your body has a pump managed by an enzyme labeled adenosine triphosphatase. It pumps sodium out of the cells while pumping potassium into the cells. All of this takes place to ensure levels required to use glucose for energy.

To regulate the proper amounts of sodium and potassium, you will hear professionals talk about the DASH diet. It stands for Dietary Approaches to Stop Hypertension. It's simple, really. Eat less salt. Eat more foods rich in potassium. Those are vegetables, fruits, seafood, and dairy. Eat baked potatoes (as opposed to peeled potatoes), plain yogurt, salmon, and bananas. The biggest thing you can do is eat fewer processed foods, fewer salty foods, and banish table salt from the table.

Serotonin--This is chemically known as 5-hydroxytryptamine. It is a monoamine neurotransmitter, fancy jargon to say it works at nerve endings to create the safe passage of information from one nerve to the next. Think of a nerve as being a long tentacle of information stretching away from the brain. Each nerve has a head, a long body called the axon, and a tail. It has to connect to the next nerve in line to transmit information from the brain down to the heart, the lungs, the legs, to every part of the body. There is a smidge of dead space between these nerves, and the neurotransmitter carries the information across that space to the next nerve.

Beyond nerve transmission, serotonin affects many parts of the body. It helps control bowel movements, nausea, and diarrhea, with a direct link to irritable bowel syndrome (IBS). It regulates anxiety and mood. With too little, you suddenly get depressed. It's no secret it is the chemical responsible for good sleep. When you are wounded, your blood platelets release serotonin to help form clots and prevent hemorrhage. It plays a role in bone health, too. High levels lead to osteoporosis, which is a catch-22 for the elderly who experience trouble sleeping. Take just the right amount. It also affects libido.

We most often stress its role in good mental health. Reduce the need for big pharma in your life by regulating your mood naturally. Normal serotonin levels mean you feel happier, calmer and more focused.

Normal levels of serotonin are measured in blood tests and should be a level of 101-283 nanograms per milliliter (ng/mL). You don't need to know or remember this, but the salient point is that it is a chemical any lab can measure. If you think you have a high or low level, ask your doctor to order a test. A low level means you need to increase it, and medicine normally goes straight to the medicine cabinet. First, try increasing your exposure to bright light. Try regular exercise. Eat your way to higher levels with eggs, cheese, turkey, nuts, salmon, tofu, and pineapple. Try meditating each day.

Conversely, the opposite effect is caused by taking medications that result in an elevated serotonin level, known as the Serotonin Syndrome. Symptoms include shivering, diarrhea, headache, confusion, and dilated pupils. Untreated, it can affect voluntary muscles, evidenced in a high fever, elevated blood pressure, a rapid or irregular heartbeat, and seizures.

When you can, eat your way to better health rather than going straight to the pharmacy and popping pills.

Sugar, sugar substitutes--Did you realize that sugar is a huge part of your diet? The daily recommended amount varies depending on which report you read, but let's say we're talking about 37.5 gm for men and 25 gm for women. That's about twelve teaspoons of sugar a day. What are most people actually eating? A person eating 2000 calories a day is probably ingesting 50 grams of sugar. Wowsers! Some researchers hypothesize the average adult is getting that 50 grams in *added sugar, hidden sugar* in addition to sweet indulgences

It's easy to recognize sugar in a can of soda. That's 39 gm in a twelve ounce can of Coke. Have that Coke with a bag of Skittles (another 47 gm) and you can see it add up. The problem is that those sweets are just the tip of the iceberg. Realize that unless you are actively avoiding sugar, you're probably eating way too much, and from sources never imagined. Almost every processed food includes sugar:

- granola
- protein bars
- yogurt
- bread
- tomato sauce
- canned soups

- processed nut butters

Become a label reader. You know to watch out for corn syrup and probably the "ose" words like fructose and maltose. Watch for fifty-six other words masquerading as sugar, things like fructose, sucrose, beet sugar, molasses, honey, caramel, carob, any kind of sugar or syrup, dextrin, dextrose, maltodextrin, D-ribose, galactose, agave nectar, turbinado.

Does it mean never having sweet treats? No. Look for stevia substitutes, like Lily chocolate. Use xylitol and other alcohol sugars, which are lower in calories and with fewer inflammatory effects on the body. Erythritol is made by a process of fermenting corn starch and it offers all the sweetness of sugar with only 5% of the calories. Sorbitol and maltitol are others. I use stevia and erythritol in 1:1 substitutions for sugar in my cookies, cakes, and bread with excellent results. Happy cooking!

Supplements--Scientists question the use of swallowing pills and supplements as a way of supporting brain health. Some push supplements and some question whether they are metabolized or excreted whole. No one offers any proof of their value. The craze for vitamins rose in the 1960s when Flintstones were peddled to children. Then One A Days became popular. These advertising campaigns legitimized supplementation and the public ran wild. Taking multivitamins evolved into taking a host of specific vitamins. I admit I've been caught up in the craze from time to time, taking E, C, B_{12} and Biotin. I couldn't help myself. It's like the world has looked through the lens of crisis medicine, and, as a result, we all skitter around like chickens with our heads cut off, pecking at food supplements in hopes of warding off maladies like heart disease and dementia.

Probiotics are one example. The FDA regulates dietary supplements, but some probiotics don't require FDA oversight. Manufacturers may claim whatever they want without a slap on the hand as long as no health claims are made. No one knows if they help or hurt, but that isn't making any difference to some of the holistic healers prescribing them or the companies making them. The better alternative is a diet rich in nutrients, one I've been describing over and over throughout this book.

Since I concentrated on eating properly, rather than popping pills, I've been healthier and calmer. I've slept better and more consistently. I've learned to heal my body with foods as nature intended. This is Coach John talking: *Eat your way to better health.*

RESOURCES

Berk, L.; Bruhjell, K.; Peters, W.; Bastian, P.; Lohman, E.; Bains, G.; Arevalo, J.; Cole, S. (2018, April 20). *Dark Chocolate Effects on Human Gene Expression.* Federation of American Societies for Experimental Biology. Abstract No. 755.1. Retrieved December 22, 2019 from https://www.fasebj.org/doi/10.1096/fasebj.2018.32.1_supplement.755.1

Borelli, L. (2017, July 7). *6 Benefits of Eating Blueberries for Brain Health, From Lowering Dementia Risk to Improving Memory.* Medical Daily. Retrieved December 22, 2019 from https://www.medicaldaily.com/6-benefits-eating-blueberries-brain-health-lowering-dementia-risk-improving-419938

Bowden Ph.D., CNS, J. (2018, August 16). *Clean Eating Is Not Disordered.* Clean Eating. Retrieved December 22, 2019 from https://www.cleaneatingmag.com/author/jonny-bowden-phd-cns

DiSalvo, D. (2017, April 27). *Why is Diet Soda So Bad For Your Brain?* Forbes. Retrieved December 22, 2019 from. https://www.forbes.com/sites/daviddisalvo/2017/04/27/why-is-diet-soda-so-bad-for-your-brain/#42bd7c885fad

Reviewed by Freeborn Ph.D., D., Cunningham, L., LoCicero MD, R, Updated by Rogers, K. (2018, October 18). White Blood Cell. (Encyclopedia Britannica. Retrieved December 22, 2019 from https://www.britannica.com/science/white-blood-cell

Greenberg Ph.D., M. (2015, February 5). *Why Our Brains Love Sugar--and Our Bodies Don't.* Psychology Today. Retrieved December 22, 2019 from https://www.psychologytoday.com/us/blog/the-mindful-self-express/201302/why-our-brains-love-sugar-and-why-our-bodies-dont

Higdon, J. (2005). Flavonoids. Oregon State University. Updated February, 2016. Retrieved December 22, 2019 from https://lpi.oregonstate.edu/mic/dietary-factors/phytochemicals/flavonoids#subclasses

Jeaveans, Christine. (2014, June 26.) How Much Sugar Do We Eat? BBC News. Retrieved December 22, 2019 from https://www.bbc.com/news

Lally, P.; van Jaarsveld, C.; Potts, H..; Wardle, J. (2009, July 16). *How Are Habits Formed: Modelling Habit Formation in the Real World.* European Journal of Social Psychology. Retrieved December 22, 2019 from https://onlinelibrary.wiley.com/doi/abs/10.1002/ejsp.674

Lappé, Frances Moore. *Diet for a Small Planet.* Ballantyne Books. New York. 1971.

Lehmen, S.; Fogoros, R. (2019, August 24). *Serving Sizes for Eighteen Fruits and Vegetables.* Very Well Fit. Retrieved December 22, 2019 from https://www.verywellfit.com/serving-sizes-for-18-fruits-and-vegetables-2506865

Levy CHHC, J. (2018, July 30). *Vitamin E Benefits the Skin, Hair, Heart, Eyes and More.* Dr. Axe. Retrieved December 22, 2019 from https://draxe.com/nutrition/vitamin-e-benefits/

Loma Linda University Health. *Dark Chocolate Boosts Memory.* Alzheimer's & Dementia Weekly. February 27, 2019. http://www.alzheimersweekly.com/2018/05/dark-chocolate-boosts-memory.html

McKay Ph.D., S. (2019, August 6). *Is Alzheimer's Disease a Women's Health Problem?* Your Brain Health. Retrieved December 22, 2019 from. http://yourbrainhealth.com.au/

Mosconi Ph.D., L. (2018, February 3). *Mind Food: What a Neuroscientist Eats.* The Times. Retrieved December 20, 2019 from https://www.thetimes.co.uk/article/mind-food-what-a-neuroscientist-eats-wd9mfz9st

Perry, D. (2018, June 7). *2 Rules for How to Cook Salmon Even Haters Will Love.* Real Simple. Retrieved December 20, 2019 from https://www.realsimple.com/food-recipes/how-to-cook-salmon-for-haters

Puckette, M.. (2016, August). Food and Wine Pairing Basics. Wine Folly. Updated October 30, 2019. Retrieved from https://winefolly.com/tutorial/getting-started-with-food-and-wine-pairing/

Rederer, M. 15 "Healthy" Foods You Won't Believe Are Full of Added Sugar. Health Prep. Retrieved December 22, 2019 from https://healthprep.com/fitness-nutrition/15-healthy-foods-you-wont-believe-are-full-of-added-sugar/?utm_source=bing&utm_medium=search&utm_campaign=328752049&utm_content=1146791188590073&utm_term=processed%20sugar&msclkid=d173b9d2037a12294431e42de10ac3f4

Shahzad MSc, A. (2018, July 24). Advances Along the Gut-Liver-Brain Axis in Alzheimer's Disease: Why Diet May Be So Impactful. Alzheimer's Association. Retrieved December 20, 2019 from https://www.alz.org/aaic/releases_2018/AAIC18-Tues-gut-liver-brain-axis.asp

Shute, Evan and Shute, Wilfred. Shute Vitamin E Protocol. Retrieved December 20, 2019 from http://www.doctoryourself.com/shute_protocol.html

Smith, K. (2017, May 13). *How to Eat More Brain Healthy Foods.* AgeRight.org. Retrieved December 20, 2019, from .http://ageright.org/2017/05/13/eating-more-brain-healthy-foods/

Sons, T. (2017, February 10). Supercharge Brain Health With These Foods. Retrieved December 20, 2019, from https://www.lifehack.org/530346/supercharge-brain-health-with-these-foods

Weiss, MD MCR, J., Woodell MD, T. (2019). Sodium Homeostasis. Chronic Disease in the Elderly. Retrieved December 22, 2019 from https://www.sciencedirect.com/topics/medicine-and-dentistry/sodium-homeostasis

Williams, R. (2012, January). Flavonoids, Cognition and Dementia: Actions, Mechanisms, and Potential Therapeutic Utility for Alzheimer Disease. Retrieved from https://www.sciencedirect.com/science/article/abs/pii/S0891584911005764

Wang, Ph.D., Y. and Shurtleff, Ph.D., D. *Probiotics: What You Need to Know.* National Center for Integrative and Complementary Health. 2012. Retrieved December 22, 2019 from https://www.sciencedirect.com/science/article/abs/pii/S0891584911005764

World Health Organization. (2013, August 28). WHO | Dementia cases set to triple by 2050 but still largely ignored. Retrieved December 20, 2019, Retrieved December 22, 2019 from https://www.who.int/mediacentre/news/releases/2012/dementia_20120411/en/

YOUR FREE GIFT

Thank you again for purchasing this book. As an additional thank you, you will receive an e-book, as a gift, and completely free.

This includes a fun and interactive daily checklist and workbook to help boost your productivity through simple activities. Life can get so busy, and this bonus booklet gives you easy and efficient tips and prompts to help you get more done, every day.

You can get the bonus booklet as follows:

To access the secret download page, open a browser window on your computer or smartphone and enter: **bonus.john-r-torrance.com**

You will be automatically directed to the download page.

Please note that this bonus booklet may be only available for download for a limited time.